Copyright © 2025 Christine Lawrence

All rights reserved.

No part of this book maybe reproduced
in any manner whatsoever without
written permission from the author except
in the case of brief quotations embodied
in critical articles and reviews.

This novel is entirely a work of fiction
inspired by the real-life stories of those who lived and worked
in the Portsmouth Borough Asylum during World War 1.
Any resemblance to actual person, living or dead, is entirely coincidental.

Thanks as always to my husband Mark, for all his patience and feedback.
Thanks to my writing community:
Jackie Green, Eileen Phyall, Margaret Jennings, Lynne Stone, Will Sutton, Helen and Richard Salsbury, Alison Habens, Tom Sykes, Annie Kirby, Loree Westron,
all at the *Portsmouth Writers' Hub, Springwood Writers, Tea Tray Creatives,*
Will Sutton's *Edit Club, Scribblers Salon* and *Write your Novel* group members,
for all the help, critiquing and support from you all.

Thanks to the *Good Mental Health Co-operative,* especially Carolyn Barber and Sarah Haskett
Thanks also to Cover artist
Joshuahlangleyart@gmail.com

ABOUT THE AUTHOR

About the author

Christine's career as a psychiatric nurse led to her working with those with drug and alcohol issues, as well as in many fields of mental health. During her career she successfully completed an MSc in Addictive Behaviour. Following her early retirement, she went back to studying and achieved a BA tons in English Literature and Creative Arts, followed by an MA in Creative Writing at Portsmouth University. She was one of the *2012 Writers to Watch* in the Portsmouth BookFest of that year and has short stories published in *Portsmouth Fairy Tales for Grown Ups, Pompey Writes, Star and Crescent* and *Day of the Dead*. She has written and performed for events including the *Victorious Festival, St. Valentine's Massacre, Portsmouth BookFest, Portsmouth DarkFest, Day of the Dead, Holmes Fest,* at several venues in Portsmouth, including The Guildhall, Portsmouth Historical Dockyard, The Kings Theatre, the Square Tower and the New Theatre Royal.

In 2017 Christine was one of the writers who took part in the *Writing Edward King* project at Portsmouth City Museum which received Arts Council Funding. She performed her writing for this project in several venues across the city. In 2018 she was one of the founders of Portsmouth's spoken word group, T'Articulation, and is now a Director of the Portsmouth Writer's Hub. In 2019 she was a co-writer for *Cursed City - Dark Tides,* a trans-media production for DarkFest. In 2021, Christine was appointed to lead workshops on the BBC/National Libraries, *Novels that Shaped our World* project, using Andrea Levy's *Small Island* as the novel to work with.

Christine's novels, *Caught in the Web, Payback, Don't Step on the Cracks, Emily,* and her collections of short stories, *Moments of Darkness* and *More Moments of Darkness,* are all available from The Book Shop at Lee-on-the-Solent, direct from the author at Lawrence.christine14@gmail.com., New to You Books, Cosham, or from Amazon.

Christine's Facebook page is https://www.facebook.com/Novelist2021

Grace

Grace

christine lawrence

THE RESEARCH

The Research

Funded by the Heritage Lottery a group of research volunteers, working with the Good Mental Health Co-operative in 2021, looked at original patient records and hospital reports from the Borough of Portsmouth Lunatic Asylum, exploring books, articles and other research linked to the Portsmouth and Hampshire area. The group partnered with other local projects looking at life during that period and remembering the sacrifices made during the Great War. The outcome of this research was a pamphlet and online hub which contains more information and source materials. The aim of the project was to raise awareness generally about the social history of mental health care, to help reduce stigma and discrimination today. (Copyright © The Good Mental Health Co-operative 2021).

https://my.creative-learning.net/bundles/heritage-ww1

The author was privileged to be a part of this research group and during the process wrote several monologues based on the lives of those who were patients in the asylum at the time. Once the project was completed she decided to continue with developing one of the monologues into a novel. *Grace* is a fictional character but she could have been one of those women who nursed in the asylum in 1918. Her story is typical of the time but is purely fictional.

Christine would like to thank the Good Mental Health Co-operative for the opportunity to take part in this project.

1

Grace opened her eyes and looked up, aware of being watched. A pigeon sat on the skylight above her bed, cooing in a most annoying way. Annoying because of the repetition of its song, and annoying that it was free. How Grace wished she were as free as that bird. It seemed to be laughing at her as it spread its wings and fluttered away. Grace stretched and sighed and climbed out of bed.

Housemaids always had a hard life, and hers was no different to many others. Her tiny attic bedroom in the home of Mr and Mrs Simpson in Craneswater Road was comfortable enough with a narrow bed, and the skylight let in the early morning sunshine. But there was no time for lying in bed and dreaming for Grace. She had duties to do. Rushing to wash in the cold-water basin beside her bed, then throwing on her maid's uniform and tidying her dark hair into her cap, she was soon tripping down the stairs to the kitchen, her first duty to make sure the kettle was filled with fresh water and that Mary had stoked the fire up when she'd woken.

Mary's room was smaller than the walk-in larder that was kept under lock and key until Mrs Amberley, the cook, arrived at seven. Grace banged on Mary's door and once she'd got up, and collected the coal from the yard, they enjoyed the few minutes alone before the older woman came in through the back door. Once she'd arrived, they knew they'd be worked off their feet.

Later that morning, Grace and Mary giggled together as they prepared the vegetables.

'Look at the size of this carrot.' Mary held it aloft. 'I'll bet you've never seen one like this.'

'You are wicked, Mary.' Grace snatched it from her and started chopping at it vigorously.

Mary nudged her. 'Be careful with that knife, Grace.'

'Stop your tomfoolery, you two,' Mrs Amberley complained. 'I need those vegetables for the soup. We haven't got all day, and Bennett, you've still not done the upstairs fireplaces.'

'Yes, Mrs Amberley. Sorry.'

Grace sighed. Working alongside Mary was the best part of the job. At least they could have a bit of a laugh together, as long as Mrs Amberley didn't keep telling them off. Everyone needed to have some fun in their life, didn't they? She picked up another carrot and scrubbed it with the vegetable brush.

The door to the back yard rattled.

'Get the door, Bennett.' Mrs Amberley stopped rolling the pastry and wiped her hands on the cloth she took from the dryer by the range.

It was Mrs James, her face as white as the scullery wall. 'Sorry to intrude but I've come to see our Mary. There's news,' she said.

'Let her in then, Bennett.' Mrs Amberley pulled a chair out from the table. 'Come in dear, and have a sit down. There's tea in the pot.'

'Thank you, I'm obliged.' She looked across at Mary and took a breath.

'Ma, what is it?' Mary pushed her unruly brown hair out of her eyes as she moved across and took her mother's hand. 'What's happened?'

'Give the poor woman a chance to take a breath.' Mrs Amberley glared at Mary. 'Pour her a cup of tea, then. And sort your cap out. Your hair is a mess.'

Mary tutted as she dried her hands on her apron, fiddled with her hair again, tucking it into her cap, then went to pour the tea. 'Sorry, Ma,' she said as she placed the full cup on the table in front of her mother. She stood and waited whilst her mother took a sip of the tea before looking up.

'It's bad news Mary, dear. Mrs Burrows called round early today to let me know and asked me to tell you.'

'Tell me what? What's happened? It's Johnny, isn't it?' She was shaking, tears of rage in her eyes. 'I knew it! Oh, why did he have to go to war?'

Her mother stood and took the girl in her arms. 'I'm so sorry. He won't be coming home.'

'Why are you sorry?' Mary pushed her away. 'It's not true, he's coming home in two weeks. We're to be wed. It's all arranged.'

'Mary. He isn't coming home. He's dead. It's awful, but it's true. Mrs Burrows had the telegram.'

'You're lying!' Mary stepped away from her mother and picked up the vegetable knife, brandishing it at the woman. 'You never liked Johnny. He's not dead. You wicked woman, telling such lies.' She lurched at her mother, screaming.

Grace found herself leaping between the two women, shouting. 'Stop! Stop it, Mary. It's your ma.'

Mary fell into Grace's arms, the knife clattering on the flagstoned floor. She sobbed and sobbed.

Grace hugged her and spoke soothingly. 'It's alright Mary,' she said. 'You'll be all right. Come and sit down now.' Realising that it was a stupid thing to say and that Mary would not be all right, at least not for a long time, Grace felt awkward but the younger woman did settle and sat at the kitchen table next to her mother.

Grace looked up and saw that Mrs Simpson, elegantly dressed already, had entered the scullery and was watching.

'What on earth is happening here?' she asked. 'I heard the noise and saw what you just did, Bennett.'

'James' sweetheart has been killed at the front,' Mrs Amberley said. 'It was a shock. I'm sure she didn't mean no harm.'

'I see. I am so sorry. I do see it must be a shock. James, go home with your mother and take some time off.'

'I don't know, Ma'am.'

'No arguments, young lady. You can't work like this.'

Mary stood and bobbed a curtsy. 'Thank you Ma'am.'

'Take as much time as you need, but be sure to come back. We need you here.' Mrs Simpson turned to the cook. 'I'm sure we can manage without her for a few days?'

'Of course, Ma'am,' Mrs Amberley sniffed and looked at Grace. 'We will manage, won't we Bennett?'

'Yes, Mrs Amberley, Ma'am.'

'Good. Then that is settled. Now, I must get on.' Mrs Simpson turned and left the room.

Mary was sobbing to herself now.

'I'm sorry Ma,' she said. 'I'm a wicked girl and should be punished. I am being punished by God. He's taken away my sweetheart and I'll never be happy again.'

'Now don't say such things,' her mother said, holding her hand. 'Come along, let's get you home now.' She stood and turned to Grace. 'Thank you Grace, for your kindness.'

Grace's knees ached, her sore hands were black with soot, a strand of hair had escaped from her cap and hung down in her eyes. She shook her head in frustration at it never being in its place. How she hated her life. When her Ma had insisted she take the position here she'd fought against it. But what else was there for a young woman like herself to do? Leaning back on her heels she turned her head to gaze out of the French windows into the finely-kept garden beyond. It was another world out there, one she knew she'd never be free to explore.

Even though the war had come and with it the promise of more interesting work for women - in the post office, on the trams, the dockyard perhaps - she doubted any of those jobs would be for her. She thought of her sister working in the munitions factory and sighed.

The draught coming through the door as it silently opened announced the arrival of her mistress. 'There you are,' she said brightly.

Embarrassed she'd been caught cleaning out the fireplace so late in the day, Grace struggled to stand and bobbed a curtsy to her mistress.

'Ma'am,' she stuttered as she tried to push the strand of hair back into place, wondering what was coming next.

'I'm glad I caught you, Bennett.'

'Sorry, Ma'am.' Grace's face flushed.

'Please don't be sorry. I wanted to thank you for the way you handled James this morning. Receiving the news about her sweetheart was a terrible thing for her to bear. You were kind and patient, and dealt with her outburst so well. Everyone deals with shocking news in a different way, I know. She is normally a timid young woman and seeing her react with such violence was most unexpected. It was only you who seemed to know how to settle her.'

'Thank you, Ma'am, but it was nothing really.'

'Nonsense. In fact, I have been thinking about you and I believe you have the makings of a good nurse.'

'Oh, no, I couldn't be a nurse. All that blood and gory stuff.'

'It's not really like that. It doesn't have to be.' She sat on the chair beside the fire. 'Listen Bennett. You know I'm a visitor to the Borough Asylum don't you? I've been thinking, you could train as a mental nurse. They desperately need women like you to join the service. I would lose you, but it seems wrong for you to waste your natural talent.'

Grace shuddered. 'The Asylum? Sorry Ma'am, but the thought of that place scares me. I couldn't ever think of working there.'

'It is not as bad as some of the stories I'm sure you've heard. It has a very modern approach to treatment and is no longer called an asylum. It's a mental hospital now. The training is exceptional, under good doctors and experienced nurses.'

Grace looked down at her feet, then took a deep breath. 'I'm grateful to you for suggesting it, but I really couldn't do it. Apart from anything else, My Ma and Pa wouldn't let me.'

'Perhaps you might talk to them both and give it some thought. You could come with me one day when I visit. That might help you to have a better understanding of what it might be like before you make up your mind.'

Thinking she'd already made up her mind, Grace bobbed a curtsy. 'Very well Ma'am. I will think about it.'

'Thank you, Bennett. Now I'll let you get on with your work.' She smiled. 'Oh, and you have soot on your nose, my dear.'

As soon as her mistress had left the room, Grace looked at herself in the mirror above the fireplace and flushed as she saw the black smudge on her face. She made to wipe it away, but her hands were still dirty. Laughing to herself she did her best with the rag in her apron pocket.

She stood for a moment longer, looking at her reflection, then shook her head. 'Nurse indeed. I think not!' and she was back on her hands and knees, cleaning the grate.

2

Grace sat in the back parlour of her parent's terraced cottage. Everything was small and cramped and she wondered as she'd done so many times before, how her Ma could stand it. Watching her now, Grace remembered when Ma was younger and didn't stoop quite as much. Her hair now grey, her face lined, she poured hot water into the teapot beside the range, and Grace remembered how her two brothers, Wilfred and Bert, her sister, Elsie and herself had somehow once fitted into this space. She shook her head, not wanting to consider that this could one day be her lot.

Her Pa sat in his usual chair, his legs stretched out but his shirt still neatly tucked in, his face clean-shaven and his boots polished. He rubbed his hands together and smiled at Grace.

'Nothing like a nice cup of Ma's tea, eh? The best in town.'

Grace smiled back, noticing the laughter lines around his eyes. 'Yes, Pa. The best in town. Still no letter from the boys at the front?'

'Nothing since they went back after Easter. We can only hope no news is good news,' Ma said. 'I'd hoped they'd be back for a few days, at least, when Teddy came home. Maybe he'll have some news, even though I don't suppose they're anywhere near.'

A knock at the front door brought Pa quickly to his feet. 'I'll get that,' he said, and was gone before Grace could stop him. Still spritely, his hair may be receding now, but he could get out of a chair pretty swiftly. Within minutes he was back in the room and Pa, never a tall man, seemed even smaller as Teddy followed him, stooping a little to fit through the doorway.

In her hurry to stand, Grace's chair tipped backwards against the wall.

'Sorry Ma,' she said in reply to the woman's tutting, and sat back down again.

Pa moved across to the stool beside the range. 'Sit down, lad.' He waved to his chair as he turned.

Grace felt the blood rushing to her face. How much more shameful could her Pa be, giving up his chair for Teddy?

The words of Mrs Simpson were at the forefront of her mind. Although she had protested that working in an asylum was not something she would ever want to do, it was tempting to bring up the prospect, to feel her way, as it were.

'There's something I want to ask you Ma, Pa.' She stood again, thinking it would be to her advantage not to be sitting. They certainly wouldn't be expecting to hear what she was about to say. Looking around at their faces, she nearly held back, her courage deserting her.

'What is it, child?' Ma was wiping her hands on her apron and watching her with a light in her eyes.

Grace hesitated, suddenly realising Ma must think she was about to announce that Teddy had proposed. Now she wished she'd spoken to her parents before he'd arrived. She shifted her feet on the spot.

'Come on, then. Out with it.' Pa looked at Teddy as if he had the answer, then back to Grace. 'Although,' he went on, 'it's usual for the man to ask for permission, first.'

'Pa! It's not that.' Grace squirmed and looked first at her ma, then her pa. Avoiding eye contact with Teddy, she looked down at the table. 'Sorry, Teddy. Oh, this is so mortifying.'

'I'm sorry, I'm sure.' Pa sniffed. 'You had better get whatever it is off your chest then and put us all out of our misery.' He looked across the room at Teddy. 'I'm sure you'd like to know what it is on her mind, too. Unless, of course, you already know.'

Grace took a deep breath. 'Something happened today and Mrs Simpson told me I would make a good nurse. She said she would put in a word for me to start my training if I wanted to.'

'You a nurse?' Ma's eyes were wide, her hands on her hips.

'Yes, me, a nurse.' Grace looked straight at her Ma. 'What is wrong with that?'

'Nothing, I suppose, if you think you could do all those tasks - like washing people, and dressing wounds.'

'It won't be like that. Not exactly. If I do it.'

'Why do you think it would be different for you? You're not special, you know.'

'I know that, Ma. But Mrs Simpson thinks I'd make a good nurse.'

'You may well do so. No doubt she knows many young ladies from good families who have taken to the vocation, more fool them. But it's not for you. How would you afford the uniform?' She turned to the range and began to pull down the airer. 'Now come and help me fold the washing.'

'They provide the uniform, don't they?' Grace moved to the range and took down a towel, folding it as she spoke. 'I'm sure they provide the uniform. I can find out. Anyway, I'm only thinking about it.'

'Well, take your time girl.' Pa looked at her and nodded. 'Whatever you decide, make sure you know what you're taking on. It won't be easy, that's all I'm saying.'

'Thank you, Pa. I will.'

'And don't agree to anything until you have spoken to me again. Us I mean.' Ma looked at Pa, shrugging her shoulders. 'It's a terrible time to go into a profession like nursing, what with the war and all those soldiers coming home maimed. I would hate to think of you seeing all that.'

'It won't be like that, Ma.' Grace kept her eyes down, busily folding one of her father's shirts.

'What do you mean child?' Ma took the shirt from her. 'Why do you think it would be so different for you?'

'I won't be working in the main hospital, that's why. Mrs Simpson is a visitor to the Asylum in Milton. She told me I would be training to be a nurse for the mental defectives. It's a new training which is recognised now.'

'Well! You can put that out of your mind, young lady.' Pa shook his head. 'No girl of mine is going to enter that place.'

'Pa, please.' Grace could feel tears filling her eyes.

'You heard your father, Grace.' Ma took her hand. 'That place is not for the likes of us. Those who work there have... reputations. They are not good girls.'

'I can't believe you really think that.' Grace looked at Teddy for support. 'Teddy, you would support me, wouldn't you?'

Teddy coughed. 'You shouldn't go against your Ma and Pa,' he said. 'Let's go for a walk, shall we? Get a bit of fresh air?'

Feeling herself about to burst with indignation, Grace walked to the door, glaring at him. 'Come on then,' she said. 'I can't stay in here a moment longer.' She slammed the door on her way out.

'Sorry,' Teddy said before he too left.

'Talk some sense into her,' Pa shouted at the closing door.

Grace was already at the front gate by the time Teddy joined her. She spun around to face him.

'I'm sorry, Teddy.' Her eyes were brimming with tears. 'I only wanted to talk about the possibilities of doing something worthwhile. More exciting than working as a parlour-maid anyway. I see how my sister's life is, working in the munitions factory and I know I don't want that either. I want more. And when Mrs Simpson said I'd make a good nurse, it made me think - maybe she could be right.'

Teddy took her hand. 'Let's walk awhile. It'll clear your head and we can talk about it as we go along.'

Heading towards the sea, a stiff wind blew as they turned the last corner, nearly taking hold of Grace's hat that she'd hastily perched on her head as she'd left the house.

'Hold tight, Grace.' Teddy linked her arm in his, laughing.

Battling against the wind, they finally found shelter in one of the viewing points that looked out at the eastern end of the Isle-of-Wight, now disappearing in the gloom. Dark clouds fought for space in the sky and in the distance, sheets of rain could be seen attacking the surface of the angry waves.

Snuggling against Teddy, Grace relaxed in his arms. 'To be honest, Teddy, I don't really know what I want. This war has turned the world upside down, not only for those who go to war, but for us remaining here also. Women are taking on so many different roles now. It makes me feel I need to do more than just be a parlour-maid.'

'It's just the war making you unsettled. You will get over this, and the war will soon be over. It can't go on forever and then we can get married.'

'Maybe we should get married now. I can't imagine life without you, Teddy. Perhaps that would be the answer. It would certainly change my life if I were to have children.' She looked at the waves and shivered.

'I don't think it would be the answer.' Teddy sighed.

'Don't you want to marry me now?'

'I do want to marry you, Grace, I really do. But not whilst this madness is still going on. The war I mean. Being married to a soldier who's away at the front won't bring you the excitement you need and long for. I would hate to know you were at home alone, worrying about me.'

'I'll do that anyway, whether we're married or not. But I suppose you're right.'

'When I go back to the front, the thought of you wanting to marry me will keep me going.'

'I love you, Teddy.' Grace leaned closer and tilted her face to his. Their lips met in a light kiss before she moved away again. 'I hope you will support me if I decide to go ahead and train as a nurse.'

Teddy pulled away and looked at her face. 'How can you be a nurse if you are to be married?'

'When the war is over. That's what you said.'

'What happens if it ends in a few months? Or even in a year? You won't want to leave nursing once you've started.'

She took his hand and squeezed it. 'I don't know, Teddy. But I'm sure I have to do something more with my life than being a maid in someone else's house.'

'But why go to that madhouse to do it? You know it has a reputation - the attendants, as well as the patients. The work will be awful, looking after those imbeciles and mad men and women. I've seen what happens in madness and it's not something I would like to think of you facing.'

'I know what people say about the place, but I also know what Mrs Simpson tells me and I want to believe that the rumours and gossip are just that. As far as the patients go, I am honestly not sure what to expect. It scares me, yes, but it excites me too. And who knows - maybe I can make a difference and help a bit.'

Teddy shook his head. 'It's a big step to take, giving up your job to try something you're not sure of.'

'I haven't made my mind up yet,' Grace said. 'I intend to think about it. I just need to know you will approve of my decision, whatever that may be.'

'Very well, I suppose you'll do it anyway.' Teddy smiled at her. 'Come here and give me a hug, my brave, wonderful girl.'

Later that night, back in her tiny room in the attic of Mrs Simpson's house, Grace lay and stared at the window, watching the changing light from the moon as the clouds still battled in the night sky. Things had certainly changed since the start of this war, and when the Zeppelin had attacked the city no-one really felt completely safe at home again. She remembered the sound of gunfire in the night and the fear of people's faces the next morning. And afterwards, all the City streets were in darkness each evening, just in case it happened again.

Grace wondered where life would take her. Should she follow this new path, or stay in the relative warmth and comfort of cleaning the parlour and serving tea for Mrs Simpson? Could she bear the boredom of this, or should she take the plunge into a new direction in her life?

3

Grace hated the feel of sweat dripping down her chin. She was now doing two people's work since Mary had been sent home over a week ago. She couldn't really imagine the grief over Mary's loss and how it could affect her so much. She'd heard of people dying from a broken heart but had never really believed there was such a thing.

'Hurry up with that hot water, Bennett.' Mrs Amberley's gruff voice brought her back down to earth with a jolt. She grabbed hold of the heavy pan, in her haste forgetting to use the oven cloths. It only took a second for the pain to sink in. She screamed at the sudden shock.

'What are you doing, girl?'

'My hand. I've burnt myself!' Grace's head was reeling.

'Come and sit down.' Grace sat at the kitchen table whilst the cook fetched the butter. 'You are a silly thing. Where was your head, eh? Dreaming of your young man I suppose.' She took the butter from the dish and blobbed in onto Grace's hand. 'There, rub that in, it'll soothe the pain and help with the healing.'

Grace looked up as Mrs Simpson entered the room. 'Whatever is going on in here now? Not more bad news I hope.'

'Bennett has burnt her hand. I was just putting butter on it to help.'

Mrs Simpson crossed the room. 'Let me see.'

'I'm sorry Ma'am, I've been clumsy.' Grace held her hand up.

'That looks very sore. I'm not sure but I think we should have that looked at.'

Mrs Amberley bristled. 'I can't lose another worker in my kitchen. Surely it will be all right with a clean bandage on it?'

'Nonsense. We can't let it get worse, and if you continue working, it will certainly do that. Come along, Bennett, I will take you to the infirmary. It won't take long, and when we get back we can decide what's to be done about your tasks.'

Mrs Amberley sniffed in disapproval as the two women left the room.

The infirmary was busy and once Grace had given her name to the attendant on the desk, she was directed to a waiting area filled with chairs, most fully occupied.

'Oh, dear, Bennett. I fear we are in for a long wait.'

Grace looked around at the crowds of people.

'Please, Ma'am, I'll be alright now. My hand feels less sore. Shouldn't we just go. All these people here, and it's only a minor burn.'

'You can never say a burn is minor. If not treated properly it will get infected. No. You must stay and wait to be seen.' She looked around. 'However, I will have to leave you. I am sorry, but I have an appointment in an hour, and I can see we won't be seen before that.' She took some coins from her purse. 'Here's some money for the doctor and your fare to come home. I should think you could make your own way on the tram?'

'Yes, of course, Ma'am, and thank you for taking care of me.'

'I will see you later this afternoon, but you must take the rest of the day off.' And she was gone through the doors and out into the street.

Grace watched as she disappeared and then looked around the room again. Why were all these people here? Surely there couldn't be this many sick folk in Portsmouth. The room was warm and it was cold outside. Perhaps some of them had come in for shelter. She realised how folk were struggling with the hardship of the war. Coal was scarce and money even more so. With the main breadwinners gone, sitting in here for an hour or two might be the only place some of these poor people had to keep warm. Children huddled into their mothers, coughing and wiping their noses on their sleeves. Older children who should be in school were there too. She'd heard of the schools closing when the masters were called up into the army. There were women teachers but fewer to go around and some of those had been enticed to work in the munitions factory or the dockyard offices. Some of the schools were taking classes only on a few days of the week, others were so full that children had to take turns in coming to class.

Grace knew how sheltered her life was, with a loving family, a good wage coming in, and herself working in such a comfortable household with a good employer. She wondered why she was feeling so unsettled and just couldn't count her blessings.

Suddenly the main doors flew open and a screaming, struggling woman was bundled in, held firmly by two constables.

'Let me go, you bloody buggers!' The woman was yelling at them, kicking out furiously as she struggled to break away. All the faces in the room were turned towards her and several were laughing, some turned away, sheltering their children in their arms.

Grace felt the excitement rising in herself as she watched. Should she be feeling like this? It was almost as if she was enjoying the drama that was unfolding in front of her.

The woman broke free and ran towards her. Standing up, Grace caught the woman in her arms. Rather than struggle to break away again, the poor woman fell into her embrace and sobbed. Taken aback at both hers and the woman's response, Grace froze for a moment, then found herself making soothing noises. 'It's alright,' she said. 'There, sit down here, next to me.'

Before the woman could sit down, the two constables had rushed over, grabbing her once again. One of them roughly clamped a pair of handcuffs on her wrist and pulled her away from Grace. 'Sorry Miss,' he said. 'We'll soon have her safely put away.'

'What do you mean? What is the matter with her?' Grace asked. 'Where are you taking her?'

'We're going to have her looked at here in the infirmary, but she's far too dangerous to stay here for long. She'll be sent to the Asylum probably. Locked up for her own good, and for the safety of the public.'

'She seems very sad, and upset,' Grace said.

'Don't know about that, Miss. We only deal with what we see, and she's mad, there's no doubt about that.' They moved away, dragging the woman between them.

Grace watched as they disappeared through some double doors that led into a corridor. She shook her head as she heard the screaming start up once more.

Riding back to Mrs Simpson's on the tram, her hand neatly bound in clean bandages, Grace's thoughts drifted back to the woman. What could have been troubling her? Grace had seen people in troubled states before, states similar to how Mary had been when she'd learned of her sweetheart's death. But this woman today seemed to be past any help, and certainly should not have been man-handled and handcuffed in the way she had been. Something had passed through Grace at the moment when she'd held the woman. It was a strong need to help, to hold her until she had felt better.

Grace began to seriously wonder if perhaps Mrs Simpson was right and she could make a good nurse for those with troubled minds.

4

Walking around Canoe Lake near to the seafront had always been a favourite for the sisters. It was one of the few places in Portsmouth that seemed to be unchanged by the war.

Elsie was horrified when Grace told her of her thoughts about working in the asylum.

'You must be insane yourself if you think there's a future working in such a place. I really can't imagine you being there, amongst all those women,' Elsie said. 'We had one at the munitions factory a few months ago and she was terribly frightening. I can't imagine you being in a place filled with people like her.'

'I know, Elsie, I know, it seems like a strange thing to want to do. I do question myself too, but there's something inside pushing me towards it. I feel that it's there, waiting for me.'

'I can't see that you can be a nurse and still want to marry Teddy. It won't work, will it? I wish you'd come to the factory and work with us. We do have fun together. Even though the work is hard and monotonous. We chat and all the girls know how to have a good time. We have every evening off, can go home to our own beds and do what we want to do in our spare time. If you were a nurse, you'd be no better off than a parlour-maid.

You'd be stuck in that asylum all day and night with probably no time to yourself.'

'And no time for Teddy? I don't know why you're so concerned about him. I know you always had a crush on him, but really? Anyway, I'm sure there would be time off. And I'd be learning new skills, something I long for. Your work is dangerous in its own way, isn't it? I wouldn't want to be handling all that dangerous material.'

'We're not supposed to talk about that.' Elsie gave her a warning look.

'Don't worry, I wouldn't tell anyone else, although I'm sure more people know than you think. I've heard people calling you a "Canary Girl" behind your back, and everyone knows what causes that.'

Elsie shrugged her shoulders. 'Maybe. Anyway, I think you should come and have a look at the place before you make up your mind. Or are you just a snob? Too good to work in a factory?'

'I can't just turn up for a tour, can I. Don't be stupid.'

'No. What I meant is you should apply for an interview to work at the factory. You don't have to make up your mind about anything, but you could have a look for yourself before you decide.'

'I suppose there'd be no harm. But I will have a look at the asylum as well. Mrs Simpson said I can go with her when she next visits.'

'Really? I don't understand your desire to do this. It's ghoulish.'

'I know, you've said. I'll do as you suggest and apply for an interview at the factory, though. I'd like to see where you work and to meet some of your friends there. And I am not a snob.'

5

Grace looked out across the harbour towards Gosport. Two weeks had passed since she last saw Elsie. The brisk wind caught her hair, almost tearing it out from beneath her hat. 'Thank heavens for hat pins,' she said out loud to herself as she boarded the chain ferry. She was feeling slightly sick as the boat rocked under her feet. Or was it the nervousness of going for an interview for a job she knew she would never take? Tucking her hands into her pockets, Grace sat firmly on the bench on the side of the small craft. She was grateful the ferry couldn't break free from the chains, otherwise she imagined that they would be halfway to the Isle of Wight by now. Or swept right out to sea and on their way to France.

But of course, this was all in her colourful mind, and before long the ferry had arrived at Priddy's Hard, the passengers all disembarking onto the firm shore once again with Grace being caught up in the small crowd. She looked about her and wondered which was the way to the factory, and should she have bothered, and why was she here wasting her afternoon off anyway?

Telling herself not to be so silly, she soon found directions to the factory office and before long was knocking on the door, waiting to be let in.

It was noisy. Women in long overalls, their hair caught up in caps, sat at their desks, writing in large ledgers. Some were working on tracing plans, others were sat at typewriters, their fingers clunking across the keys. A series of windows overlooked the factory beyond where Grace could see more rows of women, similarly dressed, all busy at their tasks, some together at tables, and others on lathes or other machinery that she was unfamiliar with. There were a few men amongst them, and one or two walking along the row, overseeing the work.

As Grace looked at the heads of the women, one of them looked up and grinned at her. It was Elsie. She gave a little wave and several of the others all turned to look at Grace. Soon they were all waving and smiling. But Grace was soon brought back to the moment by a coughing from behind her and the touch of a hand on the small of her back.

'Well, this must be Miss Bennett.' The man was tall, dressed in tweeds with a white collar and tie. His hair was greying and the lines on his forehead were set in a permanent frown. His smile didn't quite reach his eyes as he spoke, whilst holding out his hand in greeting. 'I am very pleased to meet you, Miss. I'm Mr Medford, the manager of this establishment. Please come this way and we can have a little chat.' He bowed slightly and led the way into a room at the far end.

Grace smiled as she wondered why a munitions factory would be thought of as an establishment. It sounded very grand. She noticed the ladies at their desks glancing at her as she passed.

One of them smiled and nodded as she reached the door. Their eyes met for a moment and Grace thought to herself how attractive the woman was. She looked away, embarrassed. Others just looked up quickly then kept their heads down, focusing on their work. But Mr Medford was waiting at the door.

'Come along, my dear,' he said as he held the door open. 'Welcome to my domain.'

'Thank you, Sir.'

'Please, call me Mr Medford. I like to think of my workers as part of the family, and I am sure you will soon feel a part of this family too.' He moved to sit behind the desk in the centre of the small room and indicated to Grace to take the chair facing it. He pulled a sheet of paper from one of the drawers and looked across at her, his eyes wandering from her face down to her bosom and back. 'Now, my dear, let's have a look at you. You look like you could be a strong young woman, able to take on any task?'

Grace shifted in her seat. 'I'm used to hard work Sir - sorry, Mr Medford. I've been working as a parlour-maid but I can do heavy lifting, and I'm used to carrying coals and scrubbing floors.'

'I'm sure you are,' he said as he smiled at her, then stood and walked around to the front of the desk. 'Let me look at you properly. Please stand up.'

Grace looked at him wondering why she had to stand when he'd only just asked her to sit.

'It's only that I need to see if you will fit in here. No need to be shy.' He held his hand out to her.

Ignoring his hand, Grace stood up. He took a step closer, and she realised there was no way of stepping back as she was jammed up closely to the chair. She could feel his breath on her as he spoke.

'Yes, you will do very nicely,' he said as he stepped back a pace.

'Excuse me, Mr Medford, but are you going to interview me?' Grace wondered if this was how he carried out his business when men were the only employees. 'And perhaps I could have a tour of the works?'

'I think we can dispense with the formality of questions. You will be trained and I don't expect you have any previous experience of such work, have you?'

'I would still like to have a look around before I make a decision.'

She sensed him bristling for a moment, then he moved to the door. 'Very well young lady, your wish is my command.' He ushered her through the door and soon they were walking back through the general office.

Grace could have sworn that she heard a snigger as they passed one of the desks but when she looked around no-one was looking at her. At the end of the office was the door to the workshop and once it was opened the noise of the factory blasted into Grace's awareness like a wave.

She followed behind Mr Medford as he made his way down the staircase to the factory floor. When he reached halfway down, he stopped and turned. 'This is the workshop where you will be working. These are my girls,' he announced. One or two of the women looked up, but most kept their heads down, intent on their work.

As they walked on along the rows, he suddenly stopped behind Elsie. Grace could see that her sister's back flinched as he touched her on the shoulder. 'This is your sister, I believe, Miss Bennett? Two Miss Bennett's, how will I know which is which?' He looked at Grace and grinned, his teeth glinting yellow in his hungry looking mouth.

'I'm sorry, Mr Medford. I'm not really sure this is for me,' Grace said.

'What did you say?' he shouted. 'You really will have to learn to speak up in here, my dear, or you'll never be heard above the noise.'

'Never mind,' Grace shouted back.

'Let's go back to my office where we can talk properly,' he said as he walked back to the staircase in front of her.

Grace couldn't get up the stairs quickly enough and once at the top, she turned to see Elsie looking up at her. Grace waved and swiftly left the noise of the workshop, closing the door behind her in relief. She looked around the office at all the women working there before making her way towards the room at the end, where Mr Medford was waiting.

She stopped before the door, and took a breath. 'Thank you for the tour, Mr Medford, but I don't think working here is quite right for me. I beg your pardon if I have wasted your time.'

'I'm sorry to hear that, and can assure you that you wouldn't find a better position anywhere else in Gosport or Portsmouth. Still, off you go back to your parlour-maid duties. I expect you would have found the work here too hard, a pretty young thing like you.'

'I am sure you are right, but nevertheless, I shall do my best to find the right position, which I can assure you, will not be as a mere parlour-maid.' She shook his hand and turned to sweep out of the office and soon was outside again waiting for the ferry back to Portsmouth. The sun was peeping through the clouds as she stepped aboard the boat and her heart felt lighter as she looked across the water.

6

She was glad to be back at work the next morning, and was wondering whether Mr Medford had been right and she would be better off just accepting this was to be her life. It's not so bad, she thought, at least I know where I am here. Looking around the kitchen, she sighed. The work was hard, especially as she was still doing Mary's tasks in the kitchen, peeling potatoes, keeping the range alight, washing all those pots and pans every day. Then she still had to sweep the floors upstairs, polish the furniture and keep the fires going. Mrs Simpson was a good employer and helped as much as her busy life would allow, turning down her own bed and tidying away her clothes. At least the dirties all went to the laundry once a week, so there was no heavy washing to do. Although they'd had no children, and Mr Simpson often had to work in his London office, there was still much to do for a woman of her standing in town and when she'd taken on the role of official hospital visitor, Mrs Simpson had become passionate about wanting to help young women who could be good nurses.

Mrs Amberley, the cook, was a kind soul who had taken on more of the tasks in the kitchen to save Grace from having too much to do. Still, it was hard work all the same.

'The Mistress wants a special supper tonight. She has four guests coming, so we need to be ready by four o'clock to set the table and prepare the plates for the courses. I'll need you to check the glass-wear is all spotless too.'

Grace sighed. 'I'd best get upstairs and finish the dining room, then. And I need to check the drawing room fire and run a duster across the piano too.'

'Yes, well make sure you're quick about it as I need you down here to do the veg.'

'I'll work as quick as I can,' Grace said, wiping her hands on her apron.

'I know you will, and I'm sorry. I just wish I knew when Mary's coming back to work. She can't keep off for much longer, surely.' Mrs. Amberley shook her head.

'I'll pop round and visit her when I get the chance, see how she is,' Grace replied. 'I'll be glad when she comes back too.'

'Good. Now, let's get on with it.'

It was the following afternoon and Grace had been sent on an errand to the Post Office.

'Perhaps I could make a quick visit to Mary, whilst I'm out Ma'am,' Grace suggested.

'Good idea,' Mrs Simpson said. 'I was thinking we should check in on her, but I have been so busy recently, and haven't found the time. And thinking about it, it might be nicer for her if it's you visiting rather than me.'

'I would like to see her. I'm hoping she'll welcome a visit.'

'I think it would be a good thing to do. Please give her our regards and tell her she would be welcome to come back, but only when she's fully recovered. It must have been a terrible shock.'

'Yes, Ma'am, I will. Thank you, Ma'am.'

'Let me know how you get on, won't you?'

'Of course,' and Grace left the room to go on her way.

The houses in Esslemont Road all looked the same, and soon she was standing outside Mary's home. She knocked on the door and waited, hoping someone would open the door soon as it had started to drizzle with rain. She shivered and drew her shawl around her shoulders, tucking her hands in for warmth.

The door opened and Mrs James smiled. 'It's Grace Bennett, isn't it? From Mrs Simpson's. Come in dear, and get warm.'

Grace stepped into the small passageway. Looking about she saw that the house was very similar to her own parents' abode. 'Thank you. I've come to see how Mary is.'

'Of course, come through to the parlour.' Mrs James led her to a door at the end of the passage.

Grace felt the warmth of the room as she opened the door into a cheery back-room, filled with the aroma of home baking. Mary was sat beside the range, her face lit up on seeing who the visitor was. She stood. 'It's so good to see you, Grace. I'm driving myself mad with boredom doing nothing all day. Sorry Ma.'

Grace took her hands and gave them a squeeze. 'It's good to see you too, I have missed you.' She laughed. 'And not only because there's a lot more work for me. I've missed our chats and your smiling face.'

'I think I've forgotten how to smile lately, and I miss you too.'

'Do take a seat, Grace,' Mrs James said. She was a jolly looking woman, her auburn hair in a bun, her rounded figure comfortable in a plain dress caught at the waist by a long apron. 'Yes, sit down and I'll pour some tea,' she added.

'That's very kind but please don't take any trouble. I won't be able to stay more than half an hour I'm afraid,' Grace took the chair on the other side of the range.

'It won't be any trouble. The tea is already brewed. You must have known. I'll pour it and leave you two to chat. Now keep an eye on those buns Mary. They've only just gone in and will need to come out in ten minutes.'

Left alone with their tea, the two women sat in silence for a while. Grace looked around the room and wondered how to bring up the subject of Mary's sweetheart.

'Did Mrs Simpson send you round?' Mary was the first to speak.

'Not exactly, I asked her if I could pop in. I was on an errand to the Post Office to buy some stamps and I thought it would be a good chance to see you. Mrs Amberley and I have been talking. We do miss you, but I would understand if you weren't ready to come back. It must have been a terrible shock for you, learning about your Johnny.'

'It was, and I don't suppose I'll ever recover. I've been feeling numb and for a while I couldn't even get out of bed. Ma has been patient but lately she's started to encourage me to do more. Like the baking. We don't really need the buns, what with flour being so short, but here I am, wasting time baking.'

'Do you think you'll be able to come back to work soon? Sorry, I'm sounding very selfish and it's not really that. I just think you would fare better now if you were back in your normal routine.'

Mary looked at her, then out of the window into the back yard. 'I don't know, is the honest answer. I really don't know.'

'I'm sorry, I shouldn't have pressured you. It was stupid of me. The last thing I want is for you to feel you have to do anything you're not ready for.'

'No. You're right,' Mary said. 'I have to pull myself together soon enough. I think of all the women, wives, mothers and sweethearts in this town who have lost their loved ones to the war and I realise I'm the one being selfish. I have to stop thinking about myself and get on with it. Ma tells me I'm lucky we weren't wed and I don't have children to worry about. I suppose there is some truth in that.' She shook her head as a tear fell and she wiped it away with the back of her hand.

'I'm sorry, Mary. I didn't mean to upset you,' Grace leaned forward in her chair.

'You didn't, Grace. I'm glad you came to see me and I'm glad you're encouraging me to come back to work. I have been worrying about coming back. I know I behaved very badly on that last day. I can't imagine what you all must have been thinking about me.'

'I think we all understood how terrible the shock must have been, and you won't get over it for a long time, I don't suppose. But everyone is looking forward to having you back. Me especially. I miss our working together. And I know Mrs Amberley will be more than pleased to see you. I'm a poor substitute in the kitchen, you know. Even Mrs Amberley has said that she misses your pastry.'

'Fine praise indeed! But she hardly ever lets me do such important tasks. Usually it's all the scrubbing, peeling, chopping and washing those great big pans of hers.'

'Maybe it's a time of change for all of us,' Grace said, grinning to herself.

'I doubt that. But I will come back. First thing tomorrow.'

'Wonderful, and I'm sure Mrs Simpson will be pleased to hear it too.'

As soon as Grace arrived back at the house, Mrs Simpson rang the bell.

'How was she?' she asked as soon as Grace had handed her the stamps she'd purchased. 'Poor James, I have been thinking about her.'

'I think she is very much improved Ma'am. She was pleased to see me and to hear from you and Mrs Amberley too.'

'And did you speak about her sweetheart? It must have been such a shock.'

'It was, of course, and I think it will take her a long time to come to terms with losing him. We didn't speak much about him. I think it would have re-opened a wound perhaps too soon. Still, James did say she would be happy to come back to work and has told me she'd be back tomorrow. That is, if it would suit yourself of course.'

'Really? That is good news. Have you told Mrs Amberley yet?'

'No, Ma'am. I came straight up here after coming in. I'm sure she'll be pleased though.'

'Indeed, she will,' Mrs Simpson agreed. 'Now, I am glad to have this opportunity to talk to you about something else. I most probably will regret this, as I don't want to lose you either, but I still think it would be in your interests to seriously consider my suggestion to do your nurse training.'

'I'm still thinking about it, Ma'am. I have to tell you though, that my parents don't approve. I've tried to talk to them about it and they're adamant they do not give me their blessing.'

'I'm sorry to hear that. Is there anything I can do to help persuade them?'

'Not really, Ma'am. I will make up my own mind though.'

'Well, good for you, Bennett. Good for you.' She paused then added. 'Although I would not want to encourage you to go against your parents in this.'

'Please don't worry about that, Ma'am. My parents will come round to whatever I decided in the end.'

Mrs Simpson looked at her. 'I'm visiting the asylum next Wednesday. Perhaps you would like to come along with me. I could show you some of the wards. You could meet one of the attendants, or nurses as they are now being called. Maybe that will help you to make a decision.'

Grace felt a sudden chill in her stomach. What was she getting herself into? 'I'm not sure,' she said.

'It's only a visit, Bennett. You don't have to make any decisions based on one visit. And you will be perfectly safe. There are many stories about the asylum, I know, but it's not at all terrifying.'

'I am sure you are right.' Grace looked out of the window into the well-kept garden at the rear of the house. 'Very well, I will come with you. Thank you.'

7

The day was bright and clear. Grace had worked as quickly as she could to get her morning tasks completed early enough to leave the house with Mrs Simpson at ten o'clock. She was glad of the sunshine as they left. She could not have imagined wanting to go to such a place if the skies had been dark and ominous. As the carriage approached along the tree-lined driveway, the main building of the asylum looked down upon them with the sunshine bouncing off the windows almost in a friendly way.

She felt herself tremble and hesitate as they reached the building, but Mrs Simpson led the way up the steps and ushered her through the revolving doors into the reception area.

The first thing she noticed was the smell of bees-wax polish, overlaying something else, something more pungent. She couldn't quite place it, although it was something she knew she'd never forget. Wooden panels surrounded them on every wall and to the right was a grand sweeping staircase which she was told led to a conference room. They could have been entering any country manor house in Hampshire. Not that Grace had been in any manor houses, but she had seen pictures of them in the library. She looked around in awe at the portraits on the walls of distinguished gentlemen.

They were greeted by the Medical Superintendent, the asylum Chaplain and the Matron in charge of the nurses and their patients' care.

'May I introduce Miss Bennett,' Mrs Simpson spoke to the Doctor, an imposing man despite his average height. 'This gentleman is in charge here, Doctor Devine.'

He turned to Grace. 'I am pleased to meet you, young lady. I hear you may be considering training as an attendant - or rather a nurse? We have had some success with our training of young women to become good nurses for the insane.' He offered his hand.

Grace blushed as she took it and they shook hands. 'I'm not sure yet Sir, but I am pleased to be here today. I hope I won't be in the way at all.'

'Certainly not.' He turned. 'And this is our Matron; she would be in charge of your work and your well-being, Matron Anderson. Any problems you experience should be taken to her.

'How do you do?' Grace held out her hand to the woman who took it in her firm grip. She was dressed in a red uniform and wore her lacy cap like a crown.

'Well done, young lady. I will look forward to training you.' Matron stepped back and moved to the door. 'Well we must get along. There is much to see. This way.'

The Chaplain, in a grey suit and a bashful smile, looked at Grace as he shook her hand. 'I'm the Reverend Jennings. Pleased to meet you,' he said as they hurried along behind the Matron and Dr Devine. Grace nodded to him and followed on behind.

They walked through long corridors with walls of brown and cream, doors leading off onto the various wards. Mrs Simpson walked with Grace, chatting to her along the way. 'This is the female side of the asylum. I thought it would be best to let you see this side of the building for if you did come to work here, you'd only ever be working on this side.'

'You mean, I wouldn't work with the male patients?' Grace wondered.

'That's right. Only female attendants and nurses work with female patients. You won't be working with any male staff either, except for Dr Devine, of course, and the other medical officer, Dr Blake. The asylum is completely segregated. It's for the safety of the patients, although they do get to meet on special occasions such as the regular balls which are held monthly on a Friday evening, and in church on Sundays.'

'What kinds of treatments are there for the patients?'

'Several, including medication, talking therapies, and of course, the raising of morale with physical tasks such as needlework. But you will learn all about that should you decide to join the nursing staff.'

'Here we are, ladies.' Dr Devine was at the door labelled M Ward. 'We shall begin here.' He rang the bell at the side of the door and waited. Within half a minute the door was opened to the clanking of keys and there stood a tall nurse in a crisp white apron over a dark grey dress. Her hair was neatly in place underneath a white cap which covered most of her head.

There was an unexpected quietness in the wide gallery they moved into, which was well lit by the tall windows all along one side. On the other, were several doors leading to small siderooms, the private bedrooms for the patients. A woman was mopping the floor. She looked up at them as they passed, smiled and then went back to her work.

At the far end was a wider space with chairs and tables neatly arranged. To the left of this room was a door leading to a dormitory. As they walked through the dormitory Grace could see how crowded the beds were, pushed closely together so that one would need to climb in from the foot of the bed and once in, there would be little chance of getting up again without disturbing the neighbouring patients. She wondered at how difficult it would be to make all those beds. There must have been more than fifty of them.

At the end of this room another door led to the bathroom and lavatories. The bathroom, a vast high-ceilinged room, two baths in the middle of the floor and a row of wash basins along one wall. Grace shivered at the thought of having to bathe in such a room, with other people wandering in and out without any thought to privacy or dignity.

'Where are all the patients?' she asked. 'It seems so quiet in here. Not what I was expecting.'

Dr Devine looked at her before answering. 'The ladies are all out working at their tasks. This ward is one of the quieter ones during the day. The patients have been here for a while and are suitable for moral treatment. It means that they are given worthwhile tasks to do that suit their abilities and temperament. These are designed to help raise their confidence and to relieve the insanity that brought them into the asylum.'

'I see,' said Grace. 'At least I think I do. So, insanity is not incurable then? I understood your patients were locked up for their safety and were often forgotten about by their families.'

'I believe there are different types of insanity, some of which are difficult to cure. But with many types we are able to help the patient recover and to live with their difficulties back in their own homes again. Insanity can be caused by many things. For example, the effects of war on the mind can cause what some call shell-shock. There has been some work done on this condition and many men have recovered from it completely.'

'Really? What about women's maladies? Can women recover from madness?' Grace thought about her friend Mary and the outburst she'd had when hearing about her Johnny's death. She'd wondered if Mary would ever fully recover.

'It depends on what the cause is. Insanity is not inherent in any one person, but can be caused by events in one's life. A sudden loss of a loved one, or a child, can be a trigger to bringing on madness which can be reverted back to normality if one is taken out of the situation, given good food, exercise, fresh air and something worthwhile to do.'

'The asylum helps its patients by giving them meaningful tasks to occupy their minds,' Mrs Simpson added. 'The ladies in this ward go to work in the sewing room, and the laundry, or they help the farm workers with light tasks in the fields. Some stay on the ward and do small sewing jobs here, or help with keeping the ward clean and tidy.'

'Yes,' continued Dr Devine. 'We grow all our own crops here, keep cattle and pigs and even provide food for the people of Portsmouth which has been essential during these times of war and the rationing of food.'

'That is wonderful,' Grace said.

'The men work in the woodwork shop, the farms and other workshops. We have a cobbler here, a tailor, a butcher, a baker. There are no end of places where our patients can be helped to achieve their full potential.' Dr. Devine was clearly proud of their achievements. 'Now, I think it would be a good idea for you to see one of the less settled wards. We don't want you to get the idea that it is all calm and plain sailing here.'

Grace looked at Mrs. Simpson who smiled back at her reassuringly. 'Don't worry, Bennett, it may be a shock when you first enter the ward. It's the noise mostly and it might be unexpected after being in this quieter ward. You have to remember that the patients on this ward are on the road to recovery, whilst in the one we will shortly be entering, the ladies are more disturbed, have only been in the asylum for a short while and haven't had a chance to settle in yet.'

Grace frowned.

'Don't worry too much dear. It's only fair that you see the more difficult side of the work, but you won't be working on A Ward until you have had some experience and training.'

They had soon left M Ward behind and were moving along the corridor once again.

'A Ward is always more troublesome,' the chaplain stressed. 'Please do not be alarmed. You will quickly become used to being amongst madness.'

Grace felt her stomach churning in anticipation. What had she gotten herself into?

She wondered if she could make her excuses and leave now, but it would be a shame not to see it through as well as being extremely embarrassing.

They were at the door already. She held her breath and waited.

Although she had been warned, the noise as the door opened was still a shock. More than the noise, a blast of stale hot air hit her senses. It was nothing like she'd ever before experienced. There were women everywhere it seemed. Moving about, some glaring at them, others smiling as they passed, seemingly curious as to who these strangers in their midst could be. Grace felt herself shrinking inside as she tried to stand behind the doctor and close enough to Mrs Simpson to feel safer.

The nurse who had opened the door for them marched on ahead until they reached the ward office which was at the centre of the long gallery, similar to M ward in layout but with a completely different atmosphere. 'Please do come in,' she said.

The room was small, hardly big enough to fit five people. Glass windows were on two sides, giving a view to both ends of the ward. Grace could see into the lounge area. She was told it was the Day Room, not necessarily for lounging in, although there were some comfortable chairs and sofas. A larger part of the area was furnished with tables and chairs. Some women were sitting at the tables, working on sewing tasks. Others were walking about, weaving in and out of the room and into the long gallery behind. There was a piano along one wall, but no music ready on the stand. As in M Ward, the walls were painted dark brown at the lower part and cream at the top. Grace wondered if this was a practical measure to keep the walls from looking grubby. Higher up were some framed pictures, scenes of the countryside. It certainly wasn't as forbidding as she had expected.

'Do take a seat,' the nurse indicated the chairs which had been set in the office for the visitors.

The committee were there to inspect the asylum, to ensure that treatment of the patients was good, the conditions were appropriate, and all was well with the staff. They assessed the cleanliness of the wards and checked that all the rules were kept. Grace had been told all of this by Mrs Simpson on the journey to the asylum. She sat quietly whilst the Doctor asked questions, and Mrs Simpson made notes, all the time looking out into the ward at the women and the attendant who was overseeing them.

Could this really be for me? Grace thought. It was frightening but also exciting. She wondered if she could be happy working as a parlour-maid after she'd seen what else there was a woman could do in the modern world. Suddenly, a patient rushed up to the window and thrust her face at the glass, glaring in at Grace. 'Help me! Help me! Get me out of this madhouse, please!'

Grace jumped back, immediately shocked that she would be chosen by this woman who was peering in at her, her wild eyes begging Grace to take notice. Straight away an attendant was there, shouting at the woman to stop. 'Ellie! Get away from there and behave yourself,' she said as she dragged her from the window. The woman called Ellie pulled away from the attendant's grip and threw herself into a nearby chair where she curled up and sobbed to herself. Sitting beside her, the attendant stroked the woman's hair, soothing the mad outburst from her.

Whilst all of this was happening, the rest of the women carried on as though nothing untoward was occurring. Grace looked on aghast, again wondering what she thought she was doing here.

'Are you alright Bennett?' Mrs Simpson asked. 'I hope this little scene hasn't put you off.'

Grace thought for a moment. Had it put her off? She wasn't completely sure. 'I don't know,' she admitted. 'I can see this would be very challenging work for me, but a part of me is telling me I should do it anyway.'

'You look like a robust young woman,' Doctor Devine said. 'And you seem to be intelligent and not too fazed by what you see here. Unless of course, you are a good actress.' He laughed at that.

'Thank you, Sir,' said Grace. 'I'm no actress. It's only that I am not used to such excitement in my working life, nor in my private life either. A part of me is keen to have a go at being a nurse, whilst another part of me is telling me this can't be for the likes of me.'

'You wouldn't lose anything by giving it a try, dear,' Mrs Simpson said. 'How about if I promise to keep your position open for you and you come here for a month's trial. Just to see how you fare?'

Grace glanced at the window again and realised she could see her reflection in the glass. Her eyes seemed almost as wild as the mad woman's. She turned back to Mrs Simpson. 'I really don't know if I'd be any good as a nurse,' she said.

'Nonsense. You cannot let yourself think that. But I won't try to persuade you today. We must get you home and you can take your time to think about it more fully. How does that sound to you?'

'Of course, and thank you for allowing me the chance to visit and to see what the conditions are like. I promise I will give it a lot of thought.'

Later that night, lying in her narrow bed at the top of the house in Craneswater Avenue, Grace closed her eyes, but she could still see the faces of the women in A ward, milling about. She felt herself drawn to finding out more about those poor souls. There was an excitement in her belly as she imagined herself working in that place with those people. She would be wearing the dark dress with the long white apron, her hair tidily scraped into the crisp white cap. Was it normal to feel such excitement about a job? But it would be more than just a job. People said nurses had a calling - was this what was happening to her?

8

The afternoon was cold, a bitter wind cutting through even the heaviest coat. The two sisters were walking along the promenade and chatting. The waves rushed at the shingle beach and Grace could taste the salt in the air.

'I know I'll only have a short time at home with you all,' Grace said. 'But I am looking forward to Christmas Day. We can celebrate together, and I'll be home in the afternoon for a few hours on Christmas Eve.'

'I don't know why you didn't take the job in the factory. You'd have had two whole days off and we could have more time. What happened to you anyway? I cannot understand you sometimes.'

Grace sighed. 'It didn't feel right, that's all.' She paused, then went on. 'To be honest, I felt uncomfortable with Mr Medford. I felt he was a little too familiar with me.'

'Really? Well, I'm afraid that's what he is like with all the girls. Yes, he does make me feel uncomfortable too, sometimes terribly so. A few days ago, he caught me in the yard to the lav's and as I passed him, he brushed up against me. It felt wrong but was over so quickly I hardly had time to protest. You have to get used to such behaviour when working with men.'

'Surely that can't be right?'

'Of course it's not right, but it's the way of the world. I'll just make sure I avoid such situations in the future. That's all one can do.' Elsie looked out at the sea, then back at Grace. 'I don't suppose anything like that has ever happened to you?'

'Certainly not,' Grace retorted. 'Although Mr Medford got rather too close to me in his office when I was there. I decided there and then I could never work with someone like him. Where I work, we are all women. Mr Simpson is the only male in the household and he spends most of his time working in London with the government. When he is home, I hardly see him and he always behaves like the perfect gentleman, which is what he is I suppose.'

'Well then, you are the lucky one. Perhaps you should give up all ideas of changing your job.'

'I'm still not completely sure, but I am favouring more and more on becoming a nurse. I know you don't approve, and I don't really want to keep discussing it. Let's just enjoy being together on this beautiful afternoon.'

Elsie took her arm as they walked briskly on. 'Freezing afternoon, you mean.'

'It feels good to me,' said Grace. 'Perhaps I'm just excited. Soon Teddy will be home on Christmas leave.'

'I don't know why you two don't get wed. Maybe that is what you need in your life, a young family to care for.'

Grace froze. 'Certainly not! Not yet, anyway. All right, I did think so at one time, but there's too much I want to do with my life. I admit I don't know exactly what I want to do, and one day

I would love to have children, but not whilst this awful war is still on.'

'I'm sorry, I understand you feeling like that. Do you think the war will soon be over?'

'To be honest, I don't see an end to it. Which is why I am holding back,' she said. 'But it was me who wanted to marry Teddy when he was last on leave and he talked me out of it. He was right of course. It would have been awful bringing a child into a world where there is no certainty of having two parents. What if Teddy is killed? How would I cope?'

'I think you would, whatever happened. You're a strong woman.'

'Don't you start,' Grace snapped. 'I had enough of that strong woman nonsense from Mrs Simpson when she was talking to me about working as a nurse at the asylum.'

'She's right though. But I don't want to think of you working there.'

'It's not so bad you know. It's whether I could make a difference and whether I could cope with the long hours. Oh, I don't know. Let's not talk about it anymore today. Come along, we can just catch the tram from the pier and get home in time for a cuppa before I have to get back.'

'Alright, but I will say just one more thing,' Elsie looked at her sister. 'Be careful you don't let Teddy go. He's a lovely young man, you know. A good catch, as they say.'

'I know, I know,' Grace said.

A few days later, Christmas Eve, and it was snowing. Grace looked out of the window of the drawing room and watched the white flakes falling. The trees in the front garden were beginning to be laden and everywhere was white - white sky, white ground, the walls around the garden looked like they'd been iced like a Christmas cake. Grace felt like a small child again, excited that it was snowing, excited about it being Christmas Eve but more than that, she was excited to know she would be seeing Teddy later that afternoon.

'Good morning, Bennett.' Mrs Simpson had come into the room quietly without her noticing. 'Isn't the snow beautiful? You must be quite excited this morning. Isn't your Teddy coming home on leave today?'

'Yes Ma'am. Sorry Ma'am. I was just looking out at the snow. A white Christmas!'

'It brings a kind of magic to the occasion, doesn't it?' Mrs Simpson stared out at the white scene outside. 'I do hope you have a wonderful Christmas with your family and your sweetheart.'

'Thank you, Ma'am. I hope that your Christmas is a good one, too. Mr Simpson is coming home today, too, isn't he?'

'Yes, he should be home later today.'

'I'd best get on, Ma'am. There's still lots to be done downstairs. Sorry Ma'am.' She bobbed a curtsy and left the room.

Mrs Amberley looked at Grace as she came into the kitchen. 'So there you are, girl,' she said. 'I thought you'd got lost up there.'

'It's snowing,' Grace said.

Mary screamed in delight. 'Snow, a white Christmas, magical!'

'There's no time for all that. We've still got a lot of things to get ready for the day tomorrow and you won't be going home until it's all done.'

'Can't we just go out and have a quick look, please, Mrs Amberley?'

'Oh, for goodness sake, go along then. But straight back in, no playing in the snow.'

Mary gave a little screech of delight again, wiping her hands as she skipped out of the door. Grace smiled to herself as she followed her into the back yard. She stood looking up at the sky as the flakes of snow fell onto her face and eyelashes. 'This is wonderful, Mary.'

Mary gathered a fistful of snow and threw it into the air. 'It makes me feel maybe there's some hope for the future after all.'

'I certainly hope so,' said Grace, looking up at the sky as the flakes fell onto her face. She thought of her brothers, still somewhere in a trench. Was it snowing there, too? How would they survive this war? She shook herself back to the present. 'Come along. We'll be in trouble if we don't get on with our work, and I want to get home this evening.'

Mary took her hand and squeezed it. 'I didn't think I would ever look forward to Christmas again. I'm not saying I will feel like this tomorrow, but today I feel there is some hope.'

'You have a wise head on your young shoulders, Mary, and I wish you a very pleasant, if not Merry Christmas.'

9

The train station was busy with people bustling about. Some had travelled from Chichester, while others, like Grace, were waiting for the train to come in from London. The platforms had been swept clear of snow and the skies had cleared of cloud. Bright sunshine reflected from the snow on the nearby roofs. Grace strained to see down the track, watching as it disappeared around the curve away from Fratton Station. She felt the excitement rising, hoping he would still feel the same way for her as he had before. His letters had been few and there was always doubt in Grace's mind. What if he had stopped loving her? Perhaps he's met someone else - a fancy foreign woman she could never compete with? Had the war changed him? Should she run away now whilst there was still time?

But the train was coming. It was too late to move away now with all those other people waiting for their loved ones. Grace shifted on her feet, straightened her hat which had come askew on her head, and took a deep breath. 'What will be will be,' she heard herself speaking out loud.

The engine pulled to a painful sounding halt, the station was filled with clouds of steam and soon, out of the crowds of soldiers, and the smell of burning coal, there he was, standing in front of her. Dropping his bag at his feet, he swept Grace up into his arms and swung her round in delight.

'Darling girl! It's wonderful to see you.' Holding her close, he gave her a kiss on the cheek.

'Really, Teddy,' Grace berated him as she pushed him away. 'Not here in public. Can't you wait until we are alone?'

Teddy looked about him at other couples who were embracing and laughed. 'I hardly think anyone here would be staring at us,' he said. 'I haven't stopped thinking about you and the last time we were together. You will never know how many times I've wished we'd got married before I went away.'

'I think about you all the time too, and I've missed you terribly, more than you can imagine, Teddy. But you are here now, thank heavens. Let's get you home. The family are all waiting to see you.'

Teddy's home was only a short walk from Fratton Station, in Purbrook Road. They walked together hand in hand and soon turned the corner into the street. Grace could see Mrs Evans standing outside the open front door, waving at them as they hurried along. Teddy let go of Grace's hand and quickened his pace, rushing towards his mother, throwing his bag down and taking her up in the same way he'd done with Grace at the station.

'Put me down at once,' his mother cried. 'Let's get indoors. It's freezing out here and we're letting the cold air into the house.'

'Sorry, Ma. It's so good to see you.' He picked up his bag, turned to Grace and ushered her into the house behind his mother.

A wonderful aroma of baking mince-pies was mixed with steam from a bubbling pot on the range as they entered the back parlour. 'I've been baking ready for tomorrow,' she said. 'And that's the Christmas pudding in that pot. It's made the room into quite a steam bath I am afraid. Now let's all sit down, and I will make some tea.'

'Thank you, Mrs Evans,' Grace said. 'You are so kind.'

'Not at all.' She took the kettle to fill it from the tap in the scullery leading off the back of the house. Grace felt the cold rush of air as she opened the door and glanced in at the stone-flagged floor and the stone sink against the back wall.

Grace thought about her schooldays. She had known Teddy ever since they both went to Penhale Road School. She'd hated school but had loved getting to know other children and Teddy had been her first friend when she started all those years ago. It was some time later, when they were both young adults that they had started walking out together and in the past year it was accepted that one day they would marry. Perhaps if the war hadn't got in the way they may have been married already. But things had changed now, and the world would never be the same again.

'The kettle won't take long to boil,' Mrs Evans said. 'I've some things to get on with upstairs so I'll leave you two to catch up. Perhaps you could make the tea when it's ready, Grace.'

'Yes of course, and thank you.'

'You know where the cups are, don't you?' And Mrs Evans left the room through the doorway to the staircase.

Teddy looked at Grace and grinned. 'Good old Ma, she always knows when three's a crowd.'

Grace laughed as she looked back at him. 'It is so good to have you home, Teddy. Now you may kiss me.'

'About time too,' he said, as he leaned closer to her and touched his lips to hers. 'You are a wonderful girl, Grace. I do love you so.'

'I love you too, Teddy. I wish we had more time than just a few days together. Even less than that as I have to be back at Mrs Simpson's in another hour and won't be released until tomorrow afternoon.'

'Really? I'd have thought they'd give you the whole of Christmas Day off.'

'Someone has to do for them, and Christmas Day is another day's work like any other. I'm lucky they let us have the afternoon and evening off really. Some places make their staff work all day at Christmas and don't give them time off until Boxing Day afternoon.' She looked around the room, noticing the holly decorating the mantle piece. 'At least I know you're safely home and you can enjoy Christmas morning here with your ma. And we will see each other tomorrow afternoon.'

'I suppose I must be grateful for that,' he replied.

Soon they were sipping their tea, sat at the small table. 'Should we call your ma down for a cup?' Grace asked. 'It must be very cold upstairs. It's thoughtful of her to let us have time alone, but she's been up there for at least half an hour now and I'm feeling guilty about us being in the warm whilst she's freezing.'

'Ma wouldn't mind,' Teddy said. 'But you're right of course.' He went to the door and on opening it called up into the darkness. 'Ma, won't you come down and get warm now? The tea is brewed.'

'I'm coming,' she called back and within a few minutes she was standing beside the range, warming her hands. 'It's a bitter cold Christmas Eve, isn't it? I'll be glad when the spring comes around again. This weather is hard on my old joints.'

'You shouldn't have left the warmth of the fire, Ma,' Teddy said as he passed her a steaming cup of tea.

'I know what it's like to be young and thought you two deserved a little time alone,' she replied.

'You are kind, Mrs Evans,' said Grace. 'And very thoughtful.'

They sat together, chatting about the excitement of Christmas coming, and remembering Christmases past, playing in the snow as children and how things would be different after the war was over. The minutes flew by and soon it was time for Grace to return to Mrs Simpson's house. Teddy wanted to escort her all the way to Southsea, but Grace insisted that he walk her only to the tram stop. She could happily go home safely from there and wanted him to spend as much time as he could with his Ma. He reluctantly agreed, knowing he would see her the very next day.

They hugged before she climbed aboard the tram and waved to each other as it trundled along on its way. Clouds had formed and the snow began to fall again as she rode through the streets. By the time they'd reached Craneswater Avenue and she stepped down, the fresh snow was deep enough to reach her ankles. She was grateful to have on a sturdy pair of boots but could feel the cold through the soles even during the short walk to the house.

She was very pleased to open the door into the kitchen and feel the warmth of the house envelop her, Mrs Amberley still working at the kitchen table, rolling pastry.

'Oh, there you are at last,' the cook frowned at her. 'Get your coat off and go and change your boots. You're dripping all over my floor.'

'Good evening Mrs Amberley, pleased to see you too.'

'Now don't be cheeky, young lady. Get along. I need you to help me with the baking otherwise it'll never get done. I don't want to be up all night with this.'

'Sorry Missus,' Grace said as she hurried out of the room to get changed into her working clothes.

10

Christmas morning was over in a whirl of dusting, laying and lighting fires, checking the dining table was perfect, and helping Mrs Amberley and Mary in the kitchen. They'd hardly a moment to spare to wish each other a Merry Christmas although there were small gifts passed to each other over their hastily organised breakfast. Grace had made Mrs Amberley a new scarf, and a pair of mittens for Mary. She'd been pleased to receive a jar of pickles from the cook, a luxury in these times that she would take home for her ma. Mary had given her a handkerchief which had her name embroidered on one corner. It was so beautiful and neat that Grace was taken aback at how clever Mary was with her stitching.

'Mary, you have hidden talents,' Grace had said, looking at the work. 'You should do more sewing. It is a work of art.'

Mrs Amberley agreed. 'You should show this to Mrs Simpson, Mary. She may have more work for you in this vein.' She paused. 'If that is what you want, of course. I think you may be wasted as a kitchen maid and may make a good ladies maid.'

'Thank you, Ma'am, but I'm happy with where I am at the moment. I enjoy embroidery but only as a pastime for enjoyment rather than employment. Kitchen work suits me.'

Once the main meal of dinner was done and all the plates cleared away, the dining table polished and the floor swept, Grace checked there was enough coal in the rooms and everything was in place ready for tea and a cold supper later for the Master and Mrs Simpson. Finally, she knocked on the drawing room door and was called in to speak to her employers.

'Ah, Bennett,' Mrs Simpson said as she smiled at Grace. 'Thank you for all your work this year and for helping to make this Christmas Day so lovely. I expect you would like to go and spend the rest of the day with your family, and your sweetheart?'

'Yes Ma'am. Thank you. And may I wish you both a very Happy Christmas.'

'Thank you, Bennett. Now before you go there is a small package for you on the piano. Please could you fetch it?'

Grace looked at the piano. There were three packages lined up in a row. 'Which one, Ma'am?' she asked.

'Sorry, it's the one on the left. It has your name on the label. You may open it.'

Grace was flustered, knowing that she'd not thought to prepare a gift for her employer. Opening the brown paper wrapping, she was doubly flustered to see inside a small china teacup and saucer.

'It's nothing really, just something I thought you might like to keep for yourself. For when you start your own home. Or if you decide to become a nurse, it would be nice to have something pretty to drink your tea from, wherever you are.'

Grace was overwhelmed. 'This is such a lovely, thoughtful gift,' she said. 'Thank you so much. I am sorry though as I haven't got anything for you.'

'Nonsense, Bennett. I didn't give you this for you to give me something back. It was a pleasure to give you a gift I think you will appreciate, and I'm glad you like it.'

'I do, very much. I shall take care of this, wherever my future takes me.'

'Good. Now off you go to enjoy the rest of the day with your loved ones. Oh, and please ask Mrs Amberley and James to come up when they're ready.'

Grace was tired but happy to be with her family for a few hours and was delighted with the gifts they'd exchanged. Ma was pleased with the pickles and she'd saved enough to buy new lace handkerchiefs for Ma and Elsie and gloves for her brothers and a scarf for Pa.

Ma had given her a length of ribbon and Elsie a knitted scarf. How she wished she could have seen her brothers wear their gifts but had to be happy enough with placing them in the parcel they'd prepared for the post office.

It was late that evening before Grace and Teddy could be alone again. Far too cold to sit in the front parlour, they had agreed that walking briskly would keep them warm, and as Teddy had said, when you are in love you hardly feel the cold. Of course, he was used to being out of doors. They never talked about his experiences in Belgium, but Grace had some idea from what she'd read in the newspapers.

They walked companionably, without speaking, until they reached Victoria Park. Normally, it would be a pretty place to walk, filled with flowers and shrubs, the only park in Portsmouth that wasn't given over to allotments. This evening all remained white. They found a covered shelter with a bench which was dry enough to sit for a while.

'I've been giving this a lot of thought,' Teddy said. 'I mean I've been thinking about the last time I was home on leave when we were talking about us getting wed. I have to say I think you were right and we should get married sooner. I need to know I've got a wife at home waiting for me.'

Grace hesitated before answering, then she took his hand. 'Dear Teddy,' she began. 'I am waiting here for you. I always will be waiting, but I think you were right before. It would be wrong to get married now, whilst the war's still on. The future is so uncertain and it would be a mistake. Please let us wait, as you suggested before.'

'Really?' His face dropped. 'I don't understand. Why have you changed your mind?'

'I think you were right, that's all, and I have decided that I want to develop my skills before I settle down as a wife. I've been to see the munitions factory.'

'Really? I don't like to think of you working there. It's dangerous, isn't it?'

'Elsie works there and she does well enough. But yes, I know what you mean, and I looked at it and decided it wasn't for me.'

'So what else?' He looked at her.

'Mrs Simpson has been trying to encourage me into nursing.'

'Not again? I thought you'd decided against that as well.'

'Not really, I was still thinking about it. A few weeks ago, Mrs Simpson took me to the asylum whilst she was doing her regular visit and showed me around two of the wards with Dr Devine, the medical superintendent. One of the wards was quiet and peaceful and the other was far more disturbing. But you know, since then I've been thinking about it and feel I am drawn to that type of work. The women in there are so troubled but they shouldn't be given up on. The treatments they have now are so modern and the patients are given every hope for a full recovery. I would love to think I could make a difference for them, even if only in some small way.'

'It sounds to me as if you've made up your mind, Grace. I'll worry about you being in such a place. It has a bad reputation.'

'I can't help that. Most of the staff there are good people who work hard in helping the patients. And the patients could be any one of us.'

'I hope you're right.' He paused. 'Very well, I suppose I did say I'd support you. I can't say I'm happy about it. I only hope when the war is over, you'll know what you want, and be a wife, rather than a nurse.'

'I will, I'm sure I will,' Grace squeezed his hand. 'Thank you, it means such a lot to me.'

They held each other for a while and then made their way back to the tram stop and soon they were saying goodnight in Craneswater Avenue.

Christmas leave was over all too soon and Grace was waving Teddy goodbye once again from the station. As the train disappeared along the track, Grace found herself doubting her decision. Should she have given in and taken the chance to marry

Teddy before he left? What a terrible time they were living in, when one's future was so uncertain.

Grace wiped away a tear that somehow had escaped from her eye as she watched the steam from the engine disappear into the sky.

Shaking her head, she made her way to the tram and climbed aboard to travel back to Mrs Simpson's house.

11

The snow had melted, but it remained cold. By the third week in January, Grace found herself standing once again in the entrance hall of the asylum, this time as a trainee nurse. Mrs Simpson was not with her, but Grace waited with two other young women who were also on their first day, each looking anxiously at each other.

'It looks as though we'll be spending time together.' Grace tried to break the ice between the three. 'I'm Grace Bennett.' She held her hand to the nearest woman, who was dumpy, with straw coloured hair tucked up inside her bonnet. 'Pleased to meet you,' she said. Their eyes met and Grace felt an instant attraction there. She blushed. What was happening to her lately?

'Likewise, I'm sure. And I'm Rose, Rose Jenkins.' She shook Grace's hand enthusiastically then turned to the other woman waiting.

'How d'you do?' Rose said.

'Hello, I'm happy to meet you both as well,' the other woman said. 'My name's Ethel Lang.' She was tall, as tall as Grace but more elegant, Grace thought.

'I do hope we will all become friends,' Grace said to them both. 'I suppose we'll need to rely on each other over the next few months and more.'

'We will, I'm sure,' said Rose, grinning.

The door opened and the Matron entered.

'Good morning ladies.' She stood towering over them all, looking resplendent in her red dress and high cap perched on the volumes of carefully coiffed grey hair. Her back was straight and although her girth was huge, she moved like a duchess. If Grace had not met her before whilst on her visit with Mrs Simpson, she would have been completely overwhelmed by the woman. As it was, she still felt intimidated, and could sense her two new colleagues were also in awe of her.

'Good morning Ma'am,' they said in a kind of ragged unison.

'You will address me as Matron, ladies,' she announced. She turned to Rose first. 'Now, your names, please.'

'I'm Rose Jenkins, Ma'am, I mean Matron.'

'You will be known as Jenkins here,' said Matron.

'Yes, Matron. Thank you Matron.'

Ethel stepped forward next. 'I am Lang, Ethel Lang, Matron. Pleased to meet you.'

'Thank you, Lang,' Matron replied.

She turned to Grace. 'And you are Bennett, I believe. We met briefly a few weeks ago did we not?'

'Yes, Matron,' said Grace. 'Very pleased to meet you again.'

'Now ladies, I will take you to your rooms and introduce you to some of the other nurses that you will be working with. You will be taken to the sewing room and given your uniforms which you will be expected to wear at all times unless you are off duty and away from the asylum. Someone will then take you to the training room where you will be greeted by the Senior Nurse Tutor. You will be answerable to her for the duration of your training. Later you will be introduced to the wards where you will be working. Is that all clear?'

'Yes, Matron,' they replied, this time as one.

'Follow me, then.' Matron turned away, stepping through the inner door into the long corridor beyond.

Grace remembered passing this way before and once again her senses were heightened by the atmosphere of the place. There was that strange smell she couldn't quite describe, several ladies wandered past them as they walked, some nodded to the Matron, others turned their heads away, appearing not to want to show their faces as they passed. It wasn't fear that Grace felt, more of a feeling of excitement, of knowing she was on the verge of a new adventure. Something different to anything she'd experienced before.

Rooms for the trainee nurses were at the end of a corridor, through another door. It all looked very similar to the larger wards that Grace had visited, with small rooms along one side and two bathrooms on the other. A day room was at the end with easy chairs around the edge, a table in the middle where two nurses sat in their uniforms, eating bowls of porridge. It seemed a bit late for breakfast, but apparently they were night nurses who'd come off duty only an hour before. They stood as Matron entered the room.

'Sit, sit, ladies. I would like to introduce you to some of our new intake for training. This is Bennett, Jenkins and Lang. If one of you could take them under your wing, show them their rooms and then take them to the sewing room for their uniforms, I'd be most obliged. You may leave them there and return to get your sleep. The sewing mistress will redirect the ladies to the training rooms.'

'I'll do it, Matron.' The nurse had a tired look about her eyes but they twinkled as she smiled. Her red hair was untidily stuffed under her cap and her white apron had a dark smudge down the front. Her sleeves were rolled up and she scratched her arms as she stood.

'Thank you, Brown,' Matron said. 'And do tidy up your uniform before you go. Your hair is a disgrace, you need a clean apron and your sleeves should be down and in cuffs. We can't have our nurses walking the corridors looking such a disgrace.'

'Yes, Matron. Sorry, Matron,' the nurse replied, pulling down her sleeves as she made her way to her room for a clean apron.

'I will leave you in the good hands of Brown, ladies. Good luck with your first day.'

And she swept away along the corridor and through the door into the main part of the asylum.

The other night nurse, finishing her porridge, looked up and introduced herself. 'I'm Annie Wilde,' she said. 'And she's Nellie Brown, but we all call ourselves by our surnames here. You get used to it. Matron's all right as long as you keep on her good side. She can be a hard task mistress and if you do anything wrong, she'll soon put you straight. But underneath all that I think she's a bit of a soft hearted woman really.'

'I'm Bennett, and this is Lang and Jenkins, then,' Grace was familiar with being called by her surname at work. 'My friends know me as Grace though.'

'It did feel strange at first,' Annie Wilde said. She stood, pushing her chair away from the table and smoothed out her apron. Her dark hair was sleek under the cap. 'On the wards, it's always surnames and after a while you almost forget you have a Christian name. Sometimes it can get confusing though, if there are more than one from the same family.'

'It was the same in the workhouse,' Rose said.

'It's not often that one works with two from one family at the same time,' Annie said. 'Even though it's common to have families all working here.'

Grace's room, like all the others, and the ones on the wards, was small with minimal furniture. A narrow wardrobe was against one wall, with a chest of drawers beside it. A single bed was placed along the length of the room, a desk and chair beside it and in one corner was a washstand with a towel rail on the side. There was a window which opened to a small orchard which would be beautiful in the spring. The trees now were bereft of all their leaves but there were beginnings of buds already on their branches. Grace opened the wardrobe and carefully hung her spare dress, her coat, and placed her slippers at the bottom, with her case. She would put the rest of her clothes away later. But now, it was time to be taken to the sewing room.

'Ready, ladies?' Brown was waiting for them outside. 'I'm sure you can't wait to try on your uniforms.' She laughed. 'You'll soon tire of them, I can assure you. I know I cannot wait to get into my own clothes on my time off.'

Another march along another corridor. The room was buzzing with chatter, the sound of sewing machines whirring, the smell and hiss of steam coming from the materials as they were being pressed. Some of the women were working on stitching aprons, mending dresses and petticoats, cutting out patterns for uniform dresses, for nurses, attendants, and the patients too.

Grace looked about her, noticing that some of the workers were in patient's dresses, whilst others had overalls on over their own clothes, much like those in the munitions factory had been wearing. So much activity, so much industry, she thought, and she wondered if she would have been better to have taken a job in here rather than thinking she could become a nurse.

Measured and fitted into uniforms, the new recruits were given three dresses, three aprons, three caps, three pairs of dark stockings and three chemises to wear underneath the uniforms. 'You are responsible for these uniforms, here are labels with your names on. You will sew these on yourselves. They will be laundered with the other uniforms and returned to you once clean and ironed. The nurses in the home will show you where to place your dirty laundry. Undergarments you will wash yourselves. If your uniforms ever need mending, you will notify the sewing room, unless the mending is minimal, in which case you will attend to it yourselves. Each of you will sign the ledger for your uniforms. Any questions?'

'No Miss.' Grace and the others shook their heads.

'Good. Then off you go ladies. The training rooms are only a few steps away along the main corridor.'

Soon they'd passed through another door into a room which was set up like a classroom, with rows of desks and chairs facing a blackboard. Grace's spirits dipped at the thought of being back at school, but surely this would be a school like no other she'd known before? Standing at the front beside a blackboard was a gentleman. He turned to them as they entered. She had been expecting to see Doctor Devine, but this man was younger, his full head of sandy hair swept over one eye. He was dressed in a tweed suit, the cuffs slightly frayed, and underneath he wore a white shirt with a high collar and a black bow-tie.

'Good morning ladies,' he bowed to them as he spoke. 'I am Doctor Blake. I will be responsible for some of your instruction during your training. Please take a seat and I will take you through some of the items we will be exploring during your time in this classroom.'

The three trainees looked at each other then found seats in the front row of desks. 'Are there any more of us to come?' Grace asked.

'Yes, we are expecting another seven women to join us when we start the course on Monday next. Today I am going to show you the Red Book and give you a broad outline of the lessons you will attend here. From Monday, for one week, we shall be teaching you the basics of what will be expected of you once you start on the wards. After that, you will have school sessions during your working week. You will be excused from ward duties for periods of teaching.'

'Excuse me, Sir.' Ethel Lang raised her hand. 'I have heard of the Red Book, but I'm not sure exactly what it is.'

'Please, call me Doctor. Sir is far too formal,' he replied. 'The Red Book is what is actually titled the "Handbook for the Attendants of the Insane". Quite a mouthful, I think. This will be your bible - the price of the book is two shillings and six pence. You will each be given a copy of this and the cost will be deducted from your wages. I expect you will all be reading it avidly over the next few days and weeks.'

The rest of the morning sped by and soon the recruits were being shown into the attendants' dining room. The space was filled with the noise of voices, chairs scraping the floor and cutlery against china plates. A few nurses looked up at them as they entered, each one took a tray and was given a plate full of steaming stew. Moving along the line, another server passed over a bowl of suet pudding covered in yellow custard. Grace's stomach rumbled with hunger as they made their way to an empty table.

'What do you think of the day, so far?' Rose Jenkins asked. 'There's such a lot to take in don't you think? I have no idea how I'm going to cope with all of this, and the Red Book! Have you seen some of those treatments?'

'I think it is fascinating,' Ethel Lang said. 'I, for one, cannot wait to get stuck in.'

'Me neither,' Rose answered. 'I'm just saying it's a lot to learn. That's all.'

'There is a lot to remember,' Grace agreed. 'Hopefully it won't be too much for us.' She took a spoonful of stew and chewed it slowly. 'Hmm. This stew is delicious. I'm not sure what the meat is though.'

'It's supposed to be beef. That's what it said on the menu when we came in, but there is a war on you know.' Ethel laughed. 'Could be horse meat. I suppose we'll never know.'

'You could be right,' agreed Grace. 'Anyway, it's food and it's hot and tastes nice and this suet pudding looks like it'll keep us going for a while. I hope so anyway, I'm starving.'

The rest of the meal was taken in silence as they ploughed their way through the stew and suet pudding.

Before long it was time to go back to the classroom for more instruction, this time a practical lesson from the senior nurse tutor, a stout woman with a permanent frown on her narrow face, who demonstrated how to correctly make a bed, followed by instruction on doing a bed bath, cleaning and dressing a wound, and keeping the ward area clean and tidy.

'I thought we were going to be learning about insanity,' Rose whispered to Grace. 'I know how to make a bed and clean the floor already.'

'A clean and tidy environment is conducive to good mental health.' The tutor had obviously overheard her comments. 'You cannot have one without the other. And it is good discipline for you nurses to learn this early in your training.'

'Yes, of course, I understand that,' Rose agreed. 'I didn't mean anything by it.'

'One of the things you must learn is how to know when to speak and when to hold your tongue,' the tutor said. 'Please address me as Nurse Tutor when you speak to me. I have a firm but fair way of working with my charges and consider you are all under my wing.'

'Yes, Nurse Tutor,' they all echoed.

'It is necessary for you to know the correct way to clean and dress a wound as you will be responsible for the welfare of the patients here and any first aid will be led by you as a part of the nursing staff. Our patients often need assistance with their daily activities, such as bathing, eating and drinking. It will not all be focusing on madness and behaviour. Our training is to enable you to help the patients in a way that will encompass the improvement of their physical, mental and spiritual well-being. Now, do you all understand?'

'Yes, Nurse Tutor,' was the answer from all.

'Good. Now we will talk about the recording of patients' progress.'

Some hours later Grace was relieved to sink into the easy chair in the nurses' lounge, next to Rose. The day had been so long, with far too much information to digest. Grace had thought that working as a parlour-maid was tiring, but all of this new learning was making her head ache. She was so glad that as new recruits, they would have the next two days off before starting properly in the training school on Monday.

'What a day?' Rose said. 'I never really thought this would ever happen. I've always wanted to do something different with my life and although for the first years after school, I've worked at making beds and mopping the floors of the workhouse infirmary, I've always hoped I'd do more.'

'I'm not quite sure how I got here, to be honest,' Grace said. 'But here I am.'

'It's exciting, isn't it?' Rose said. 'I was anxious yesterday and wondered if I'd fit in. It's a big step-up from working in the workhouse.'

'So how do you feel now? I think you fit in, as you call it.' Grace smiled. 'You certainly do with me, anyway.'

'I feel really good, I think. We were all nervous, weren't we? But that made it even more exciting, starting together. I can see we'll all be friends for a lifetime. Hope so, anyway.'

'All in the same boat and all scared to death.'

'Well, we've got through day one and now have the weekend to get our heads around our new lives. What will you do over the weekend?'

'I'm going to spend it at home with my parents and my sister. And maybe take a look at the notes from today.'

'So, I'll see you on Monday then.'

12

When the war started Rose had wondered about working in the dockyard or perhaps as a Land Girl but really she thought the attraction was only so she could be amongst other women. Women like herself perhaps? She'd always known she was a bit different from other girls. There was one thing she knew she'd never wanted to be and that was a housewife, nor a mother to children. It wasn't that she didn't particularly like children, she just didn't want any of her own. When she'd told her ma the way she felt, Ma had laughed at her and told her she'd have to put up with her lot the same as all women did. This made Rose even more determined.

Her Pa was a stockily built man who worked in the coal yard at the docks. He didn't say much at the best of times. Rose was frightened of her Pa - he wasn't a kind man. She'd felt the back of his hand across her head on many occasion, usually on a Friday night when he rolled home from the pub three sheets to the wind, as Ma would describe him. They learned to stay out of his way when he'd been drinking. It was a relief when Rose knew she'd be living-in at the Asylum.

It wasn't that Rose didn't like men, of course she did. There were many of them from school that she'd kept in touch with, although most of them had all gone to the front, one by one. They were all good blokes, men you could have a good laugh with, but nothing more than that for her, not so far anyway. It wasn't that she'd not had any young man interested in her either. She'd been told she was pretty and she certainly had the full figure of a woman from a young age, but she wasn't interested in walking out with anyone.

There were her female friends, school friends, and people she'd met since working. Some of the women workers were cruel, but others were kind enough to the inmates and were good fun to spend time with after working hours were done. Then one day, she'd been invited to a house party of one of the women. That's where she'd realised that you could be happy without a man in your life.

At first it was scary and she'd had to wrestle with all she'd been taught as a child. The Rector in their church had spoken about "unnatural practices" and she wondered whether she'd sinned when she'd let a woman kiss her. Talking to her new friends helped to ease these fears and she'd soon realised there was nothing wrong in liking women and she knew some who lived together even closer than merely good friends.

When she was told about the asylum and that they were starting to train people to be nurses for the insane, something lit up in her mind, and it seemed her eyes were opening to a new future. It was exciting, a way forward for her, learning new skills and living with other independent women, and perhaps doing something good for others. She had not been thinking about finding love in such a place - it was a new environment with new challenges that attracted her.

When Rose had arrived at the asylum the day before, she'd wondered whether she'd done the right thing in giving up her safe job in the workhouse. Then she'd met the other ladies who'd arrived on the same day. She could see how nervous they all were and felt a camaraderie between the three, a kind of bond that would be hard to break in the future. Ethel Lang was someone she felt she'd rely on to help with her studies, something she was completely new to, but it was when she turned to look at Grace Bennett that something special happened to Rose. She felt herself gasping at the light that seemed to emanate from Grace's eyes as she smiled. When Grace shook her hand Rose could feel herself becoming hot and hoped she wasn't blushing.

She wondered how she'd cope with working and living under the same roof as this woman and told herself not to be stupid. 'You're here to work and learn,' she told herself. 'You know nothing about this woman, and it's not very likely she'd ever feel the same.'

13

The tram to Fratton was full. The weather still cold, with a cruel wind blowing, tempered by the bright sunshine. Grace looked out of the window as they travelled on their way, wishing for the spring to hurry up and arrive.

There were so many crammed onto the tram, shoppers on their way to Charlotte Street on the other side of the island, or perhaps to Fratton Road to buy their weekend supplies. For the past year, shops had less and less in them and it was only since the rationing of food had begun, there was just enough to go around for everyone. Previously, Grace remembered the long queues outside the bakers and butchers in the main thoroughfare, customers hoping the store wouldn't sell out before they reached the door. There was a great deal of unrest as many knew about the friends of the shopkeepers who would be served through the back door.

Clive Road, in contrast, was quiet enough. A horse-drawn wagon clopped along, the driver an elderly man, his clothes and skin blackened with dust from the bags of coal he delivered along the way.

Grace picked up her pace, eager to get home. Ma was there, waiting at the door, her face a picture of relief to see her daughter again so soon. She gave the young woman a hug and drew her into the house, out of the cold.

'Dear Grace,' she said. 'I haven't stopped thinking about you since you left here yesterday morning. How did you cope?'

'I coped very well, Ma, and I've met some nice young women too. They're sensible ladies who have been well brought up, so you needn't worry that I will be in bad company.'

'What about the patients? It can't be easy.'

'I haven't been with any patients yet. Yesterday we spent the day settling in. We were given uniforms and instructions in a classroom. My room is small but big enough for me with even a little desk so I can study when I'm not working on the wards. It is so exciting, Ma. I know I am going to love my work.'

'I hope you do.' Her ma went to the range. 'Now take your things to your room, settle yourself in and then come down and we can have a proper chat. I have missed you.'

'Oh, Ma! I've only been gone for one night, and before that I was hardly ever here. You only saw me for a few hours each week. This won't be much different.'

'Except it is different as you will be behind those high walls, locked in with all those mad people.'

'I will get used to it and so will you,' Grace assured her as she made her way up the stairs to the old familiar bedroom she'd shared with Elsie. She'd only had time to unpack her small bag and lay out her nightdress on the bed ready for later, when she heard a knock on the front door. Soon her Ma was calling her down and there in the parlour was Mrs Evans, her face white and pinched. Grace felt slightly sick wondering what the news would be.

'I've had a telegram, about Teddy. It's not good news.' Her hands were shaking.

'He's not...' Grace began, the words stuck in her throat.

'No, dear. He is alive, thank God. But, he is maimed. The telegram says he is returning home. I've also received a visit from an officer who told me he is to be cared for in the Queen Alexander Hospital where he will be rehabilitated.'

'Rehabilitated? What are his injuries?' Grace asked. 'They must be severe ones.'

'Oh my dear girl - he has lost both his legs and his sight is affected although they hope it's only a temporary loss. His sight I mean. It's unbearable, my darling boy.' She sobbed as she spoke.

Grace felt herself swaying, her legs were jelly, her head was light and her stomach churned. 'Oh, poor Teddy, poor, poor Teddy,' she wailed.

'Sit down Grace.' Her mother took her arm and eased her into the chair beside the range. 'You must be strong, for his sake.' She went into the scullery and came back with a bottle of sherry left over from a long past Christmas, together with three small glasses.

Pouring the wine, she passed a glass to Grace. 'Here, my girl, drink this. It'll help with the shock. Mrs Evans? I'm sure you could do with one as well, I know I could.'

'Thank you, I'm much obliged. I feel as though my life has turned on its head. I know I should expect the worse and so many young men won't be coming back at all. But I can't bear the thought of my Teddy being maimed.'

Grace sipped her sherry. Her mind was numbed as she tried not to imagine what Teddy must be going through. Her poor, strong, man, would he ever be strong again? And how could she carry on with her new life as a nurse when Teddy came home? She had promised to marry him but what would life be like with a disabled husband? What would she be expected to do? It was a terrible thought, but she loved him and knew she would have to stand by him. She felt selfish and ashamed at even thinking these things.

'When do you suppose he will be transferred to the hospital?' she asked.

'It'll be soon.' Mrs Evans said. 'On the very next transport ship back. Probably in the next week or so. I can see it's a great shock for you and certainly not what you thought would be the beginning of your life together. I know you'd planned to marry when this awful war was over, but things will be different now.'

'I've promised to marry Teddy, and I can't see that will change.' Grace stared into the open door of the range at the flames there. 'I will keep my word. I know life might be hard, but I love him terribly.'

'Words are cheap.' Mrs Evans cradled her sherry, then drank it down. 'You should have married when you had the chance. I should go now. I have things I must get on with.' She placed the empty glass on the table and turned to Grace. 'I'll be the first to have any news and as soon as Teddy is home in Portsmouth, I'll let you know.'

'Thank you, Mrs Evans,' Grace said as she stood.

Mrs Evans embraced her quickly and then spoke to Grace's mother. 'Thank you for the sherry, Bertha, it was needed. And please do drop by to see me, too, anytime you have to spare.'

'I will, and I'm here to help if ever you need anything. I'll see you out.' The two women passed through into the narrow passageway. Grace was left to stare into the fire, fear flickering inside her like the flames as they licked the coals.

Within minutes her ma was back in the room. 'What will you do now?' she asked. 'You will have to give up your ideas of training in the asylum if you really intend to marry Teddy.'

'I know, Ma. It's not something I wanted to do so soon. I do want to marry him but we'd planned to wait until the war was over. Now it seems like Teddy's war is over sooner than expected. I don't want to give up my plans to be a nurse.' She paused, looking up at her ma. 'Life has other plans for me it seems.'

'Would you listen to my advice, Grace?'

'What's that, Ma? I know you don't approve of me working in the asylum.'

'You're right, I didn't want you to embark on such a career, as you call it. However, I am proud of you for standing up for what you believe in and for pursuing this calling. I just want you to consider very hard before you commit yourself to marriage to Teddy. It will be very difficult for you both. Marriage is never easy at the best of times and believe me, having a man who would be relying on you to support him in every way, is not something I would wish on my daughter.'

'Ma! But I love Teddy and have promised to marry him. Surely you don't think I should break that promise? If we had married before he'd gone away, then I wouldn't have any choice but to stand by him. In sickness and in health, after all.'

'But you didn't make that oath, though did you? Perhaps it was a good thing after all.'

'I can't believe you're saying this, Ma.' Grace looked at her ma's face which was lined with worry.

'Please don't get me wrong, Grace. You're my daughter. I still think of you as my little girl and want to be sure you are happy and protected. I know I can't do that anymore, but I just don't want you to get yourself into a situation that causes you no end of pain.'

'I will be all right, Ma. But thank you for caring about me.'

'I'll get on with preparing the dinner then.' Ma went into the scullery and began to scrub the potatoes.

14

It was after a sleepless night that Grace came down the next morning. Elsie had come in late the evening before, had climbed into bed beside her and had fallen asleep within minutes. She was already gone when Grace woke up. Her ma was in the kitchen, preparing pastry for a meat pie that would be their main meal later in the day. She looked up as Grace entered the room.

'Morning, Ma. Where's Pa?'

'He gone to the allotment. There's not much to be done this time of year but I think he just enjoys getting outside for a few hours. It's hard work in the dockyard where he spends so much time in the sheds. A bit of fresh air and digging does him good.'

'He must have gone out early, I didn't even hear him leaving.'

'He did. I think he enjoys being with his cronies more than anything to be honest.'

'That's probably true. Can I help you with anything this morning? I'm sorry I slept so late, but I had a restless night.'

'I'm sure you did, and no thank you. I can cope with this although you could fetch me the pastry brush from the drawer. Are you going to church this morning?'

Grace passed her the brush. 'I am, Ma. Will you come with me? I could do with a bit of company.'

'I've got too much to do here. Where's Elsie? You should wake up the lazy girl and get her to go with you.'

'She's not here. She must have got up really early if you missed her. She came in late last night and hardly said a word to me before she fell asleep. Her snoring was keeping me awake.'

'Really? I can't imagine what is going on with that girl. She's been acting strangely lately. I think maybe there's a young man involved. Has she shared anything with you?'

'No, not really, Ma.' Grace perched on the edge of the dresser, trying to recall what Elsie had told her.

'What do you mean, not really? If you know something you should tell me.'

'No, it's nothing, nothing at all. I expect she'll tell us soon enough.' Grace stepped into the scullery, looking into the larder. 'Is there anything I can eat before I go to church?'

'There's a pot of porridge on the range. Have some of that - it'll keep you warm. That church is pretty cold at the best of times.'

The church was cold. Ma had been perfectly right and Grace was glad of the porridge she'd eaten and the warm scarf and gloves she wore. Teddy was on her mind as she prayed and sang the hymns. She was afraid of how she'd react when she saw him and couldn't quite imagine how they'd cope. The hospital would surely keep him there for a long while to get him ready to face the civilian world again. Would he get his full eyesight back or would she be looking after a husband who couldn't see, nor walk? She'd seen soldiers in the town without legs, some of them swinging along on crutches, others in bath chairs. She'd seen those with bandaged eyes, being helped along by a nurse, too. Was this really the future she'd hoped for?

Grace looked around the congregation, seeing uniformed men on leave, able-bodied men, standing alongside their wives and mothers, holding their heads up high. Suddenly she felt sorry for them, knowing they, too could be maimed or killed the next time they went back to the front line. What a waste of lives, she thought.

After the service, she made her way out and walked across the churchyard towards her home. It was warmer in the sunshine than it had been inside the church. Reaching the far corner of the grassy ground, she noticed the familiar young woman sitting on the bench by the wall.

'Elsie, what on earth are you doing, sitting here in the cold?' Grace sat down next to her. 'I was going to ask you to come to church with me, but you'd gone out already.'

'Oh, Grace. I woke up early and couldn't get back to sleep so I just got up and I've been walking about for the past three hours.'

'Something must have happened. Was it something at the factory? You came in very late last night. I tried to speak to you, but you looked so tired and then went straight to sleep.'

Elsie looked across the graves into the distance. 'I couldn't face church this morning. Sorry.'

'You can tell me, Elsie. What is it?'

'I can't talk about it, I'm so ashamed.'

'Whatever it is, I'm sure we can sort it out. Nothing could be so bad.'

'It is bad.' Elsie took a deep breath and let out a sigh. 'Mr Medford has been at it again. He caught me after all the other girls had left last night and, oh, I can't tell you Grace.'

'I knew that man could not be trusted. What did he do?' Grace took her hand. 'I'm sorry, you don't have to tell me, but if you could bring yourself to talk about it we may be able to do something, perhaps?'

'There is nothing to be done. He tried to molest me but I did push him away and shouted at him to leave me alone. Then he said I shouldn't tell anyone, or I'd lose my position. He said I should be good to him as well, or I'd be sorry. I don't know what to do.'

'You must speak to someone about it. Report him.'

'There is no-one to report him to, Grace.' She shook her head. 'Anyway no-one would take it seriously. I've been taught you have to expect this when you work in the man's world. Even though there are more women in the factory now, it's still a man's place.'

'I don't know how you can stay there.' Grace squeezed Elsie's hand.

'You just have to get on with it, really, Grace. Now let's change the subject. How's life in the asylum? That must be an eye-opener for you after your quiet life as a parlour-maid.'

'I have only had one day so far, so it's early days but I think I am going to like it. But I have news for you too. Not good news I'm afraid, and it will change everything.'

'What could possibly have happened now?' Elsie frowned at her sister as she spoke.

'It's Teddy. He's been injured - very badly as it happens. He has lost both his legs and his eyesight is affected too. He is being transferred to the Queen Alexandra Hospital in the next week or so. The war is over for him, and it looks like my nursing career could be too.'

Elsie's face paled. 'Oh, my dear, that makes my little problem seem nothing. Lost his legs! That is terrible news. How will he manage?'

Grace wiped a tear from her cheek that had somehow escaped. She felt an overwhelming fear rising once again. She'd tried to keep it at bay but there it was, always trying to come to the fore. 'I promised I would marry him, and so I will. We were going to wed at the end of the war, but I see he'll need me now. I admit the prospect of it all scares me but it's my duty.'

'I don't know why you didn't marry him when you had the chance, Grace. You shouldn't be doing it out of duty. Teddy is a lovely man. But would you really want you to give up your nursing at this stage? I mean, you've barely begun.'

'I plan to keep at it until we can work out our future. I expect he'll be in treatment and rehabilitation at first so I can carry on for a while at least. I will have to speak to the Matron to see if I can do that without committing to the job on a long term-basis. I really don't know yet what will happen. It's all too difficult to think about.'

'I suppose you'll need to wait until Teddy's home.'

'I just hope it'll be soon.' Grace stood up. 'Are you going to come home with me for some dinner? Ma's wondering where you are.'

'Yes, I'm coming. But no more talk about Mr Medford though. I just want to forget that man and my work for one day.'

They linked arms and left the churchyard together. 'I'm starving,' said Elsie. 'I missed breakfast and last night's supper.'

'Ma's making a meat pie. No-one makes pastry like her. Now you've made me hungry too.'

'At least we've got our Ma and Pa, and each other, whatever happens, eh?'

'And our brothers, Alfred and Bert. Even though they couldn't get leave at Christmas, they still wrote to us. And we must keep hoping they come through this war unharmed, although that seems less and less likely as the months go by.'

'Don't even think that, Grace. They have to come home. I couldn't bear it if they didn't.'

'Sorry. Come on, let's get home then.'

15

Arriving back at the asylum that evening, Grace sat on her bed, wondering again what the future would hold for both herself, Elsie, their brothers, and Teddy, too. She'd hung her civilian clothes in the wardrobe and donned her night gown. Not feeling ready to face her new friends, she turned off the light, climbed into the bed and tried to sleep.

Somehow, sleep came to her eventually and the morning was there all too soon. Someone was banging on her door. It was Rose.

'Come on lazy-bones, time to get ready for our first proper day in training school,' she said as she came into the room. 'You'll miss breakfast if you don't hurry.'

Grace sat up and stretched. 'I won't be long,' she said and pulled herself out of bed.

'It's exciting, isn't it?' Rose was dancing on the spot. 'I can't wait to get stuck in, can you?'

'Yes, yes, but just let me get dressed, won't you?'

'I will, I will,' and Rose swept out of the room, slamming the door behind her.

Grace smiled to herself as she quickly got herself ready for the day.

The classroom was already half filled with trainees. The nurse tutor was waiting to greet Grace, Ethel and Rose as they entered.

'Do hurry along ladies. We have much to cover today. I am pleased to see you are all dressed in your uniforms. Please ensure you always present in a neat and tidy way. Make sure your hair is completely covered with your cap and your aprons are clean. I will expect your footwear to be well polished as well. We have to give a good impression to the patients here. Remember you are all role models for the ladies you will be caring for on the wards.'

Grace looked down at her boots. She hadn't given herself enough time to clean them. She hoped Nurse Tutor wouldn't notice but suspected she would. Tucking her feet under the chair, she turned her attention back to the front of the room.

'I trust you all had time to peruse your handbooks over the weekend,' Nurse Tutor said. 'Those of you who were given them on Friday should be a step ahead of the others. Are there any questions?'

Ethel Lang raised her hand. 'On Friday you said this was to be our bible. But are there any other books we should be reading?'

'A very good question and yes, there will be other books recommended for you. Although at this stage, I would advise you to focus on the Red Book. It has guidance on all the questions you will need for your examinations although that is some way off as yet. For the time being I would advise you to watch, listen and learn from working on the wards. This week we shall be studying the rudiments of nursing care to prepare you for then.'

'Thank you, Nurse Tutor,' Ethel Lang said.

'Now ladies, follow me into the practical room. We will work in pairs and practice how to bandage a sprain on the ankle and then how to use a triangle bandage for a broken arm.'

Grace linked her arm through Rose's. 'Work with me, won't you?' she said as they followed the others into the practical room.

The rest of the week passed quickly with Grace trying her best to remember everything she'd been taught. Reading through her notes at the end of the Saturday morning, the last day of the teaching week, she realised there was still so much to learn, as well as so much of what she'd learnt that she didn't really understand yet and wondered if she ever would. Then it was Saturday afternoon, and they were being released home for the rest of the weekend. As she walked along Asylum Road towards the tram stop, Grace wondered how Teddy was. She'd not heard anything yet as to whether he was back in England, although he was on her mind all the time. Of course, the easiest way to find out would be to call on his mother in Purbrook Road, so once the tram had arrived at Fratton Station, she made a detour and soon reached her destination.

Mrs Evans opened the door. 'You'd better come in,' she said.

'I won't stop for long,' Grace said. 'I'm on my way home and Ma is expecting me but I needed to know if there is any news yet about Teddy.'

Mrs Evans led the way into the parlour. 'I would have told you earlier, but had no way whilst you were in the asylum. Teddy arrived at the hospital on Thursday. I was able to see him briefly yesterday. He is,' she hesitated. 'He is very much changed. You should prepare yourself for the worst shock.'

'Surely the worst would be his death?' Grace said. 'I mean, he is alive and that's everything isn't it?'

'I know I am wrong in saying this and perhaps I should keep my counsel, but now I've seen him and how he's suffering, I wonder if it would have been kinder...'

'Kinder? Kinder for who?' Grace was horrified.

'Yes, kinder, for him, and for all of us.' Mrs Evans sat heavily in her chair. 'Of course, I can't help thinking if you'd married before, he'd have been more careful.'

'You're blaming me? I am sorry, Mrs Evans, it must have been a horror for you to see him like that.' Grace sat on the edge of the other chair and leaned forward slightly. 'But in time, you might see there is still hope for the future for him. We must be brave and do our best to keep positive.'

'I hope you'll keep that strength when you see him for yourself. Somehow I doubt it.'

'How can you say that? I would like to see him as soon as possible. What are the visiting times? Would there be visiting on Sunday, tomorrow? I won't have any time during the week or for the foreseeable future. I start on the wards on Monday and will have very little time free after that.'

'So my Teddy is not your priority, even now.' She paused. 'Visiting on Sundays is from two until three in the afternoon. He's allowed only two visitors at a time, but you must see him, of course. You may come with me.'

'Thank you, Mrs Evans. I am much obliged. I can call for you after one tomorrow and we will walk to the tram station together. Would that suit you?'

'Of course.' She smiled at Grace and took her hand. 'Tomorrow then.'

'Tomorrow. Now I should be on my way to see my ma and the family.'

Grace walked quickly away, wondering if things would ever be the same. Had she imagined the change in Mrs Evans?

The house was filled with noise when she arrived home a short while later. Ma and Elsie were laughing as they chatted together. Her Pa had only just come in before Grace and was in the scullery pulling off his work-boots.

'This is what I miss,' Grace said. 'Coming home to you all, the happy sound of laughter and knowing all is how it should be in the world. One could almost believe that the war wasn't happening out there.'

'Come and give me a hug then,' her pa called from the back room. 'It's good to see you, girl.'

She hugged him as he stood there in his socks. 'Come through to the warmth Pa,' Grace said. 'Warm up your toes.'

'I will, but let me put my other boots on first. I've been wearing those work boots all day and need some comfort for me old feet.'

'And I want a hug too,' Ma called from the parlour.

'And don't forget me, Grace,' Elsie said.

'All these hugs,' Grace looked around and laughed. 'You'd think we hadn't seen each other for months. It's only a week since I was home.'

'Yes, yes, we know,' Ma said. 'But you've been behind those high walls, locked away and it seems as though you've been gone forever already. It was different when you were at Mrs Simpson's. We knew we could call in and see you if needs be, but we can't now, can we?'

'True I suppose. Come here then.' And she took both her Ma and Elsie in a huge hug. She felt suddenly overwhelmed with emotion thinking about how much life would be altered from now on. Wiping away a tear, she pulled away from the two women.

'I popped in to see Mrs Evans on the way home,' she said. 'Teddy's back. He's in the hospital, Queen Alexandra that is. Mrs Evans and me are going to visit him tomorrow afternoon.'

'Oh dear, Grace. Will you be alright?' Ma asked.

'I don't exactly know, Ma. To be honest, I'm quite afraid of what it'll be like. I thought all last week that I'm strong and can face anything, but now it's come closer, I'm not sure.'

'Shall I come with you?' Ma suggested.

'That's a lovely thought, but Mrs Evans will be with me and only two people are allowed to visit at a time. We'll support each other no doubt. Although I sensed disapproval from her.'

'Poor Teddy.' Elsie glared at her sister. 'I don't blame her for being like that with you. If it had been me…'

'If it had been you? Well, it wasn't you, was it? I know you've always had a soft spot for him, but he only ever wanted me, didn't he?' Grace snapped.

'Stop it, you two,' Ma said. 'What awful things to say.'

'Sorry Ma. I only hope Teddy will be pleased to see me and I'm strong enough not to react when I see his injuries. It will be difficult, no doubt.'

'Life can be difficult I'm afraid, and no more so than in times of war,' Ma said. 'Now, no more of this talk, we need to clear the table for supper. Pa, the water's hot for your wash. I'll fetch you a clean towel.' She bustled about getting things ready. 'Lay the table Elsie, won't you? Grace, take your bag upstairs out of the way.'

'Yes Ma,' they said together as Grace took up her bag and went upstairs.

16

After church the next morning, Elsie and Grace took the tram to the pier and disembarked for a walk along the promenade. It had changed since the early days of the war but still remained a favourite place to walk, the air brisk and the sound of the waves on the shingle was pure music.

They walked in silence for a while, arms linked, until Grace spoke. 'Come along, Elsie, we've talked a lot about Teddy and me since I got home. Now it's your turn. How have things been for you?'

'Oh, I don't want to talk about it to be truthful. Let's just walk for a while and enjoy the sea air.'

'If that's what you really want. Then we will.'

Soon they'd walked along to the far end of Eastney beach. 'Tell me about your work,' Elsie said as they turned to walk back along the way they'd come. 'Is it really grim, like I imagine? What are the other attendants like, and the patients?'

Grace chuckled. 'It's not so grim, to be honest, although I haven't had much time on the wards yet. Most of what I've been doing has been in the classroom. The other trainees are nice enough. I've made friends with a couple of them. It's early days but I think I'll do all right.'

'There must be a lot to learn.'

'We have to study a handbook which has been specially prepared for the instruction of attendants of the insane! Doesn't it sound awful?'

'Oh? Yes, it would put me off if I had to read that.'

'We've been told it's to be our bible whilst doing the training. It's not as bad as it sounds though. It describes the functions of the body and all about good nutrition and general nursing, of course. We have to know how to treat general ill-health as well as madness.'

'Functions of the body? Ugh, I don't think I want to know all about those kind of things.'

'It's just as well you're not going to be a nurse then, isn't it?' Grace said as she grinned back at her sister. 'I must say, my eyes are being opened every day I'm there.'

'We'd better get going or we'll be late for dinner.' Elsie said.

'Yes, I need to be at Mrs Evans' just after one to get to the hospital in time.'

'I'm sorry for what I said about you and Teddy yesterday,' Elsie said as she squeezed her sister's arm. 'Although I can't understand why you're still planning to be a nurse. You can't do both, can you?'

'It's all such a shock, to be honest, Elsie. I don't really know what I want anymore.'

The tram to the hospital was full. Women in their Sunday best with worried faces, some with their families around them. Grace wondered whether all those children would be allowed in the wards. She doubted it but still they would go. As they neared the bottom of Portsdown Hill, Grace's stomach was churning. She was glad she'd not eaten much, she'd been unable to if the truth were told, and when the tram stopped outside the gates of the hospital, her legs trembled as they disembarked.

The corridor was long and seemed to go on forever. Mrs Evans linked her arm through Grace's as they walked. 'Are you sure you want to do this?' she whispered.

'Yes, of course,' Grace answered, lifting her head and pulling her back straight as she walked with a purpose in her step. She noticed the fine portraits of unknown gentlemen on the walls and of course, of Queen Alexandra. There were landscapes too, of ships in Portsmouth Harbour, views across to the Isle of Wight, distracting the visitors as they passed.

At last they reached the ward. The doors opened at a push and once inside, the beds stretched along each side, patients sitting or lying under pristine white sheets and pale blue blankets, all neatly tucked in. Grace noticed the "hospital corners" she'd been taught in the practical room the previous week as she scanned the rows looking for Teddy.

'He's right at the other end, on the left.' Mrs Evans led the way past several who already had visitors beside their beds. Grace tried not to stare at them as she passed and wondered how all these families would ever get back to normal.

And there he was, her own dear Teddy, but unrecognisable with bandages covering his eyes. The blankets covering him were stretched over a frame and she shuddered to think of what might remain of his legs. How would he ever manage?

'Ma, is that you?' He turned his head in their direction. When he smiled, it was his own crooked smile. Something was missing and Grace realised that he'd always smiled with his eyes. She hoped so much that he would be able to use those eyes again one day.

'Yes, Teddy, I'm here, and I've brought along Grace to see you too.' She looked at Grace.

'What!' Teddy snapped back at her. 'Ma, you should have asked me before you did that.'

'Now don't be like that, Teddy. Grace cares for you. She worries. It's not right for you to push her away.'

Grace reached out and touched his hand as she spoke. 'Dear Teddy,' she whispered.

'Don't touch me!' He whipped his hand away in anger. 'Get out, go on, bugger off!'

Grace recoiled and stepped back. Her stomach flipped.

Mrs Evans spoke. 'Teddy, hush, please keep your voice down and mind your language. Everyone is staring at us.'

'So, get used to it, Ma,' Teddy snapped. 'You'd better go, and tell Grace not to come again.'

'I'm still here, Teddy,' Grace said, trying to disguise the lump in her throat. 'And I won't stop coming to see you. How can I?'

'You won't be let in so don't trouble yourself.' He turned his head away.

The two women sat for a while in silence. Grace fought to keep the tears from flowing. She looked around the ward at the other families, wondering if anyone else was experiencing such painful feelings as she was.

'Teddy,' Mrs Evans tried again. 'Teddy, you must be tired and hurting. It's not the time to say things you may regret.'

'No, Ma, I just want you both to go and let me be. And Grace, you must stay away.'

'Very well,' his mother agreed. 'We will go now. But this is not the end of the matter.'

Grace watched in silence as his Ma kissed him on the cheek then she stood, her back straight as she took Grace's arm. They walked briskly down the ward, passing all the other visitors as they each pretended not to be looking at the two broken women.

The tram ride home was taken in silence. Grace stared out of the window, not trusting herself to speak.

At last they reached Fratton and soon were walking through the streets towards Purbrook Road. At the end of the road, Mrs Evans stopped. 'Would you like to come in?

'No thank you, Mrs Evans.' Grace tried not to look at the woman. 'I need to get home.' She ignored the hand reaching out to her and turned away.

'I'm sorry it's come to this.'

Turning to face the older woman, Grace forced a smile. 'I won't give up on Teddy. I only need some time to think now.'

'Of course, of course. I do understand. But remember how young you are. Perhaps Teddy is right. It would be best for you.'

'I told you, I won't give up.' And Grace walked away briskly towards her home.

17

The next few days flowed swiftly on for Grace, with so much to learn and so much to think about in her new life as a trainee nurse. She barely had time to let her future with Teddy to interfere with her days. The nights were another matter. Beset with dreams of her young man being maimed, with her dragging him out of the mud and mire that he seemed to be always trapped in. Every morning she woke, her thoughts fighting with how could she carry on nursing as though nothing had happened, wishing that Teddy was not maimed, was still at the front and would be home soon.

Planning to visit him again as soon as she could, Grace put her mind to her work. Working with Rose was indeed a Godsend for her and kept her mind away from Teddy. One morning Rose and Grace were allocated to do the morning bathing. They were shown the bath book and told how each patient's name in the book had to be ticked off to ensure that their hair was washed, nails clipped, and any issues noted.

Grace had been shocked when she first saw the bathroom, although it wasn't that much different to the bathroom at the workhouse so Rose was used to seeing the two bath-tubs set in the centre of a room, with easy access all around the bath.

Rose put the plug in the first bath and turned on the taps. 'Come on, Grace, let's get this done, we've got a whole list of ladies to do.'

'I don't like this much,' Grace said, as she moved to fill the other bath. 'No dignity for our ladies, is there?'

'It's no different to using the communal bath house. Some of us only ever have baths with other people in the room.' She laughed. 'Of course, you're so posh down your end of town, eh.'

'We are certainly not posh!'

'Posher than me anyway.' Rose flicked water at Grace.

'Oi! Don't start that, you.' Grace scooped a handful of water and hurled it across at Rose, laughing.

'That's it! Now you've asked for it.' Rose took up a glass beaker and filled it from her bath, slinging it towards Grace, who screamed as she ducked. Soon the two women were both soaked and both laughing like a couple of children.

The door to the bathroom opening stopped their frivolity as they realised that Sister Biggs was standing there. 'Bennett. Jenkins. Stop this at once!'

Grace and Rose stood almost to attention, each trying hard not to laugh.

Sister Biggs continued. 'Get on with your duties, young ladies. And when you have finished, go and change into dry uniforms before coming to my office. I will not have this kind of behaviour on my ward. We are not here for fun.' And she swept from the room.

'Did you see she was trying not to laugh?' Rose said as she grabbed a towel and dabbed at her dress.

'I think you're right,' said Grace. '"Not here for fun", she said. But there's nothing wrong with having fun while we can, is there?'

'No need to take everything seriously, is there, Grace?'

'You are so right, Rose. Oh, I am glad we are working together. You probably have saved my life, you know.'

'That's a bit drastic, but I do enjoy working with you as well.'

Before long another two weeks had passed, with enough time off to get to the hospital and back. It was a shock when the Nurse Tutor came to see her on the ward and told her that her mother was waiting in the hospital entrance hall. It could only be bad news, surely, but Grace was not prepared when she saw the panic in her mother's eyes.

'What's happened, Ma?' Grace sat on one of the straight-backed chairs placed against the wall and took her mother's hand. 'Is it Teddy?'

Ma shook her head. 'It's Elsie. She's had a brainstorm. She was arrested. I don't know what's been going on. She attacked her boss and they've certified her. She's here in the asylum. I don't know what to do.'

'Slow down, Ma. What do you mean? How can they certify her?'

'I don't understand it myself. I had to come and see you. Can you help her? Get her home?'

'Oh, Ma. Of course I will do what I can, if I can do anything. But, what about her boss, Mr Medford, isn't it? I never liked him. Is he... is he hurt?

'As far as I know, he isn't badly hurt. I tried to get Elsie to tell me what happened, what led to it, but she was, well, she was disturbed and then the Constable turned up and they took her away. Mr Medford said she'd turned into a mad woman, for no reason, he said.'

'I wouldn't take his word for anything, Ma. Surely even if Elsie's in here, she'll be soon proved sane and they'll let her go,'

'Or she'll be charged with assault and go to prison.' Ma was wringing her hands.

'She might not go to prison, Ma. She can't.'

'What can I do?' The tears were showing in Ma's eyes now.

'You can visit her. And I will go and see her too. I'll do whatever I can to help her out of this. Please don't worry too much. The stories you hear about this place are not always true. I'll do whatever I can to make sure she is well cared for, I promise.'

'I will worry, of course, but I feel better since I've seen you.'

'I'm glad Ma. And it's good to see you. I've missed you.'

Nurse Tutor was sympathetic but reluctant to allow Grace to visit her sister on the assessment ward.

'It's not a good idea to get involved at this stage. Not good for you nor your sister. You could easily make things worse.' Nevertheless she arranged for Grace to spend her short break on the ward with Elsie.

Grace made her way to the far end of the asylum, fretting as she walked briskly, wishing she had a longer break, but also relieved that soon she would see for herself how her dear sister was.

She heard the screams even before the attendant opened door. Hoping it wasn't Elsie, Grace followed her guide down the long gallery, remembering the day she'd visited with Mrs Simpson all those weeks ago. Finally they reached a dormitory.

'Miss Bennett, you have a visitor.' The attendant looked back at Grace. 'She's settled now, shouldn't be any trouble.'

Grace stiffened and looked at the woman. 'She's my sister.'

'Didn't mean anything by it, I'm sure. You should have seen her when she got here, that's all I'm saying.'

'Sorry.' Grace turned away and walked towards the bed where Elsie was curled up like a baby. 'Elsie, it's me.' She reached her hand to touch her sister's shoulder.

Elsie looked up at her. Her face was red and puffy, her eyes staring up at Grace. 'Oh, dear,' she said. 'What have I done?'

Grace sat on the bed and took Elsie in her arms. 'It will be alright, I promise. But what happened?'

'They gave me some medicine. I can't think properly. I just want to go home.'

'Elsie, they say you attacked Mr Medford. What did he do to you? I know you wouldn't have attacked him for no reason.'

'I can't tell you. I can't remember, I don't want to remember.'

'Elsie, this is important. I know it must be painful, but you need to tell me.'

'I don't want to think about it anymore. I'm safe in here.'

Grace took a deep breath. 'You can't think that. You can't want to stay in here. They could keep you in here for a long time. And if they decide there's nothing much wrong with you, you will be charged with a crime and that could be worse.'

'I don't understand. I think I am mad. I must be to have done what I did.'

'Just tell me what happened please.' Grace sat up and looked around the dormitory. 'You can't want to spend your life in here. If you tell the truth, there may be ways you can be helped to get out and to maybe face the court with a lesser charge - even perhaps be found innocent - if it was in self-defence.'

'Self-defence?'

'Yes. If you were attacked first, or something happened to make you defend yourself.'

'They won't believe me. Why would they? He said I led him on. He said such terrible things about me. I asked for it.' Elsie shook her head. 'I didn't lead him on, Grace, I didn't. But they won't believe me. That man is an upstanding member of the community. That's what he said to me. No-one will take my word over his.'

'I wouldn't be too sure about that. What about the other girls in the factory? They must have had trouble with him in the past. Did anyone ever see anything. I know you told me he'd been a nuisance to you before.'

'Nuisance! That's not the half of it.'

'Sorry, I didn't mean to make less of it.'

'I know you didn't mean to, but it makes it seem trivial. I don't think anyone will take it seriously. Being pestered by men is part of life, isn't it? They think they can do what they want. You just have to grin and bear it.'

'But it's not right. And the world is changing, Elsie. We shouldn't put up with that sort of thing anymore.'

'Why? Just because we're doing men's jobs now? You can't really believe life will change for us. Wait until they all come back at the end of this war - if it ever happens. Then we'll be expected to give up our work and go home to the kitchen. That's what we are told, anyway. We're only there for the duration.'

'Maybe, but I have to believe some things are changing for the better for us.'

'Men will always have more rights than us. And we won't have any choice.'

They sat in silence for a few moments, Grace deep in thought. Finally she spoke. 'So, Mr Medford attacked you? Tell me what happened.'

'He followed me into the storeroom, Grace. He had me trapped in there and told me if I screamed I'd be given my cards. I didn't know what to do but when he placed his hands on me,' she paused, sobbing. 'He had his hand inside my blouse - ripped the buttons. I couldn't bear it. I pushed him away. He went for me, again, this time he was trying to push up my skirts. I didn't scream but I bit him, managed to get out of the room and ran up the stairs. I thought I'd be safe once I got back into the main office, but he followed me. He moved so fast, grabbed my foot halfway up the staircase. I held onto the rail and kicked out at him. He fell.'

'Someone must have seen it. One of the girls?'

'It was tea time. They all go outside for fresh air, away from the stink of the cordite. No-one would have seen or heard a thing.'

Grace left a short time later, making her way back to her own ward, trying to work out how she could resolve poor Elsie's plight. She had to get her out of this nightmare somehow.

18

Rose had been thinking about Grace a lot, in between trying to keep her mind on other things - the studying and all the learning new skills on the ward. Making beds and mopping floors she was expert at, but there was so much more to this job. She was a natural at calming mad people, or so Sister Biggs had told her. It hadn't stopped the woman from picking on her whenever she got the chance though. Rose wondered why women went into this lark if they had no patience with others.

It was at night she lay in her bed thinking about Grace. It was so frustrating feeling like this and not being able to tell anyone. Rose had no idea how to show her friend what she felt. She suspected Grace would probably run a mile if she knew.

So, she'd have to take things very slowly, develop their friendship and then see what might develop. She had doubts on her plan of course, convincing herself she'd get nowhere but a friendship would be better than nothing. She told herself they had the same sense of fun. There was indeed hope. Working together nearly every day was enough to keep her going.

One afternoon, on her off duty time, and sick of all these thoughts running through her head which were stopping her from being able to study properly, she threw her book down on her bed and made her way out for a walk.

The bright crisp afternoon air cleared her head as she walked towards the end of Asylum Road, past the fields around the asylum. She stood and stared a moment at the herd of dairy cows in the meadow before going on to the end where the beginning of the disused canal was. Sitting for a while, her legs dangled from the bank as she gazed across the water to Hayling Island. She looked into the distance but there were no answers there, only gulls screaming at her from the sky.

Rose knew about Grace's sister and how worried she must be about her. 'Perhaps there's some way I could help,' she wondered out loud. 'I can't change how I feel about Grace, and it may not be the right time to show my feelings, but I can be a friend to her, can't I?'

Standing up again, she brushed the grass from her skirts and strode off along the edge of the harbour, intent on walking off the feelings of frustration. She watched the waves lapping on the shore, everything seemed so peaceful here. You'd never know the turmoil the world was in, was one of the thoughts in her mind. She wondered what Elsie's story was too. Would she be able to go home soon, or would she be a long term patient, destined to stay in the asylum now she was in. Rosie knew this still happened to many people who found themselves in the place, despite the modern treatments and the determination of the medical officer to try and cure people.

After walking for almost an hour, Rose checked her watch and realised she'd need to get back to work. Along the way, passing the public house, on a whim, she went to the off-licence hatch and bought herself four bottles of brown ale. Berating herself for being too much like her Pa, she justified it as being for Grace, that they'd both need something to cheer themselves up with after a long day working on the ward. Of course, she'd have to get the bottles in without being seen by the House Sister. Thank goodness for deep pockets in her uniform was her thought as she went through the door into the nurses home, carefully trying to avoid a clanking sound, and soon they were tucked away in the bag at the bottom of her wardrobe.

Later that evening, Rose sat on Grace's bed and pulled out the bottles of ale she had hidden in her bag.

'Have you got a mug in here?' She asked.

Grace was at her desk, her head in her hands. She looked up. 'Mug? What on earth?'

'I think you need a little tipple after the day you've had.' Rose jumped up and found the small pot that Grace kept her pencils in, tipped out the contents and poured the ale, passing it to Grace. 'Bottoms up,' she said.

'Really, Rose, you are terrible. What if we get caught? You know the rules about drinking.'

'Rules are made to break. Anyway we won't get caught. Come on, have a drink. It'll make you feel better, for a while anyway.' She laughed and took a swig from the bottle.

Grace took a sip of her drink, making a face. 'I don't drink anymore really,' she said.

'Well it's about time you did. We all need something to unwind with and a little beer don't do any harm to no-one. Or so me old Dad said.'

'You never talk about your family.'

'Nope, you don't want to know.'

'Alright. We won't then. If you don't want to.'

'We don't have to talk about anything, but I'm all ears if you want to tell me what's going on with you.'

'It's my sister, Elsie. She's in A Ward. Well you probably know about it already. I know how people have been gossiping.'

'Yes, I did hear. I also heard she was attacked first by a certain Mr Medford, from the munitions factory. I know some of the girls from there. He's not a nice man, that one. Thinks he's untouchable.'

'Elsie told me what happened but no-one would believe her side of things. He told the police that Elsie did it without him provoking her.'

'We'll soon see about that. I can ask around and see what I can do. Now drink your beer; there's another one in my bag.'

Grace sighed. 'You are a good friend, Rose. I really do appreciate you.'

'Well, I ain't going anywhere Grace.' She looked around the room. 'Who'd have thought we'd be in this place, eh?'

'I know. But at least we can leave whenever we want.' Grace lifted her mug. 'Here's to us, and to getting Elsie out.'

'Yeah, cheers to that.'

19

Grace expected to have a sleepless night, but the tipple had certainly seemed to help her relax and soon it was the morning. A few moments of peace as she woke soon flashed away as she remembered her dear sister who was locked in the ward at the end of that long corridor. She knew there'd be no chance of another visit today, and anyway Grace had other things she needed to do. First, though, she had to get to her duties and soon she was dressed in her uniform and back in the ward, helping to wake the patients, and preparing breakfasts.

She stirred the porridge, wondering about the instructions she'd read in the handbook. The chapter on nutrition and feeding fuel to the body made her smile to herself at the mess she was stirring. How was this supposed to keep a person nourished? Still, she thought, the women on this ward seemed to manage well enough on the diet. A bowl of porridge and a piece of bread for breakfast was filling enough with another chunk of bread and sometimes cheese at midday and a bowl of watery stew for supper. Of course there was always the suet pudding, with rhubarb, something that grew in profusion in the asylum gardens, an occasional treat but one that always seemed to be welcome.

'Wake up Bennett!' Sister Biggs was standing in the doorway to the kitchen, Her apron gleaming white and her cap starched and lacy. 'You'll stir the bottom out of that pot. In the meantime, the patients are going hungry.'

'Sorry, Sister.' Grace hurried to serve the gooey mess into bowls and place them on the wooden trolley.

'And when you've done with that, come to the clinic room and help with the medicines. And don't take all day.' Sister Biggs moved swiftly away along the gallery.

Grace looked around the dining room as she passed out the bowls, wondering about each of the patients in turn. Although they all seemed to be similar, it was only really because of the clothes they wore. Grey dresses, some ill-fitting, with only one or two women in their own clothing. These were the private patients, who paid for their treatment and the board they received. Their food was of higher quality. They still had the porridge for breakfast, as everyone else did, but at supper time, they were served decent meat and vegetables. All the women were troubled in their own way, and Grace wondered about their stories. How had they ended up in here? She was curious, so made up her mind to ask Sister if she could look at some of their notes.

In the clinic room, Sister Biggs was waiting.

'Sorry, Sister,' Grace said.

'You will have to be quicker at your duties. We haven't got all day, Bennett. Now, this is for Joan Hendry. It's Lithium Bromide which is essential for Mrs Hendry. She suffers from acute mania with depression and this is the only medication that can keep her stable. We hope before long she will be fully recovered and can go home again, but only time will tell. Now, you know which lady is Mrs Hendry, I hope.'

'Yes, Sister.'

'Off you go then.'

Grace thought it would be easy. Mrs Hendry was there, still sitting at the breakfast table, and all seemed calm, but as she approached, the woman suddenly leapt from her chair, screaming. The teacup she had in her hand was flung at Grace, hitting her on the front of her uniform. Shocked, Grace jumped back just in time as Mrs Hendry threw herself across the table.

'Get that stuff away from me, you bitch!' she yelled, and pushed Grace in the shoulder. The medicine glass slipped from her hand and smashed, the sticky syrup and broken glass spreading across the wooden floor.

Before she could even wonder what had happened, two attendants were there, grappling with Mrs Hendry and holding her in a vice grip whilst she still screamed abuse at Grace. 'I'll kill you! Get off me, let me get at her!'

Pushed to the floor with force, Mrs Hendry was smacked in the face by one of the attendants whilst the other shouted, 'Shut your gob, you bloody cow.' Then all seemed to stand still.

Sister Biggs was at the clinic door. 'Take her to her room and calm her down. And mind your language.' She spoke quietly and clearly, despite the noise in the room. Other patients who had begun to pace about, moved away as Mrs Hendry was lifted from the floor and taken firmly to her room.

'Bennett,' Sister Biggs spoke. 'Clean up that mess, change your apron and then come here. There's another dose for Mrs

Hendry waiting.' She turned back into the clinic, closing the door behind her.

Grace swept and mopped the sticky floor. She realised she was shaking. What on earth had happened? Would she ever get used to the uncertainty of this work? And the way those attendants had pushed the poor woman to the floor, smacking her and that awful swearing. It was hardly a caring way to deal with a person who was in torment, was it? But she couldn't stop now, she was determined to succeed, and with the war going on, there could only be more need for nurses who were prepared to help those with troubled minds. She only hoped she'd not become like those other attendants. Was she being naive, thinking she could make a difference?

20

Having already decided to spend her few hours off that afternoon trying to help Elsie, Grace walked briskly to Mrs Simpson's house in Southsea. As she walked, she let the morning's happenings run through her mind again. She'd known work in the asylum wouldn't be easy and all the stories she'd heard, the warnings from Ma, were in the forefront of her mind, but today was the first time she'd been in the thick of it herself. She wasn't hurt, coming away from it with nothing but a tea stain on her white apron. She remembered shaking, the fear, the not knowing how to deal with it, but underneath there was something else. Was it excitement? One thing was certain - her life as a nurse would never be dull.

At the kitchen door of the house in Craneswater Avenue, Grace paused before she knocked. Was she doing the right thing by going to Mrs Simpson? She'd been wonderful before, helping and encouraging Grace, but would she be able to or even be interested in helping Elsie?

Shaking her head, she tapped on the door. Almost immediately it opened and there stood Mary, her face beaming. 'Grace. Oh, it's good to see you. Come in. What a lovely surprise.'

'It's good to see you too, come here and give me a hug.' Grace stepped in and the two women embraced.

'It's Grace, Mrs Amberley, come to see us.' Mary led her into the room where Mrs Amberley was sitting at the kitchen table.

'We've just made some tea. Sit down.' Mrs Amberley took up the teapot and began to pour tea into a clean cup even before Grace could answer.

'Thank you. I will have a cuppa please.' She sat down opposite the older woman. 'It's good to be back. I hope all is well with you both.'

'Yes, dear, we are getting along well enough.' Mrs. Amberley smiled as she spoke. 'And we have another helper. Mary's our new parlourmaid, in your place, and we have a new scullery girl, Sarah. It's her afternoon off but she's a good worker. What about you? How are you managing at that place?'

'It's, interesting. Hard work and challenging at times, but I enjoy it. I'm glad you have more help now, and congratulations to you Mary. You will do well.' She paused. 'Actually, I was hoping to see Mrs Simpson whilst I am here. I need to ask her a favour.'

'Oh, la-de-dah, asking favours of the lady of the house now? It must be something important.' Mrs Amberley laughed.

'Yes, it is. But I'd rather not talk about it if you don't mind. No offence meant, but it's very personal and not my story to tell.'

'Don't worry yourself, I was only jesting. To be honest, I think it's wonderful that Mrs S helped you to find your situation in the asylum, much as I don't approve of young ladies working in that place. I can see it was the right thing for you. I just hope you haven't made the wrong choice, that's all.'

'It's not an easy job, but it feels right.'

'Mary, will you pop upstairs and let the mistress know she has a visitor. But let's have our tea first. How is your young man, Grace?'

Grace didn't quite know how to tell them about Teddy. With Mary sitting there, having lost her own young man, it seemed the wrong thing to do. But there was so much of this kind of news about in these times, she knew she couldn't avoid it.

'He's home, but unfortunately, he's been badly injured. I am grateful to have him home, and alive, but whilst he is in hospital, I haven't been able to see much of him.' She paused and looked at Mary. 'I am so sorry, Mary, I know you'd have been more than glad to have Johnny home in any state, but at the moment Teddy won't see me. He's lost both of his legs and his sight is impaired. I know he will recover and a man can get used to having no legs, but he's broken at the moment. He's called off our engagement.'

'I am so sorry,' Mary said. She had a tear in her eye and wiped it away with her apron.

'I won't believe he doesn't want me anymore. Don't worry, I haven't given up.'

'Good girl,' Mrs Amberley turned to Mary. 'Is there any cake in the larder? I think we need something to give us all a boost.'

'And then I'll tell the mistress you're here,' Mary took out the cake and placed it on the table.

The tea and cake over, Grace was called upstairs.

'Tell me about your training,' Mrs Simpson began.

'The work's hard but very interesting. I love helping on the wards with the ladies although sometimes it can be a little fraught. This morning there was a situation which was quite alarming at the time, but afterwards the Sister explained to me why the lady behaves in the way she does sometimes. A little understanding is so important I think.'

'You're certainly correct in that. I knew you'd be a good nurse. You have a natural manner with people who are troubled. But how are you, yourself?'

'I am well, but I worry about my sweetheart, Teddy, who is in the Queen Alexandra Hospital.' She told Mrs Simpson what happened and how Teddy refused to see her.

'That is so sad, but perhaps, in time, he will come around.'

'Maybe.' Grace looked at her hands, then back at Mrs Simpson. 'But that isn't what I've come to see you about.'

'Oh! So this isn't only a social call then?' Mrs Simpson smiled as she spoke.

'I would have come soon anyway, mainly to thank you for all you've already done for me.' Grace paused. 'Only, I am worried about my sister, Elsie. She is a patient in A Ward. I don't believe there is anything wrong with her, but she's accused of attacking her boss, Mr Medford. He's a man with a reputation for behaving in an ungentlemanly way towards the women in his charge. I had experience of how he is myself when I went for an interview at the factory some time ago. Elsie had also previously told me about a time when he assaulted her. She told me what happened on this occasion, and I am sure she acted in self defence.'

'But why is she in the asylum? Was she arrested?'

'She was, but she was so angry and reacted in an unseemly way apparently.' Grace picked at the thread on her dress. 'They deemed she was mad and sent her to the asylum. But if it's proved she's not insane, she will most likely go to prison so she could be in a worse situation.'

'What do you think I can do to help?'

'I don't know, really. I didn't know who to turn to. You have influence and know people who may be able to help. We can't afford to pay a solicitor, and I couldn't bear to see my sister in prison, or in the asylum. I don't know what's worse. I really don't.'

'Hmm, I may be able to help. But I will have to think about it, who to reach out to.'

'Thank you so much. Apart from anything else, that man should be stopped. It's terrible to think a man in power should take advantage of innocent young women, and whilst they are all doing their best to help in the war effort, too.'

'You're right. I can't abide men like that. There are too many of them still about. We will do what we can. But not all men are the same. There are many good ones in the world.'

'I know, of course. Mr Medford is in the minority I'm sure. He just seems so sure of himself. When I spoke to Elsie she said there were no witnesses but I've been to the factory and can't believe that no-one saw what happened. I wonder if people are too afraid to speak up. No-one wants to lose their job or to have their working day made more difficult if they did.'

'Leave it with me, Grace. I will do my best.' Mrs Simpson stood. 'Now, sadly I have to get ready for a meeting at the Town Hall. Do call again whenever you can. I want to hear more about your nursing, and I really hope things do improve with your young man too.'

Standing, Grace took Mrs Simpson's hand. 'Thank you again. I know you will do what you can. And please don't worry about me, everything will work out, I'm sure.'

21

Soon enough Grace's afternoon off was over and she was back on duty. There was a little more hope within her as she walked along the ward gallery that evening, doing the rounds to make sure all was well with the ladies. Supper was over, although the aroma of stewed mutton still hung on the air. The patients were quiet and there was no sign of the disturbance of that morning. She looked in at Mrs Hendry's room. The woman was already tucked up in bed and snoring loudly. 'Thank goodness for that,' Grace whispered.

The evening duties on this ward were simple. All of the patients were able to get themselves to bed, which they all seemed keen to do as soon as the evening drinks were cleared away. There was a medication round at eight o'clock. The day nurse went off duty and afterwards the attendants and nurses were allowed to sit quietly in the gallery, to sew or to read before the night attendant arrived. It was the ideal time to use for studying the notes from the nursing school and to have a look at the handbook they'd been told they needed to know from cover to cover.

Grace sighed as she opened the book. 'So much to learn,' she said to herself.

Approaching footsteps alerted her to Rose who was wiping her hands on her apron as she walked. 'Talking to yourself?' Rose said. 'First sign of madness they say.'

'All this reading we have to do. So much to know. There's never any time to do it all,' she said. 'How are we supposed to cope?'

'Stop moaning, Grace. You know you love it. The reading, the learning, the work.'

'I do. But the days are so long.'

'At least you had the afternoon off today. I've been here since six this morning.'

'Sorry. I know, but there's always other things to do and I don't want to spend my afternoon off studying. Not all the time anyway.'

'What did you do then?'

'I've been so worried about Elsie, so I went to see my old employer, Mrs Simpson. I thought she might be able to help, her being an official visitor and she has so many useful connections.' She looked at Rose. 'I know you said you knew some girls who worked in the munitions factory and you might be able to speak to them, but having someone like Mrs Simpson on our side can only help, don't you think?'

'Of course. The more the merrier, eh?'

'Mrs Simpson may be able to get Elsie a solicitor and if we could find a witness, that would help wouldn't it? Someone must have seen something.'

'I'm sure they did. It'll be hard though. No-one wants to get into trouble.'

'If no-one says anything, who will be the next victim?'

'You're right. I will do what I can, I've said before. He won't get away with it.'

Grace reached across and took Rosie's hand. 'Thank you, I don't know what I'd do without you, Rose.'

It was only meant to be a quick squeeze of the hand, but Grace was reluctant to let go and when she turned to look at Rose, the other woman smiled. Their eyes met for a moment, as some kind of understanding flashed between them. 'We're good for each other, I think,' Rose said quietly.

They both sat in silence for a while, to a background of the sleeping sounds of women in the nearby dormitory. The feel of Rose's hand in hers was comforting to Grace.

'Tell me about Teddy again.' Rose asked, taking her hand away. 'Do you think…'

'That there's a future with him?' Grace's hand felt empty. 'I thought so. I'm not the kind of woman to give up on a man, but, and I feel so guilty even admitting this, I'm not sure anymore. I don't want to give up my work here, my training. Now I've started, I know it's right for me. People at home think I'm mad, I know they do, but to me, it just feels right.'

She stopped and looked around the ward, now in semi-darkness with only the lamp on the table casting shadows. The empty tea cup that had been left there reminded her how thirsty she was.

Rose seemed to have read her mind. 'About time we had a cuppa,' she said as she stood.

'Thanks Rose. Don't tread on too many cockroaches.'

Rose laughed. 'I'm used to them,' she said. 'They soon scatter from my big feet.'

Cockroaches were certainly a part of the evening shifts on the ward, as they all seemed to come out as soon as the daylight faded. Grace shuddered. She could hear them scuttling away as Rose walked.

Grace was deep in thought when Rose returned and sat at the table again. 'How much reading have you done,' she asked. 'Not much, I'm thinking.'

'I've got a lot on my mind.'

'Of course you have, you idiot. I was only joking. But come on, test me on the functions of the lungs. I can never keep anything in my head. I read and read, and it just goes in one side and out the other.'

'I know. I'm the same. And who'd have thought we'd have to learn so much about the human body? I believed it would only be about how to calm people down, things like that.'

'I suppose it's obvious once you start to think about it. If you are healthy in your body, it follows that your mind is better?'

'It depends a lot on other things though. What about the effect the war has on you, worrying about our families, the men away, even our future? How long is this war going to go on for? Food is becoming less and less for a start. How can mothers put good food on the table if there's none in the shops?' She sighed and looked around the gallery. 'I mean look at this lot in here. How many more are there outside who could do with a time away from all the worry?'

'I hadn't really thought much about that, but you are right. We're quite lucky in here, with the asylum farm feeding us. Although a lot of our farm produce will go to feed the troops.'

Grace shook her head. 'I hope it doesn't go on for much longer. It's wearing me down to be truthful. I worry about my brothers. I couldn't bear it if one of them came home like Teddy did, or even worse, not at all.'

'There's not much point in dwelling on it though. Come on, the function of the lungs.

22

They were becoming closer. This was wonderful and at the same time agony for Rose. She wanted to tell Grace her feelings, but was terrified. Would the time ever be right? When Grace had taken her hand and held on for that few minutes longer than was necessary, Rose's heart had been thumping so loudly she was certain Grace could hear it. Then when their eyes had met, it was almost too much altogether. She'd had to take her hand away and ask about Grace's sweetheart. Rose knew she had to be realistic about this but she couldn't help hoping all the same. Moving away to make the tea had given her time to get her feet grounded again although it seemed that Grace's future with Teddy was limited.

At least Rose could help her friend with her sister's plight. The very next day she had off she decided to go the munitions factory herself and meet up with a couple of her old pals. She knew Marg and Peggy still worked there. Making her way across on the ferry helped to clear her head. The sea air was perfect for clarifying things. Her feelings for Grace had been weighing her down ever since the first day they met. She'd have to pull herself together and get on with what she'd joined the nursing school for, to learn new skills and to be of use to people.

All the same, helping Grace's sister was doing something good, wasn't it? And there was always the hope that in time, Grace would get closer to her. As friends, of course, she told herself.

Rose sat outside the factory gates and waited. She knew the women would all come out at twelve noon for their break and she would catch her two old friends as soon as they left. She looked at her watch, only ten minutes to wait. Over by the gate, the watchman was staring at her. She stared back, not feeling intimidated at all. 'It's still a free country,' she said to herself. 'I can sit where I like.'

At last the gates opened and a group of workers were pushing their way through. Rose stood and waved as soon as she saw Marg and Peggy. They came across to her.

'Rose?' Marg said. 'This is a surprise.'

'Are you here to get a job?' asked Peggy. 'I didn't think you wanted to work here.'

'No. I've come to see the pair of you, actually. I'm hoping you can help me.'

'Well it's nice to see you anyway,' Marg said. 'We should get together outside of work. But, I can't think how we can help you.'

'Look. A friend of mine's sister worked here. Elsie Bennett.'

'Oh, her,' Peggy said. 'She's not here anymore. Went mad and got taken to the nut house.'

'I know that. She's in the asylum. I work there now.' Rose said. 'She was assaulted by your boss. But I expect you know that too, don't you?'

Marg and Peggy looked at each other. Peggy shook her head.

'That was what she told the police I expect,' Marg said. 'But it's not true. She can't prove it anyway.'

'Someone must have witnessed something,' Rose insisted.

'We were all out here, on our break,' Peggy said. 'It was all over by the time we got back.'

'Every single one of you was out here?' Rose asked again. 'And no-one saw anything?'

'That's right,' Peggy agreed.

'Well I'm sorry, but I can't believe that, Peggy. What about other times? It wasn't the first I don't suppose.'

'Look, Rose,' Marg said. 'It's more than our jobs are worth to say anything against Mr Medford. I agree he's always been a bit... you know, but you learn how to avoid it, if you're clever.'

'So you let him prey on your work mates?' Rose shook her head. 'I can't believe it.'

'Sorry, life is hard enough these days.' Peggy said. 'We do what we can but need our jobs.'

'What happened to "all for one and one for all"?' Rose looked at them in disgust.

'Don't look like that, Rose,' said Marg. 'We can't afford to lose our jobs. We've both got kids and with the men away, life's not easy.'

'Sorry. I didn't mean to be so...'

'Never mind, and I'm sorry that your friend's in trouble, but we can't help.'

'I'm sorry too,' said Peggy. 'I hope we'll still be friends with you, Rose.'

'Of course,' Rose replied. She stood and gave each woman a hug. 'And we'll meet up soon, although nurse training takes most of my time now, what with the shifts on the wards and the learning from books. Whoever would have thought it of me, eh?'

'I'm sure you'll do well, Rose,' said Marg. 'You always were the brainy one in class.'

'Was I?' Rose frowned. 'I never thought that.'

'Well good luck with it anyway. Although I couldn't do what you're doing, working with dangerous mad people.'

'They're hardly dangerous,' Rose said. 'Some of the stories that come out of the asylum are completely exaggerated you know. Most of the ladies I look after are confused and sad. A few are over-excited and sometimes out of control, but they do get better. Most of them, anyway. And Elsie will get better and go home in time.'

'Well rather you than me, anyway,' Peggy said.

All the way back to the nurses' home, Rose was berating herself, wishing she'd been able to handle her friends in a different way. Perhaps if she'd tried harder, they may have offered to act as witnesses, but realistically, she knew that wouldn't happen. Her heart was dragging her down with its heaviness as she arrived back.

Grace was on duty for the rest of the day, something that Rose was glad of. She decided she'd keep to herself her visit to the munitions factory. There was no point in upsetting Grace even more, and hopefully, her old mistress, Mrs Simpson would be able to help.

23

It was a full two weeks and Grace had heard nothing from Mrs Simpson. She'd tried not to worry and spent as much of her free time as possible reading from the handbook. Of course, there were lectures to go to and daily tutorials in between ward duties and whenever she could she managed to drop in to see Elsie in A Ward. It was so frustrating, seeing her sister who was improving, but was kept in, still waiting to find out what would happen next.

Finally, Grace could wait no longer. Another precious afternoon off arrived as she caught the tram to The Hard, and jumped on the passenger ferry to Gosport. Her memory cast shudders of the time she'd been this way before and she wondered what she thought she could achieve by this journey but knew she just had to try. There was an ominous feeling in the air as the wind across the water caught her hair and whipped it across her eyes.

At last arriving at Priddy's Hard, she marched straight to the factory building. 'I've an appointment with Mr Medford,' she announced at the gate, smiling at the man on duty.

He grinned at her. 'I remember you, Miss,' he said as he let her through.

Well that was easy, she thought, and without hesitating she swiftly carried on walking to the building which housed the munitions girls. She pushed open the door and marched up the stairs to the main office. As she entered, several faces turned to stare at her. Although she felt the blood rush to her head, giving her the rosy blush of embarrassment, this was not going to stop her. Without further ado she entered the inner office ready to face Mr Medford.

The office was empty. Feeling deflated, Grace took a deep breath and stormed back out of the room. She looked around at the women who were still staring at her.

'Where is he?' she demanded. 'Mr Medford, where is he?'

With no reply from the amazed faces, Grace strode back along the row and when she reached the door to the workshop, she turned to the room. 'He can't be far, can he? Don't worry, I'll soon find him.'

She stood at the top of the staircase, looking down at the workers below. Everyone was busy, heads down, the noise of the room so loud that no-one had noticed she was standing there, watching. Scanning the room, Grace saw there was a gap between the women sitting at the tables. Now she knew where Mr Medford would most likely be.

Moving swiftly down the stairs, Grace nodded to a couple of the women who'd now noticed her, and swept past the tables to the storeroom at the end. She tried the door only to find it was locked. There was no key in the door but she could hear noises from within.

Knocking hard, she shouted, 'Mr Medford. Get out here now. I am not going away until you come out. I know what despicable things you're up to.'

There was a brief pause before the door burst open and Mr Medford pushed his way out, forcing Grace backwards and away from the door. She caught a glimpse of a young woman in a state of undress before the man slammed the door behind him.

'Who the hell do you think you are, forcing your way in here. This is a top-secret factory and you are trespassing. I could have you arrested. There is a war on and you are on a very dangerous path.'

'You are disgusting! Behaving in a most ungentlemanly way at such a time. I know I won't get anywhere by speaking to you, but I can only try. I'm here to beg you to withdraw charges you have made about my sister, Elsie. She has suffered enough, don't you think?'

'Your sister! She is nothing but a slut. She attacked me when she'd had enough of me. Oh, yes, she was happy enough to oblige when it suited her. She had special treatment over the other girls.'

'How dare you. You are a liar, Mr Medford.' Grace looked past him at the women working at the tables, many of them watching with open mouths. 'And you lot. Some of you called yourselves friends of Elsie, I know you did. Will none of you step forward? Someone must have witnessed what happened to Elsie that day.'

Mr Medford gave a snort into the silence. 'You see, they know who looks after them, don't you ladies?' He turned back to Grace. 'You're wasting your time, and mine, coming here, disrupting the factory. Now, I'd advise you to get out before you're very sorry.'

He turned and started to make his way back up the stairs. Grace stood for a moment, her eyes looking over the women, many of whom now had their heads down again.

'Alright,' she said to the room. 'I understand why you're afraid to speak up. Just think about which one of you will be in his clutches next. Is it really worth it?' She followed him up the stairs.

Suddenly he spun around and gave her a look that sent a chill through her. Grace stepped back and felt herself losing her balance. It happened so quickly but she saved herself by grabbing a hold onto the rail. That was when she noticed that he was holding a spanner in his hand and as he turned he rapped her on the knuckles with it. Tumbling down the stairs, the last thing Grace saw before falling into a faint, was Mrs Simpson watching from the window of the office above.

Grace woke up with Mrs Simpson and a gentleman kneeling beside her. The noise of the factory had subsided and several of the women were standing beside the tables looking concerned. Others were talking quietly to each other.

Mrs Simpson spoke first. 'Bennett, are you alright? What on earth are you doing here?'

'I had to try and make him change his mind. I've only made things worse,' Grace groaned.

'Never mind that. Let's get you up, slowly now. I don't think you've broken any bones but you can never be too careful.' She turned to the gentleman. 'Come along, give the girl a hand,

George. Oh, I beg your pardon, Bennett. This is my friend, Mr James.'

Soon they had helped Grace up the stairs and out through the front door of the building.

'Wait here, Bennett,' instructed Mrs Simpson. 'George and I have some business first with Mr Medford.'

Grace sat by the water, gazing across to the dockyard. Her mind was filled with what ifs. Even so, she was determined not to let that man win. She wondered how they could get out of this turmoil they were in. Not only in their personal lives - herself, Teddy, Elsie, her dear friend, Rose and all the troubled souls at the asylum. It seemed to her to reflect the wider picture of what was happening in the world. She thought about herself, her own choices in the past year. Was she using the madness of working with the insane as a way to deny what was going on in Europe? Her work was certainly taking her mind away from those horrors. She felt an overwhelming guilt at the lack of time she'd spent thinking about her brothers. How were Wilfred and Bert faring? Thinking about them was too hard.

'Come along, Bennett,' Mrs Simpson's voice broke into Grace's thoughts. 'Let's get you back across the ferry and home.'

Grace stood. 'What did he say?' she asked. 'Have I made it worse.'

'I don't think you will have anything more to worry about from that gentleman,' Mrs Simpson smiled grimly. 'He would be foolish if he tried to take this any further.'

24

Time passed and still there was no news about Elsie. Grace wondered if she'd imagined what Mrs Simpson had said about Mr Medford. 'They all stand together, don't they,' she said to herself. 'Poor Elsie, what will become of her?'

Grace's daily work continued. She was relieved that Mrs Hendry seemed to be more settled and now there were some new ladies on the ward. She learned about the admission process of writing the new patient's notes, how the doctor assessed and diagnosed each one, and what treatment was best. Being a new patient in such a setting could not be easy for the ladies at such a time of confusion for them. Grace realised she seemed to have a way to help settle them sometimes, whilst at others, nothing seemed to help until the patient was given a draught to help them sleep.

Mrs Pullman was a private patient. She'd only recently had her first baby and somehow this had caused a madness. She believed she was poisoning her child with her milk and had stopped feeding the poor little mite. Finally, her husband, a lieutenant in the navy, had asked for her to be admitted whilst the baby was being cared for by a nanny under the supervision of his own mother at home. Mrs Pullman's own mother was nowhere nearby to help.

Grace had no experience of caring for a baby, nor childbirth, but thought she felt Mrs Pullman's pain, realising it was just another part of women's lot, being expected to be good wives and mothers, but without any real training for it. She thought of her own ma and was grateful for having such a loving, caring person in her life.

One morning early, just after the breakfast tables had been vacated by most of the ladies, Grace was brought down to earth with a loud crashing noise coming from the dining room. She ran towards the sound of an endless screaming, fleetingly wondering where the other attendants were. Sister was in the clinic in the middle of dressing a wound, and the others were in the bathroom supervising the morning baths. The shock of the sight that greeted Grace at the scene didn't really come back to her until much later. For now, she was horrified to see two women on the floor beside an over-turned table, crockery in pieces all around. Mrs Hendry was on her back with Mrs Pullman sitting astride her as she gripped the other woman by the hair and repeatedly smashed her head into the floor.

Hesitating for only a second, Grace shouted, 'Stop it, Mrs Pullman, stop it!' whilst she grasped at Mrs Pullman's arm to try and pull her off.

Mrs Pullman, letting go of the other woman, swung around to punch Grace in the face, then pushing her away, she got to her feet and ran down the corridor to her room, banging the door behind her.

'She's got a broken cup with her,' shouted one of the other ladies who'd been watching at a safe distance. 'I saw her pick it up. She's got it with her.'

Grace, still on the floor, feeling dazed and ashamed that she'd let this happen to her, tried to get up.

Sister Biggs appeared beside her. 'What on earth is going on here?' she demanded.

'Mrs Pullman was attacking Mrs Hendry.' Grace struggled to her feet. 'She ran to her room but might have a broken cup with her.'

'I see.' Sister looked down at Mrs Hendry. 'Are you alright? Come along, let's get you up on your feet. Bennett, help her into a chair.'

Soon, Mrs Hendry was sitting up and Rose, with two other attendants had appeared from the bathrooms. 'Jenkins, take care of her. We need to make sure Mrs Pullman is safe.'

'What happened?' Rose was asking. 'Are you alright, Bennett?'

'She is perfectly well.' Sister barked as she turned to Grace. 'Follow me, Nurse Bennett.'

The sight that greeted them on opening the door was one Grace would never forget. It was the blood that was most shocking, spurting like a fountain from Mrs Pullman's left arm as she sat on the middle of her bed, gripping the broken crockery in her hand as she sliced into herself. Grace wanted to rush in and stop her but Sister Biggs gently raised her hand to stop her at the same time as she spoke to the distressed woman on the bed.

'Mrs Pullman, it's alright my dear. It's all over now, you can stop it now.'

'Don't come any closer,' Mrs Pullman screamed. 'You are the devil, like everyone else in here.'

'It's me, Sister Biggs. You know me. I am here to help make you better. To keep you safe.' Her soothing voice seemed to calm the very air in the room as Mrs Pullman slowly ceased cutting herself. 'Here, let me help you.'

As Mrs Pullman slumped onto the bed, dropping the sharp fragment of crockery, Sister Biggs moved forward, taking up the pillow and pulling the pillow-case from it, wrapping it around the woman's arm to stop the flow of blood.

Grace looked around the room, now covered in splatters of bright red blood. She suddenly felt sick.

'Bennett. Go and fetch Dr Blake. Tell him we need his services. I will remain here until you return.'

The Doctor's office was only a short walk along the main corridor and soon Grace had returned with him. She'd quickly told him what had happened and he gave instructions as they reached the ward. 'We will need a wound stitching kit. Do you know how to organise that?' He asked.

'Yes Doctor,' Grace replied. She showed Dr Blake to Mrs Pullman's room and went straight to the clinic.

Sister Biggs was soon beside her. 'We need something to sedate Mrs Pullman as well,' she said. 'You lay up the trolley for the stitching and I will organise her medication.'

Watching the Doctor sew Mrs Pullman's arm, Grace was both fascinated and disgusted. How could someone do that to themselves? And yet, how interesting the human body was. She could see the flesh underneath the skin, all the way to the bone. Would it ever really heal? The scar would be terrible and she fleetingly thought it was lucky for the woman that long gloves were so fashionable. It would be hard to hide such a wound from the world without gloves.

The stitching took some time to complete, but Mrs Pullman was sedated now and her eyes were glazed. Finally, the patching up was done, and the Doctor and Sister Biggs prepared to leave the room.

'Mrs Pullman will need to have a clean bed,' Sister said. 'Bennett, put her in the spare bed in the dormitory for now. I will instruct the maids to clean this room before she comes back. You will have to stay beside her until then.'

'Yes, Sister.'

'Put her in a bath chair, we don't want any more incidents today, do we?'

Soon enough Mrs Pullman was safely in a dormitory bed, with Grace sat beside her, watching the woman's breathing, the troubled frown on her face gradually receding. It was only then that Grace felt herself shaking. What had she brought herself to? A question that kept coming up every time something like this happened. Was this really for her? As she watched the sleeping woman, she felt herself relax, the shaking subsided and was replaced by a warm glow that she had somehow achieved something, learnt something from the older Sister who had remained so calm and yet so completely in charge during the whole incident. 'Can I ever be like her?' she wondered.

'I'll bet you could do with one of these?' Rose burst into the nurses' lounge later that evening. 'What a flipping day?'

Grace looked up from her reading. 'I know. I'm trying not to think too much about it.'

'Sorry.' Rose waved two bottles of ale. 'I've got just the thing to take your mind off it.'

Grace laughed. 'You are so bad for me.'

'Bad as each other. But you know it's what you need.'

'All right, I give in.' Grace agreed. 'But not out here where anyone can see. You know we're not allowed alcohol in the nurses' home.'

'Better than drinking on the streets, isn't it?'

'All the same.'

'Come to my room then,' Rose grinned. 'And bring a mug. Unless you want to swig from the bottle.'

'I'm not a degenerate!'

'Really? Oh that's a disappointment.'

'Honestly, Rose, you are terrible.'

'I know, but you love me, don't you?'

Grace blushed. 'Stop it.'

'Only joking,' Rose turned and walked towards her room. 'Come on then, if you're coming.'

'I am, and I've something better to drink out of. I'd forgotten Mrs Simpson gave me a very nice tea-cup and saucer when I left her employ. I will drink my beer out of that.'

'Oh hoity-toity,' Rose laughed.

25

The next morning, finally a note arrived from her friend and ex-employer, inviting Grace to call at the house in Craneswater Road. She replied to the note immediately and on her next afternoon off she made her way to her old place of work. This time she rang the front doorbell which was answered by her old friend, Mary. 'You look very smart, Mary,' she whispered as she was shown into the drawing room.

'I'm glad you could come,' Mrs Simpson greeted her guest. 'I have good news about your sister. Mr Medford has finally withdrawn his complaint.'

'Really? That's good news. Will he lose his position? The man is a menace and should be sacked.'

'Sadly, at the time of war, he is needed. And besides, seeing him getting just desserts is something beyond even my influence.' Mrs Simpson smiled. 'Let's just be glad that your sister will be able to get on with her life. I'm sure she will be discharged from the ward soon. I hear she is doing well.'

'I'm so grateful for your help, whatever it is you have done to persuade that man to back down. Thank you.'

'You are most welcome. Now tell me about how you're getting on.'

Later that week, Elsie was released from the asylum and the following Wednesday Grace made her way home on her afternoon off to help welcome her younger sister home. Approaching the familiar street with excitement in her heart, she was passing Purbrook Road. Something made her glance along the street, thoughts of Teddy in her mind, and there he was. She was sure it was him, sitting in a bath chair outside his home. But who was with him? Grace was taken aback as she watched her sister, standing beside her Teddy, smiling at him, no eyes for what else may be happening in the street.

Her thoughts in confusion, Grace made her way towards the two of them. Elsie saw her first. She looked at Teddy and then waved to Grace. Taking a few steps to her sister, Elsie held out her arms. 'Dear Grace,' she said, 'I am so happy to see you. You've heard my news then?'

'That you have been released? Yes, I've been so worried about you. I thought you'd never be home again.'

'I think it might be thanks to you, Grace. I heard what happened at the factory.'

'That man is a menace and should be locked up.' Grace turned to Teddy who was sat there watching them both.

'Teddy, it's good to see you home.' She paused. 'Are you still having treatment? How are your eyes?'

'My eyes are better, thank you.' He spoke in a pleasant enough manner like one would to a friend rather than a sweetheart.

'That is good news,' Grace shifted on her feet. 'I have missed you,' she added.

'I'm sorry, Grace,' he said. 'I was rude to you when you visited me, but it still stands. What I said, I mean.'

'I don't know what to say,' Grace looked at Teddy then turned to Elsie. 'I have to go, Ma is expecting me. Are you going home?'

'Of course, I will walk with you.' Elsie turned to Teddy. 'I'll speak to you tomorrow?'

'I look forward to that. Goodbye, Grace.'

Elsie walked arm in arm with Grace down the street. As soon as they turned the corner, Grace spoke.

'What is going on?' she asked.

'I don't know what you mean.'

'Between you and Teddy. I saw the way you two were looking at each other. There's a spark between you. I know there is.'

'Nonsense. I just feel sorry for him.'

'Really? There's a difference between feeling sorry for someone and what I saw in your faces.'

'Why do you care? He is not your property?'

Grace stopped walking and turned to her sister. 'Why do I care? I am aware he is no longer mine. Although I had believed he would change his mind.'

'But you didn't want him. He told me you stopped visiting him. He assumed you'd changed your mind.'

'No! That is not true.' Grace was aghast. 'Elsie, he told me that he wanted to end our engagement and I wasn't welcome to visit him again. I still want him, more than ever now.'

'If that's true, why haven't you tried harder to see him?' Elsie began to walk again.

Grace hurried to catch up. 'It must be some sort of mistake. He did say those things to me, really he did. You can ask his ma if you don't believe me. She was there with me at the time.'

'Alright. I will take your word for it. But Teddy tells me he is free now, so what will you do about it?'

Grace hesitated. 'I don't know. I should speak to him.' She sighed to herself. 'I will speak to him.'

'I think you should, but please, Grace, be sure of what you really want before you do.'

'Don't worry, Elsie. I am sure.' And they continued their walk home together.

The celebration of Elsie's homecoming was going on late into the evening but Grace needed to be back at the nurses home by nine o'clock. Saying her goodbyes on the doorstep, she walked back to Fratton station alone, thinking about their earlier conversation and what she'd witnessed between Elsie and Teddy. As she passed the end of Purbrook Road, she glanced towards his home, wondering what she should do and what she really wanted. Elsie had been right. She owed it to Teddy to be sure of what exactly she wanted her future to be before she had the right to speak to him. One thing was sure, Teddy wouldn't be going back to the front in the near future and probably not ever. If she chose to stand by him, she would have to give up any thought of a career in nursing. All nurses had to be single women and that wasn't going to change anytime in the near future.

Soon Grace was back in the nurses home. Her heart lifted as soon as she entered and saw Rose was still up. The other nurses were all in their rooms.

'You're back, and just in time.' Rose stood as she spoke. 'I was about to make a pot of tea. You will join me?'

'Thank you. It's been quite a day.'

'So come to the kitchen and tell me all about it.'

'I saw Teddy.' Grace blurted her news.

'Teddy? Really?' Rose lifted the boiled kettle from the gas stove. She looked at Grace. 'And…?'

'He was with my sister. They were together outside his house. It was a surprise to be honest and now I don't know whether I'm on my head or my heels.'

'When you say, "together", what do you mean exactly?'

'I mean they were together in the street, but I could see there was something more there than friendship. I asked Elsie about it and she didn't deny it. He'd told her I didn't want him anymore. That's not how it happened, it was his choice. I need to speak to him, but now I'm not sure what I want anymore.'

'A bit of a muddle then.' Rose took the pot of tea and two mugs with some milk in a little jug and carried them through to the sitting room. 'It's late. You need to have some sleep. It may be more clear in the morning. Here, drink your tea.'

'I just wish I knew what to do.'

'We can talk more about this properly when you've had a bit more time to think about it.'

'I'm not sure I will sleep much tonight.'

'Once your head hits that pillow it will come soon enough,' Rose said as she stood up from the table. 'Goodnight, Grace.'

'Goodnight.'

Grace watched as Rose made her way to her room. She smiled to herself at the thought of having such a friend.

26

Grace lay awake, all the events of the day churning over and over in her head. What did she want? The question became so much harder to answer as each day passed. There was so much to consider: what were her true feelings for Teddy? Did he love her still? Was there a spark between him and Elsie? Was being a nurse more important to Grace than being Teddy's wife? Did the thought of being with a man with no legs matter? Could she ever cope with giving up nursing? And then there was her friendship with Rose. Grace had never had such a closeness with a woman before. It seemed like something special, maybe frightening, was happening.

As the hours passed, Grace told herself she needed more rest than answers now, but it was only when she'd made the decision to go and meet with Teddy for a proper conversation that she managed to relax and allow the sleep to come.

Grace's next day off was over a week away. There was only work, study, and more work to keep her occupied. She tried not to think too much about her decisions, hoping the answers would come in good time.

Another new lady was admitted to the ward and Sister Biggs announced Grace would be responsible for her well-being.

'You will greet the patient, try to make her feel at ease, and complete the admission nursing form.' She handed a sheet of paper to Grace. 'Once completed, show her to the bed in the dormitory. We will need to keep her under observation of course, until we know more about her behaviour.'

'Yes, Sister.'

'Her notes from the workhouse say she can be violent, so be wary, and don't take any nonsense from her.'

'No, Sister.'

'There's no need to be alarmed, Bennett. I wouldn't ask you to take her on if I didn't think you had it in you. Just be firm but kind, and you won't go wrong. Her name is Mrs Smith. Gladys Smith. She is widowed and not long delivered of a child which has left her unhinged. A sad but all the more familiar predicament for young women since the start of the war, I am sorry to say.'

'That is sad,' Grace said, thinking of her own situation and how terrible it was for Teddy. 'Will this war never end?' she sighed.

'All wars end eventually, Bennett.' Sister Biggs said. 'And we nurses are left to pick up the pieces afterwards. Now, Mrs Smith will be here later this morning so you'd best get on with finishing your normal duties before she arrives. Once she is here, you will need to keep an eye on her for the rest of the day.'

Mrs Smith was sitting alone in the sunshine of the day room. She'd been brought in by attendants from the workhouse.

'Hello, my dear,' Grace said as she sat beside the new patient. 'I'm to be your nurse today. My name is Bennett.' She hesitated. 'But you may call me nurse.'

There was no response from the young woman.

'I know your name is Mrs Smith - Gladys Smith. I need to ask a few more questions of you, if you don't mind.'

Mrs Smith looked across at the piano which was prepared for someone to sit and play, the lid opened and music on the stand. Grace thought she was about to speak, but she only shook her head.

'I know you must be afraid, being brought in here.' Grace tried to reassure her. 'It can be quite frightening the first time, but it's not so bad.' She held out the paper Sister Biggs had given her. 'I must complete this form. It's so we can help you with any treatment you might need so you can recover. But you will need to answer some of my questions.'

Mrs Smith shifted in her chair. She looked toward the window.

'Would you like to move to the seat beside the window?' Grace asked. 'We could look out at the fields. If you like,' she added.

Mrs Smith stood.

'You would?' Grace stood too. 'Very well, lead the way.'

They sat looking out across the gardens where they could see the trees in the distance that encircled the fields. The walls of the asylum stood between the gardens and the fields but were low enough at that point to see the ploughed earth beyond. Grace wondered what Mrs Smith must be thinking, being unable to leave this place and wander in the countryside by herself. Was she feeling despondent being in here, or relieved that the real world was left behind?

'Mrs Smith,' she began again. 'I am going to complete this form as much as I can for the moment. I know your name and have your home address and other information from your notes from the workhouse. The other things I need to ask, we can work on later.' She paused, hoping for a response. 'Now, I want you to know that I am here to help you, as all the nurses and doctors are in here. We all want you to get well enough to go home. So remember, I am here for you. I'll show you to your bed now. We'll put you in the dormitory so we can keep an eye on you more easily. You'll be with other women. It is quite full in the dormitory but you'll be safe in there.'

Mrs Smith's first night in the ward was not as happy as it should have been. The following morning when Grace arrived for duty she discovered that the young woman had been involved in an incident in the night with a neighbouring patient. It was unclear as to who had been the instigator of this, but needless to say, Mrs Smith had been removed to a side room.

After receiving the handover from the night nurses, Grace made her way to the room and unlocked the door.

Mrs Smith was hunched on her bed, looking at Grace in fear as she entered.

'Please, don't be afraid,' Grace said. 'It will be alright, really it will.' She held out her hands to the frightened woman to show that she had nothing hidden. 'I am only here to help you.'

Mrs Smith sat up and stared at the wall.

'They said at the workhouse that you couldn't speak,' Grace said. 'Perhaps speaking is something that feels like too much at the moment?'

Mrs Smith looked at Grace but said nothing.

Grace tried again. 'Please, I'm only here to help you. I can see you're not ready to talk yet, but I'll come back and try again later.'

Mrs Smith sank back onto the pillow and remained quiet. Grace smiled at her. 'You must rest now,' she said. 'I have work to do on the ward but I will look in on you to make sure you don't need anything. We'll bring you in some breakfast later too. I'll lock your door again so you won't be disturbed. But I will come back.'

Sister Biggs was waiting for Grace in the office. 'Now you'd best write up the notes before you forget anything,' she said. 'And be quick about it. We're all behind with the morning tasks.'

'Yes, Sister.' Grace sat at the desk. 'Although she wouldn't speak to me, so I'm not sure what to write.'

'You must write an account of what you observed, Bennett,' Sister said. 'I popped along and looked in the window at you. Don't worry, you will soon gain her trust.' And she swept out of the room.

Grace picked up the pen and began to write. 'Where to start?' she wondered. She knew from what she'd learnt in the training sessions you could only write the facts and your impressions on the behaviour. You could not make diagnoses. And once you'd written down anything it would be there for all to see with no room for corrections. She'd read some of the previous notes on patients and was horrified at how some of the attendants made judgements on people that couldn't possibly be correct. She hoped she'd never be as jaded as some of the older attendants were.

27

It was a bright but cold morning when Grace next left the asylum building. As she walked she noticed how the year was moving on. There were the first signs of daffodils in the gardens she passed and although many of the trees were still bare, there was definitely the feel of winter coming to an end. Green shoots of new leaves were beginning to sprout, and the air smelt of optimism.

Soon she was standing outside Teddy's house in Purbrook Road. Grace had given much thought to what she was going to say but now she was here, she hesitated to knock on the door. She'd realised her work was very important to her but her feelings for Teddy remained strong. Finally, she knocked, and the door was immediately opened by Mrs Evans.

'I wondered whether you were going to knock or go away again. I saw you from the window as you passed. Come in.' She opened the door wide for Grace to enter.

'I'm sorry, Mrs Evans, I wasn't sure...'

'Never mind. Just come in. I'll tell Teddy you're here. I know you two need to talk.'

'I was hoping he'd see me,' Grace said. 'But I'll wait here in the hall if you don't mind. I really don't want to impose on him.'

'Nonsense. He owes it to you to see you at least. But wait here if you wish.' And she turned towards the back parlour.

Grace felt the gush of warm air and the usual aroma of baking as the door opened and closed. She waited, trying not to listen through the thin walls.

Finally, the door opened again and Mrs Evans ushered her in. Teddy sat beside the range in his bath-chair. He looked at Grace. 'Forgive me for not standing,' he said.

'Of course,' Grace stuttered then realised he was being sarcastic.

'Are you going to sit down, then?' He looked at the other chair. 'Or just look down on me?'

'Sorry,' Grace said and she sat in the chair opposite. 'Look Teddy...'

'It's something that I can still do,' he said. 'Just about.'

'Yes, it's wonderful you have your sight back now, at least.'

'At least. That doesn't make me a catch anymore though, does it?'

'Teddy, please don't.' Grace leaned forward. 'I know you must be hurting terribly but I still love you. I haven't given up hope that we can be together.' She paused. 'If that's what you want, I mean.'

'What I want? Do you actually think I have a choice anymore? I am only half a man now and can never be whole again. Is that what you really want? It's not up to me is it?'

'Of course it is.' Grace hesitated. 'I gave you my word before you went away that I would wait for you. I haven't broken my word. I do still want you.'

'Then why do you hesitate? And why has it taken you so long to come to see me? I've been home for weeks now. You have made it clear to me what's important to you.'

'But you told me not to visit. You said I shouldn't come.'

'I would never have said that.' He paused. 'You didn't even try.'

'I couldn't leave my duties before. You understand duties, don't you?'

'I certainly do understand duties. I'm the one who's been on the front line after all.' He glared at her. 'But you, you have been following your wish to become a nurse. You're able to leave at any time, only you choose not to. So now you come to me asking me what I want. I will tell you. I want a wife who will be there for me, not just doing her duty, but wanting to be with me whatever the circumstances. Not being put second to her career.'

'Times are different during a war, Teddy. You know that.' Grace sighed. 'You can't expect me to leave nursing now. Although if that's what you want, then I will.'

'Of course it's not what I want. What I wanted is for you to be how you were before I went away. When I was the centre of your world, things were clearer then. We both knew what we wanted of our future together. What's happened to me has changed me and your new career has changed you too. I honestly don't think I want you anymore. Not how you are now.'

Grace flinched at the bitterness of his words. 'You haven't even given us a chance to get to know each other again. It's only been a matter of a few months. We can't have both changed so much in so little time.'

'It's not the time, it's what's happened. I'm sorry.'

'I'm sorry too,' Grace said as she blinked back the tears that threatened to fall. She looked around the room, at the neat curtains at the window, the checked tablecloth, depicting everything she thought she'd always wanted out of life. 'I'd better go. I hope we can still be friends,' she added.

'I'm sure we can,' Teddy said. He looked away.

'What about Elsie?' Grace said. 'I noticed there's something of a spark between you two.'

'She's been there for me. When I needed someone to lean on.'

'When I wasn't.' Grace felt the sting in his voice. 'Well I am happy for you both. I hope you look after each other.' She stood. 'I should go.'

Mrs Evans was still waiting in the hallway. She smiled at Grace and took her hand. 'I am so sorry,' she said. 'But I don't understand you young people.'

'It's all right.' It was only when she was in the street that Grace allowed the tears to flow. But if she were truthful to herself, with the tears was also a feeling of relief.

With the rest of the day off before her, Grace found herself climbing onto the tram and taking the journey through the town and up to the bottom of Portsdown Hill. Glad now of her warm jacket, she stepped from the tram into the blustery winds and made off at a brisk pace towards the top of the hill where she knew there were seats looking out over the town below.

As she walked, memories of the past flooded into her mind. She remembered the last time she'd been here, with her brothers and Elsie. They were still youngsters then, with no thought of a war to come which would change all their lives. With her brothers still in Europe, she thought about how lucky they were to be alive after so many of their pals had perished in the past year. But were they still alive? The family hadn't heard from either of them since Christmas, and they could have been injured, or lost. She had no idea and could only hope.

Reaching the top, now walking along the flat area where the funfair once had been held, watching the sheep in the distance as they grazed with no idea of the turmoil going on in the world of humans, Grace smiled to herself, trying to shake away dark thoughts of her brothers' fates. She thought about Teddy and how he was going to manage in the future. Her emotions were troubled indeed. She couldn't help but feel guilty to have chosen nursing over her sweetheart. But she told herself it was his choice. She would have stood by him if he'd only let her. And she was glad he had Elsie.

A passing cloud sent a chill over the length of Grace's spine, together with a feeling she was being watched. She stopped and spun around. The ground was covered in gorse shrubs and in the distance the sheep seemed untroubled still. There was no-one else around. She was alone. 'I must be going mad,' she said out loud. 'They said madness might be catching, I'd better be careful.'

Laughing to herself she walked on and eventually reached the viewing point where she sat looking out across Portsmouth. Even in the middle of war, the view was special. From here, you could almost believe nothing had changed. She could see the spire of St Mary's Church and the rows of houses beyond, where her own home was. Nearer were the roofs of the Queen Alexandra Hospital where Teddy had been brought only a few weeks before.

In the distance she could see the walls of the asylum, the clock tower and the green of the fields where some of the patients were allowed to work. On the other side of Portsea Island were the docks where her pa worked and across the water in Gosport was Priddy's Hard and the munitions factory.

Thinking about Priddy's Hard and all that had happened there brought another shiver along Grace's spine. She shook her head. 'I'm not thinking about that anymore,' she told herself. 'It's over now and Elsie is safe from that man.'

Across the Solent was the Isle of Wight. The sky was clear and you could see every detail of this side of the island, something that only happened occasionally, the view often being covered in mist from the sea. It was so peaceful today, but Grace couldn't shake off the feeling she was being watched. Looking around again, there was a movement beside a shrub but as she stared, she was sure she'd imagined it. Angry that thoughts of Mr Medford was spoiling her day off, she stood up and shouted towards where she'd thought she'd seen someone, 'You are not scaring me! Leave me alone!' Immediately feeling silly at shouting to the wilderness Grace shook her head as she walked swiftly towards the shrub. Of course there was no-one there.

Taking the tram back to Fratton Station, Grace still had time to call in to see her ma and take a walk with her sister.

They strolled towards St Mary's Church as they talked.

'I've been to see Teddy this morning,' Grace began. 'We have come to an agreement.'

Elsie shrugged her shoulders. 'Really? And why are you telling me?'

'Elsie, let's not pretend anymore. I know you have feelings for him. When I think back to before the war, you always had a fondness for him, you know you did.'

'So, what if that's true?'

Grace stopped walking and turned to her sister. 'I'm not judging you, Elsie. I don't blame you, nor Teddy. None of us can help our feelings, I know that. I just want you to know I will always love Teddy, but I realise it's for the best we break off our engagement. We talked this morning and agreed we would stay friends.'

'Stay friends, but you will always love him?'

'I mean, I will always be fond of him. We were very close for a long time, you know that.'

'How close?' Elsie frowned as she spoke.

'Not that close. Don't worry, we didn't...'

'Never mind. I don't want to know.' Elsie took Grace's arm. 'You are my sister and dearest friend. I am sorry it hasn't worked out for you but, yes, I am pleased too.' She paused. 'Are you sure you're all right?'

'I feel - sad it hasn't worked out, but I feel relieved too that Teddy is safe and he has you. Are you sure you can cope with his injuries though?'

'I love him. I know it might be difficult, but we will manage.'

'I love you, dear Elsie. You'll always be my little sister. I know things have been difficult between us at times, and we don't always agree on things. But remember, anything you want help with, I am always here for you.'

28

Grace sat in the nurses' sitting room later, thinking about all that had happened. She felt at home in the surroundings she was in, with the bustle of the other trainees around her. She also felt a weight was lifted now she'd finally made some decisions about her future.

Ethel was sitting at one of the tables, her attention on the books she was surrounded by. Grace felt a little guilty she'd allowed herself to become so distracted as she realised she'd been neglecting her own studies.

'Look at you, Lang,' she said. 'Always with your head in a book.'

Ethel looked up. 'I know, I'm the boring one, but I do struggle to remember anything.'

'How are you getting on in the ward?' Grace asked. Ethel was also on M Ward but the women weren't always on duty at the same time.

'I think I'm doing fairly well, although it's hard to tell with Sister Biggs. She's always telling me I'm useless.'

'Really, I'm sure she doesn't mean it. It's just her way, isn't it?'

'Does she do that to you?'

'Sometimes,' Grace thought for a moment. 'Although I have found her quite encouraging.'

'It's just me then.' Ethel sighed.

'I'm sure it's not. I just haven't been caught out yet,' Grace grimaced. 'I feel like I'm completely out of my depth most of the time. The work can be frightening, can't it?'

'Very. I sometimes wonder what I'm doing here and if I can last much longer.'

'I know how you feel, and yet, being here I feel completely at home as well.'

'I can't say I do. I just keep thinking that if I do the reading, learn all the practical lessons in the classroom, one day it will become clear and I'll know exactly what I'm doing.'

'Hmm, I'm not sure that will ever happen for me. There is so much to learn.'

'Exactly, so if you don't mind, I'm going to get on with my studies.' Ethel smiled and turned back to her reading.

Grace sighed to herself and went into the kitchen. She stood at the window, looking out into the dark evening. There was a chill in the air coming through the gaps in the window frame. The building was less than fifty years old and had not been built for warmth, rather to let in light and fresh air. Of course there was warmth beside the fireplaces but not in places like this little kitchen which was only designed to make cups of tea for the nurses. Main meals were taken in the staff dining room.

Other nurses were sitting about on the sofas in the lounge. Grace called out to let them know there was tea in the pot. She'd noticed some who'd started their training earlier than Grace and her friends: Nellie Brown, with her fiery red hair and freckles, and Annie Wilde whose sleek black hair was in contrast to Nellie's. They'd been reading their study books as well as Ethel but both looked pleased to be disturbed by the promise of a cup of tea.

'Thanks Grace,' Nellie said. 'Or should I call you Bennett?'

'I hate all this surnames only,' Annie Wilde said. 'I am Annie to my friends and I hope I can call you lot my friends.'

'I suppose I wouldn't like it either if my name was Wilde,' Nellie laughed.

'Anyone know where Rose is?' Grace asked. She'd have liked to have shared the outcome of the day with her.

'She got into a bit of bother on the ward today and Sister made her stay to help clear up the mess.' Annie said.

'Really? What happened? Is she alright?'

'I think so. It was another new patient who didn't want to be here. Rose had to restrain the woman and by the time they got her to a side-room, some of the other patients decided to get involved and things got smashed up. Rose should be back soon. It wasn't as bad as it sounds. I think Sister Biggs was in a bad mood and had to pick on someone to blame.' Annie shrugged her shoulders. 'I've seen that side of her before. She has her favourites too.'

'She's been alright with me, mostly,' Grace said.

'As I say, she has her favourites.' Annie said. 'She's alright with me but I've seen her picking on some of the others.'

It was another half an hour before Rose arrived from the ward. She looked worn out as she sat on the sofa with the others.

Soon the other women were making their way one by one to their bedrooms and Grace and Rose were left alone.

'I heard you had a difficult day,' Grace said. 'Are you all right?'

'Of course. I'm tough. But what about you? Did you have a good day off?'

'It was - eventful. I made some decisions and saw Teddy. We parted as friends but have called off our engagement.'

'I'm sorry,' Rose said.

'I'm sorry too, but I'm sure it was the right thing to do. And I've spoken to my sister, Elsie. It appears she and Teddy have feelings for each other. I've...'

'Really? What?'

Grace paused.

'Grace? What were you about to say?'

'I've given them my blessing. I know, I have no right to either way, but it's important to me we are all good friends. My sister and me, we're close, and Teddy will always be important too. We went through a lot together. You know we've been walking out since school.'

'It must be sad for you at the moment but it's probably the right thing?'

'It is, I think.' Grace looked at Rose. 'Anyway, it's done now and no going back.'

'Good for you.' Rose took Grace's hand. 'Come on, we need to celebrate. I've got a beer in my room.'

Grace hesitated only for a moment. 'Why not?' she said. 'Although I'm not really sure what we're celebrating.'

'Decisions my dear. Decisions. Fetch your fancy teacup then.'

Grace sat on the edge of Rose's bed. The ale she was supping had already gone to her head. 'I should go to bed,' she said.

'Don't go yet, you haven't finished your drink. Come here.' Rose took Grace's hand and pulled her closer.

'What are you doing?' Grace wasn't sure whether she felt uncomfortable or excited.

'I just need a hug, that's all.' Rose looked at Grace and smiled. 'It's been an awful day and sometimes a hug helps.'

Grace shifted closer and gave her an awkward hug. 'Are you all right?' she asked.

'Much better now, thank you. This is what I need. It's so nice being close like this.'

Grace felt Rose's hand on the back of her neck, stroking her. She wasn't sure what was happening but felt herself relaxing a little. 'That's lovely,' she whispered.

Rose turned to look at her face. They were so close, Grace glanced into Rose's eyes then turned away. 'Look at me again, Grace,' Rose said. 'Have you ever kissed a woman? On the lips, I mean.'

'No.'

'Look at me.'

'I can't,' Grace shook her head.

'Please,' Rose took her by the chin and gently turned Grace's face to her own again. She moved a little closer and their lips met, gently at first, then Grace felt herself give in to the rising passion she felt.

It was when Rose gave a little moan that Grace felt herself recoil. 'What are we doing?' She pushed herself away, sitting back on the edge of the bed.

'I'm sorry,' Rose looked flustered as she too, sat up. 'I didn't mean to upset you.'

'I wasn't. I'm not,' Grace said. 'I'm sorry too. I've never done that before. I've always been told it's wrong.'

'It's not wrong if you liked it. I did, didn't you?'

Grace stood. 'Yes, I did. I've been thinking about you a lot but it's too much. I don't know. Please don't ask me.'

'Oh, Grace, don't go like this. Can't we just talk about it?'

'What is there to say? We've both had a drink and this, whatever it is, will not happen again. I won't let it.'

'Please, don't say that. I know you're upset and it's a shock to you, of course, but I have strong feelings for you and I think you feel the same about me. You are just afraid. It's something you've not done before.'

'Have you done this before?'

'Yes, I have. And there is nothing wrong in loving someone, is there?'

'But you are a woman. And so am I.' Grace stepped towards the door. 'It's unnatural.'

'No, it's not. Not to me anyway, and I hope you could feel the same, in time.'

Grace opened the door. 'I can't. I'm not ready.' And she ran from the room.

29

Grace's lips stung as she dashed along the corridor. Hesitating at her room, she turned once to look back at Rose's closed door and then carried on walking quickly to the exit into the gardens. The cold air stunned her as she stepped out into the night, catching her breath, but nothing could send her back indoors whilst she felt like this. The gardens were empty of everything but the wind in the trees and this seemed to soothe Grace's mind as she walked, trying to work out what her true feelings were.

She valued Rose's friendship and couldn't abide the thought of losing it. Had what they'd just done spoilt their friendship? What was it anyway? Grace was confused. It had been a very long and heartbreaking day. The meeting with Teddy affected her more than she could admit. They'd been sweethearts for such a long time. It seemed like she'd been walking through the day in a daze trying hard not to let her feelings come to the surface and then after one drink with Rosie, all had come to the fore and something had been released that she didn't understand.

Looking around her, Grace could see she'd reached a gate leading to the outside of the asylum. She'd been told about this gate and expected it would be locked. She tried the latch anyway and pushed against the wood. It groaned and creaked but soon opened and she was looking out across the fields towards the distant road.

Without hesitation Grace slipped through and began to walk along the outside wall towards Asylum Road. The cold of the night was welcome as Grace strode out, leaving her troubles far behind her whilst she mulled over in her mind all that had happened.

Her thoughts again turned to Elsie and Teddy. She wondered again how Elsie would cope with a crippled man to care for. She seemed to really love Teddy - perhaps it would be the best thing for all of them with Elsie at least safe and happy with a good man, and Teddy would be part of the family.

'But could I manage knowing we were once to be married? To see them together over the years?' Grace still loved Teddy very much indeed. Life was painful at times and so confusing. Why should women have to choose between careers and marriage? It was so unfair. She acknowledged a certain feeling of jealousy that Elsie and Teddy at least knew what they wanted and would have it with each other.

The road was empty, the pub at the end of the road in darkness. The only sounds were Grace's footsteps as her boots struck against the cobbles and the gentle lapping of the sea on the shore of Langstone. She was heading towards the old lock entrance to the canal that once ran all the way to Landport in Portsmouth. This was long out of use but there still remained an old bench which looked out across the harbour.

Something made Grace stop walking. She paused and looked back along the road. She could have sworn she'd heard footsteps echoing back to hers. But she could see no-one following her.

'You're imagining things,' she told herself. 'Twice in one day.'

Moving on, Grace soon reached the bench looking out across to Hayling Island. She remembered times, when as a girl, her parents would take the family on the ferry boat from Eastney Point across to the island where they'd have a picnic and play on the sand. It had always been a rare treat away from the pebbled beach in Southsea. Such a day of memories, Grace sighed to herself, thinking and wishing times could still be that simple.

'If only this stupid war hadn't started,' she spoke to the wind. 'Maybe life could have been so much easier then.'

'Yes, and then women like you would be kept in your place.'

She jumped in fear and looked around, recognising the man's deep voice, The night was so dark she could only make out his shadow, a few feet behind her.

'What are you doing here?' she shook as she spoke. 'You've been following me. Who are you?'

'Don't you recognise me?' He stepped a little closer. Grace stood and backed away. 'Mr Medford, I thought it was you! Why are you here? Haven't you done enough mischief?' She looked around to see if there was anyone else about, but the shore was deserted of people.

'Oh so you do recognise me then. I wondered when you'd realise.' He gave a little sneer. 'Now we're alone at last, I think it's time we had a little chat, don't you?'

'I have nothing more to say to you.' Grace made to walk away but he grabbed her arm and swung her round to face him.

'No you don't, young lady. You owe me.' He pulled her closer.

'Let me go, you brute!' Grace struggled to get away. 'You'll be sorry if you don't.'

'Will I indeed?' He laughed in her face as he gripped her even tighter.

'You must be mad if you think you can bully me and get away with it.' She kicked his shin, hoping he'd let go but his grasp was too firm. 'Let me go. Help, help,' she screamed as loudly as she was able, hoping that the nearby innkeeper would hear.

Mr Medford was laughing at her. 'You won't be heard, silly girl. The pub has been closed for the past week. They've gone away. We are all alone.' He pulled her closer still as she sobbed in frustration. 'Now don't cry, I don't like it when they cry. Come on, I know all about you nurses, especially the lunatic attendants. I know what you like.'

He let go of one of her arms and grabbed her about the head, pulling her in for a kiss. Grace felt his hot breath on her face, the smell making her gag. Taking the opportunity of having one hand free, she made a fist and punched him in the stomach. Immediately he let go of her, doubling up in pain.

Grace gave him a kick for good measure before she turned and ran, the only thing in her mind was to get as far away from him as possible. The ground was uneven and she stumbled as she ran, but the terror in her heart kept her somehow on her feet and soon she'd reached the very end of the canal. She could go no further without climbing down to the roughly pebbled beach below. Taking the opportunity to look back she saw Medford wasn't in sight. He could be anywhere, perhaps hiding behind one of the small boats that were pulled up nearby above the shoreline.

Grace realised she was still in great danger. There were a few houseboats moored nearby but all was silent apart from the gentle lapping of the sea and the sound of the wooden hulls knocking against the planks of the walkway.

Suddenly she saw a movement as he loomed out of the darkness and into her sight. He was still a fair way off but there was no way she could avoid him without going back the way she'd come. Standing on the edge of the canal, Grace could see in the gloom the outline of an ancient ladder, left there from the days when the canal was in use. She glanced back again and then slipped onto the top of rung of the ladder. Soon she was halfway down. Maybe if she stayed there, he might not see her. She'd hide there until he went away.

She held her breath and waited. Would it work?

She was soon answered as she heard the thundering of his footsteps and the shout. 'I know you're down there you silly bitch. You can't escape.' He was getting closer. 'You might as well give in now. You know you'll love it when you finally give in. We can have a nice cuddle. I've got some brandy here to warm you up, too.'

Grace felt sick at the thought. She scrambled further down the ladder and before long her feet reached the bottom. The ground was slippery with mud from the flats and she found herself sliding about.

She looked up. Medford leaned over the side of the canal wall. He was laughing. 'Silly, silly woman. Shall I just wait here until you've had enough in that mud bath? I must say, I like a bit of mud on a woman. Makes you even more of a challenge to grasp hold of, nice and slippery, if you get my meaning?'

'You are disgusting!' Grace yelled up at him. 'I will never give in.' She looked around in desperation. There was only one other way out and that was towards the tide which was far out at the moment. If she went that way, there would be a chance of getting ashore out of sight of that awful man.

Moving across the slime was hard enough when it was on the brick base of the canal floor but once her feet found the mud flats it would be more dangerous, she knew, but she had little choice. There had been stories about people being stuck in the flats hereabouts. With one last look back to where Medford was waiting, she took a few steps forward. If only she could get to the shore just around the other side she'd stand a chance of running from him.

Just a few more steps. So far it had been firm underfoot. A few more steps, she kept saying to herself as each one sank further and further into the mud. She could feel the weight of her long skirts pulling her down as the mire and water soaked into her clothes. 'Damn these long dresses,' she swore. But she was so determined to escape she kept on going.

Looking up, she could see the shore was only a few feet from where she now stood. She cast her eyes back to where she'd last seen Medford, leaning over the canal side. There was no sign of him now. The flicker of fear she felt gave her a burst of energy and she took another step forward. Too hasty. Too late to go back as she felt herself being pulled into the mire.

She screamed.

30

The more she struggled, the faster Grace was being sucked deeper into the mud. She knew there was only one thing left to do, call for help from Mr Medford. Before she could open her mouth, there he was, standing on the nearby bank. He was laughing at her.

'Please, Mr Medford, help me. Please.' Her arms reached towards him.

'Now you want me?' He stood with his arms folded, a smirk on his face. 'Tell, me, young madam, why should I help you, eh?'

'You won't leave me here like this, will you?' Grace knew time was not on her side. The tide would be coming in before long and the night was cold. Being stuck in a mud pit was bad enough, but without being able to get out before being surrounded by the sea would surely be the end of her.

'Give me one good reason why I should save you?'

'You aren't really a bad person, are you? You didn't mean to hurt me did you?' She struggled again and felt herself sinking a little deeper into the sludge. 'Look, I know I've caused trouble for you, but I can put in a good word if that's what you want. Please, help me out and we can talk.'

'Pah! I don't want to talk to you. You must be insane if you think that's what I want. No. You being in there'll save me the trouble of getting my hands dirty.' He took a few steps away then turned back. 'I'll give you a tip before I go. The more you struggle, the quicker your end'll be. Goodnight sweetheart.'

He was laughing as he walked away. Grace stared at his back until he finally disappeared into the night. She felt the panic rising along with a complete loneliness, with just the sound of the sea which was slowly moving closer and the rustle of leaves from the trees nearby. Of course, Mr Medford was right about struggling. Grace remembered her pa telling her that once, a long time ago it seemed. She looked at the sky and tried to slow her breathing. The moon was pushing through the clouds, succeeding to shine every now and again as the wind came in from the sea.

She thought about some of the things that had happened in the past twenty-four hours. How she wished she could go back in time to the morning when she'd gone to see Teddy. She wondered if the day would have turned out differently if he'd still wanted her. If only she'd decided to give up nursing and be the woman he wanted her to be, maybe none of this would have happened.

She was trying not to think about Rose and any feelings she may have for her friend. Whatever happened now, nothing mattered anymore. Grace had little chance of getting out of this awful predicament. Life was so hard sometimes, she thought, so hard, but worth fighting for. But how to fight when whatever she did, however hard she struggled, things would only get worse. She closed her eyes.

A dog barking brought her back to the present. A little brown dog had come to her rescue, bringing a surge of hope with it. 'Hello, little dog,' Grace said, holding out her hand. 'Where did you come from?'

The dog kept barking and ran in circles. Grace looked around to see if there was anyone else nearby. Surely the dog would belong to someone, someone who was out walking and who lived close to the shore. 'Where's your master?' Grace asked, hopefully, then called out. 'Help, help me. I'm stuck in the mud flat, please anyone, help me.'

With no reply, her hopes sagged. Looking around again, she realised the dog had disappeared too. 'No, please don't you abandon me,' Grace spoke to the air around her. 'I don't believe this, it's too awful.' She closed her eyes again. 'Please, help me,' she prayed. To whom, she had no idea, it was just something one did when there was no way out, wasn't it?

It seemed as though hours had passed, though it must have only been minutes. She heard a bark. The dog was coming back. Grace called out again, hoping it had brought help. Surely she couldn't be that lucky. But then there was the silhouette of someone on the bank. It looked like a man. Not Medford back again, come back to gloat and to watch as she suffered? She shook her head.

Suddenly the clouds shifted and the moon shone fully on the shadow's face. It was a woman, surely. A woman's face on a man's body? But so many women were wearing men's clothing these days it being much more practical.

'What on Earth?' the woman spoke. 'Are you all right?'

'No, I'm stuck, please help me. I'm so cold.'

'Of course, what a stupid question. I can see you are not all right. Hold on. I'll be back.' And the woman ran along the bank, returning with a long branch from one of the trees. 'I think this will be strong enough to hold you. Grab the end.' She stepped onto the pebbled beach and thrust the branch towards Grace who managed to grasp hold of it with both hands.

'Pull yourself out if you can. You might have to crawl along holding the branch once you get your legs freed. Can you do it?' She held onto to the other end and tried to help by pulling against Grace. It was a struggle but finally she was on the shore, lying on her back barely able to catch her breath.

'Well, well, thank goodness for that.' The stranger looked down at Grace. 'Whatever were you doing in there anyway? It's hardly the time nor the place for a dip in the sea.'

Grace shook her head, unable to speak.

'What's the matter with me? Come on lovely, let me help you up. You need to get warm, never mind my questions.' She got down to her knees and soon was helping Grace to stand. 'I live in the houseboat just along the water's edge there. There's a hot cuppa for you waiting.'

'I'm covered in mud,' Grace said.

'Mud is something we are used to. Come along.'

They stumbled along together, the little dog racing ahead and back again until they reached an old ramshackle wooden boat. Soon inside, Grace felt the warmth wrap around her as she was helped onto a colourful sofa.

'I'm Georgia by the way,' the woman said. 'The kettle's already on so tea won't be long.'

'Thank you. I don't know how long I'd have lasted…'

'Never mind that now. Let's just get you warmed up inside and out. Now, you take those wet things off. I'll get you some dry clothes.' She moved to the end of the room and through a doorway. Grace could hear her talking. 'It's a poor soul I've rescued from the mud. I need to borrow some clothes.'

Grace hesitated to peel off her wet things knowing she was in a stranger's home, and what if the man in the other room came in? She waited, but when the door opened again although it wasn't Georgia who came through, it wasn't a man either.

'Hello dear,' an older woman entered, looking as though she'd only just woken. 'I had a feeling we wouldn't sleep well tonight. As soon as I knew it was a full moon.'

Grace frowned. 'I'm so sorry, I'll leave you in peace. I didn't mean to intrude.'

'Don't be daft. I don't mean anything by it. Georgia's bringing out some dry things for you. I'll be back in a tick.' The woman went out through the door to the deck.

Grace could feel the boat rocking as the woman jumped ashore. She was only left alone for a few minutes before Georgia was back with a woollen dress. 'Here, put this on. Oh and have you got a name? I can't keep calling you young lady, or whatever.'

'I'm Grace. Grace Bennett. Thank you for this. You are very kind.'

The outside door opened and the dog came leaping in followed by the other woman. 'Oh, and this is Dora. We live here together, as you've probably worked out for yourself. And Scamp, the dog.'

'Pleased to meet you Dora, Scamp, and you too Georgia. I am so grateful for the trouble you've taken for me.'

'Nonsense.'

Grace quickly changed into the dry clothes. She'd taken her muddy wet boots off and they were beside the outside door. 'Oh dear,' she said. 'My boots are ruined, and I've made a terrible mess in your home.'

'It's only mud,' Dora said. 'Pleased to meet you too Grace. Is there any toast, Georgia?'

The tea was welcome and hot. And so was the toast which Grace hadn't realised she was hungry for until she smelt it toasting and saw the butter melting into the slice that Georgia had placed in front of her. 'Real butter?' This was something she didn't have very often, not since the rationing had started.

'We save it for emergencies and special occasions, and I think this is definitely one if not both of those.' Dora said as she licked the butter from her fingers. 'Now, ladies, I am absolutely ready for sleep now. You will have to excuse me.'

'I should go,' Grace tried to get to her feet but her legs gave way. 'I need to get back.'

'No you don't. You shall stay here until the morning. The sofa makes a good bed, and we have more blankets.' Georgia was already bustling about in a cupboard, bringing out pillows and a rough looking blanket. 'It's not much but you'll be cosy.'

'But I'll get into trouble if I'm not back before morning,' Grace said.

The two women looked at each other. 'You from the asylum?' Dora asked.

'Yes, I am, but I'm not an inmate. Really.'

'No more questions until the morning. Now settle down and rest.'

The two women left Grace alone with the dog, Grace wondering what on earth had she brought herself to now. They were such friendly women, but they obviously thought she was an escapee from the asylum, which she supposed she was, but not as they assumed. People at the nurses' home would miss her in the morning. She'd be in trouble with the Home Sister for sure and with Sister Biggs on the ward. Would this be the end of her very short career as a nurse?

31

What an idiot! Rose was so angry with herself. She'd frightened Grace off and there would be no going back to how they were before. Stung by Grace's words had stopped her from chasing after her friend. It was when Rose heard the garden door banging that she jumped up and followed down the corridor herself, past the other bedrooms and to the door.

Once outside in the night air, Rose stopped and looked around. There was a wind in the trees and she heard a distant owl hoot but no sound of footsteps. The path led away to the right and wound through the small orchard to the left. This seemed the most likely way Grace would have taken, although she was unsure why. She'd not spent much time in the garden before, only sitting on the bench by the door for a few minutes a few weeks ago, but she knew Grace liked walking in the garden.

Clouds were flitting across the sky, blocking out the moonlight fleetingly as she walked. She felt sick at the thought that she'd spoilt anything between Grace and herself and wished with all her being that she could turn back the clock.

Soon she'd walked the whole perimeter of the garden and still no sign of Grace. She'd walked past the old gate which led out into the fields, but it had always been locked in case of any inmate escaping so she'd walked on, never thinking that Grace could have got out that way. She sat on the seat for a while, listening to the wind and noises of foxes screeching to each other, an eerie sound indeed which gave her the shivers. She took another turn around the garden. Surely Grace must be out here somewhere, but the garden was empty. She must have gone back indoors.

Rose made her way back to her bedroom. She stood outside Grace's door for a while, listening and wondering whether she should knock. Deciding it would be best to leave her be, she took herself to bed where she lay awake for long into the early hours of the night.

When she woke and it was still only four in the morning, she gave up trying to rest and got up, going quietly to Grace's room. Tapping gently, she opened the door and looked in. The bed was empty and had not been slept in. Rose's mind reeled. Had Grace been out all night? Cursing herself for not checking before, Rose couldn't think straight. Where could she have gone? Had she left the asylum, gone home? Would she come back? So many questions and no answers.

Rose went back to her room, knowing she could do nothing else now until the morning, when she hoped all would become clear. She only hoped Grace would return and would be all right. She could have spoilt her chance to continue her training if she was found to have left the nursing home without permission. But if she returned before she was discovered missing, all could be well after all. And then again, what if she had been hurt by someone? One thing was for certain was Rose would not sleep any more this night.

32

Sunlight on her face woke Grace from a dream. Or was it the dog licking her? She stretched, wondering where she was and what this little dog was doing in bed with her. Inner knives attacked her stomach as the reality of her situation came to mind.

'Well, little dog, I seem to have got myself into a bit of a mess, haven't I?' She stroked him. 'Thank you for rescuing me last night, but I need to get back.'

She wondered what the time was and stood, looking around for her own clothes. They hung on a chair next to the stove, still covered in mud but now dried. She hoped the mud would brush off before she got back to the nurse's home. 'What a mess,' she thought.

The inner door opened, and Georgia appeared. 'Good morning, Grace, isn't it?'

'Yes, and you're Georgia. I have to thank you again for saving me and taking me in last night. And your friend of course - Dora?'

'That's right. And you are more than welcome. This is a difficult time, especially for women. We should all support each other.'

'I'm still grateful to you. But I should be getting back to the asylum. We're not really meant to be out after nine at night.'

'You should have breakfast before you leave. I'm just making some porridge.'

'I shouldn't, really. I'll be in trouble when they find out I'm not in my room. If I go now there's a chance I can slip in the way I came without anyone knowing I've been missing.'

Georgia busied herself at the stove. 'I'm sorry. It's none of my business but would you mind telling me how you came to be in the asylum? You don't appear to be…'

'Insane? Oh, well I'm not. Although you would think so, wouldn't you? I mean, why would a person be wandering about the mud flats in the middle of the night?'

'So, what is your story?' Georgia paused. 'I'm sorry, I'm being very, very nosy. Take no notice of me.'

'I don't mind at all. I can understand how you'd be curious. I'm a trainee nurse in fact, and last night I suppose you could say I escaped for what I thought was going to be a short walk to clear my head.'

'Oh, I am so sorry,' Georgia said. 'We thought you must have been an escapee inmate.'

'I guessed that, but no, although some of my friends and family think I am mad.'

'Yes, well, we know all about how family don't understand us, don't we Dora?' She spoke to the other woman who had appeared from the inner room.

'We do, indeed,' said Dora. The woman was dressed in a floral gown which reached to just above the ankles, her hair was plaited around her head, her weathered face smiled at Georgia. 'That's why we ended up living on this houseboat.' She looked at Grace. 'Did you sleep well, young lady? I'm sorry it was only on the couch and with Scamp by the looks of it.' She shooed the dog off the couch and sat down.

'I was very comfortable thank you. But I really should go back to the asylum now.'

'So, you're a trainee nurse, are you? I heard what you said before.'

'I am, yes and I'm going to be in trouble when I get back.' As much as she wanted to leave, Grace was reluctant. She wondered why. 'You both have been so kind to me, but I would like to get to know you. Can I visit again, please? I'd like to thank you properly.'

'Oh, enough of that. But you are welcome to visit us again,' Dora said. 'Georgia has to work on the trams most days, but you must come for supper one evening, and you'd be welcome to pop in any time you need to get away, to clear your head or whatever you want to call it.'

'Working at the asylum must be challenging,' Georgia said. 'Dora is right, you'd be welcome to come at any time.'

Grace smiled at the two women. 'Do you have a job, too, Dora?' she asked.

'My dear, I am an artist. I have a studio on the bank of the harbour, just a few feet from here. Well, it's actually an old boat shed. I own it and now it's my studio. You'd be welcome to see my works whenever you have time.'

'Thank you,' Grace said. 'Now, please, I must go. I'm sorry I can't stay for breakfast, but I promise I will pop in to visit again.'

Once on the shore, she turned to look at the houseboat. The two ladies were standing on the wooden deck. 'See you soon,' they called in unison. Grace waved and hurried back along Asylum Road to face what the outcome of her night away would bring.

She'd only gone a short way when the thought of Medford was in her head again. She'd almost forgotten about him with the relief of being saved from the mud and meeting the two women. But he was sure to be around somewhere. Even if he'd not stayed all night, she knew he'd be back once he realised she wasn't out of the way. Suddenly there were shadows everywhere, watching her. Telling herself she was being ridiculous, Grace nevertheless broke into a run and soon arrived at the asylum walls. Slipping along the side wall, she soon found the gate that she'd managed to escape through the night before.

It was with a great relief that she stepped through into the grounds again. Wondering if she should tell someone to lock the door in case someone got out who perhaps shouldn't be at large. She shook her head and decided to say nothing. In the back of her mind was the thought that she may need this way out again before long.

Entering the nurses' home, Grace saw it was still very early. Just enough time to get to her room, change into her uniform and make it to the ward. She was opening her door when Rose appeared from the kitchen.

'Where have you been?' she hissed. 'You were out all night. I was so worried.'

'You didn't tell anyone, did you?'

'Of course not. What do you think I am?' Rose glared at her. 'But what happened? I looked in the garden and you'd gone. Who have you been with?'

'I haven't been with anyone. At least that's not what happened,' Grace said. 'Well, I was with someone but I was safe. In the end anyway. Look there's no time now. I need to change and get on duty.'

'Of course. But can we talk later? About what happened before, I mean, and what happened to you after, of course. Are you sure you're all right? Why are you so muddy?'

'I can't tell you now. But I will.'

She entered her room and did her best to tidy her hair and have a quick wash. Soon she was in her clean uniform. She looked at her clothes on the bed. 'You will have to be sorted out later,' she told the dress. There wasn't much she could do with her boots other than brush off as much of the dirt as she could before she left for the ward. 'Sister Biggs will have my guts for garters when she sees the state of these. But needs must, there's no more time.'

It was fortunate the day passed without any further calamities or excitements. The ladies on the ward seemed settled. Grace's new patient, Gladys, was now working in the laundry and those left behind appeared to be content to sit and work at their sewing tasks.

The trainees were expected at the nursing school at ten o'clock for the lecture from the Doctor. Today they were to learn all about the function of the circulatory system, nutrition and things to be specially observed.

Grace had previously read the section in the handbook on this subject and was already noticing the way different patients approached their meals, how some bolted their food, and others were reluctant to go to the dinner table. One or two ladies were in states of delusion, whereby they believed that the food was either poisoned or had been tampered with in some way. She had learned ways to help those ladies be more confident in eating, allowing them to watch the food being served and making sure that they were able to eat at their own pace, and in a quieter part of the dining room. This only worked occasionally of course, as the delusions were invariably deep rooted, but in time, hopefully they would begin to improve and feel more comfortable in eating.

In the classroom, they moved on to the observation of the digestive system and in particular the bowels. To be sitting in a room full of trainee nurses, being talked to by a man about the kinds of things to notice when inspecting the patient's bowel movement was slightly uncomfortable for Grace. As a maid, she was used to emptying chamber pots and cleaning up after her Mistress, but the thought of looking through a stool, as they were laughingly called, to see if the patient had constipation, worms, or had been eating their clothing and worse, was something that would never leave her. But she knew it was important as problems with the bowels could definitely have a great impact on a person's mental health.

The lecture certainly took her mind off her own troubles but she was glad to get back to the ward ready to serve the lunches. Rose walked beside her along the corridor.

'That was interesting, wasn't it?' Rose screwed up her face as she spoke.

'I know. I'd read all of what he was saying already, but to hear him speaking of those things, it turned my stomach a bit if I'm honest.'

'Certainly food for thought,' Rose said, then laughed. 'Oh my, food for thought!'

'That's awful, Rose,' Grace looked at her. Her lips twitched. 'But funny too.'

Rose took her arm and they giggled their way along until they reached the ward door. 'Are we all right?' she asked.

'Of course. We are friends,' Grace took out her keys and opened the door.

'Friends?' Rose frowned as she stepped through into the ward.

'Friends are good. Isn't that enough for you?'

'I suppose. Come on then, lots of work to do.'

Grace had already walked away and was halfway to the dining room when Rose called after her.

'Can we still talk later?'

Grace shrugged her shoulders and kept walking.

33

Finally, after a long day, Grace finished writing her notes and left the ward. She was the last of the day staff to leave, having been caught up with her written work. She knew she was actually avoiding the moment when she'd have to sit down with Rose again for the talk. She owed it to her friend to try and work out what was going on between them. But Grace was afraid of her feelings. She was confused and wished she had someone she could talk to about it. But who? Perhaps her sister would understand. But there' would be no chance today. She couldn't risk leaving the asylum on a second night.

The nurses' home was already quiet when she entered the door and walked down to the kitchen. Only Ethel was still up.

'Oh, there you are Grace,' she said. 'I'm just making a drink. Do you want one or are you going straight to bed?'

'That would be welcome, thank you.' Grace looked out into the lounge. 'Has everyone else gone to bed?

'Yes, only me left up. Have you had a good day? You look tired.'

'It's been a long day. But a good one, I think.'

'I'm finding the work very hard, aren't you?' Ethel said. 'And all the studying too.. I still don't know if I'll ever make it as a trained nurse.'

'I'm sure you will. You are good with the ladies. Very kind and patient. I don't know why we call them patients, as they seldom are.' She laughed. 'But I mean it, you will make a good nurse.'

'I hope so. I really want to do this.'

'Me too.' Grace paused. 'Yes, I do. Do you know, I was unsure at first and over the last few weeks I've been wondering why I'm doing it, but today, talking to you, I now feel sure. It's the right thing for me.'

'I'm glad to have helped.' Ethel handed her a cup. 'I'm off to bed now. I need my rest. Goodnight.'

'Goodnight.'

Grace stood for a moment in the kitchen, looking our of the window into the dark of the evening, then made up her mind.

She knocked gently on Rose's door then quietly turned the handle. She heard Rose calling out, 'Come in.'

Rose was sitting at her desk, still in her uniform. She looked at Grace and smiled.

'I thought you might have already gone to bed.' Grace said. 'I've got tea. Would you like me to fetch you a cup?'

Rose shook her head. 'No thanks. I've already had some and don't want to be up and down all night.'

'May I sit down?' Grace looked at the still neatly made bed. There were no other places to sit in the room.

'Please. Of course. You don't have to ask.' Rose stood and turned her chair so that it faced the bed. 'Would you rather sit here. I can take the bed.'

Grace moved to the other side of the room and sat on the chair. Her teacup rattled in the saucer. 'Oh dear, I'm shaking,' she said.

'I'm sorry things have come to this between us.' Rose sat on the edge of the bed. 'The last thing I want is to lose you as a friend or to make you feel awkward.'

'You haven't really. I'm just very confused. All of this is new to me.' Grace looked at Rose. 'And I need to tell you what happened last night.'

'Of course, I'm sorry. This is not about me, I know, but I felt terrible when you ran off last night. And then you didn't come back. I thought you were out in the garden, but you'd gone. Where did you go?'

She told Rose about Mr Medford, and the mud and the two women on the house-boat. It all seemed unbelievable to her now, but it did happen.

'You must be exhausted.'

'I am a bit, and I've still got to try and brush the mud from my clothes too. And my boots are still dirty.'

'I'm just glad you're all right. And I'm sorry about everything.'

'Grace smiled and squeezed Rose's hand. 'Let's take it a day at a time, shall we?' She kissed Rose on the cheek and left the room.

Lying in her bed a short while later, Grace looked up at her dress, now hanging on the wardrobe door, the mud brushed from it. She would wear it tomorrow when she finished her morning shift. She planned to meet Elsie for a shopping afternoon in Palmerston Road. Thinking about Else and Teddy as she lay there, she wondered once again if she'd made the right decision.

The following afternoon was warmer now the spring had finally arrived. As Grace waited for Elsie by the tram station, she perched on the bench and was busy day-dreaming about all that had happened over the past few weeks. She hadn't noticed the tram arrive until the driver stepped off onto the pavement.

'Penny for 'em?' It was the familiar voice of her saviour, Georgia. 'You were miles away.'

Grace stood. 'I am so sorry. I didn't even realise the tram had arrived.' She noticed the clothes Georgia was wearing. 'Of course, you drive the tram. How brave of you.'

Georgia laughed. 'Nowhere near as brave as working as an asylum nurse,' she said. 'Driving a tram is easy. And it's fun being always in the front.'

'Really? I suppose, but what about being in charge of all those passengers? Responsible for them, I mean.'

'They're mostly all right. Obviously there are some who don't approve of a woman doing a man's job, but there aren't many men left at home, are there? We're doing war work.'

'I do admire you.'

'It's hard work, and sometimes people can be very rude, and speak to me like I owe them something. and I suppose I do. I owe them a safe journey.'

'It's a good thing to be doing. You could be working in a shop. or an office, or getting married with a few little ones to take care of.'

'There's no chance of that, I'm afraid. Getting married I mean, and I don't think I'd suit working in a shop or an office. Unless I was the boss, of course.' She laughed.

'The war won't go on forever, hopefully,' Grace said.

'The trouble is, as soon as it is over, I'll lose my job and it'll be given to a man. Probably one with no experience of driving a tram either. Then what will I do?'

'Do you have a young man at the front? Surely you will someone to care for you?'

'Huh! No, of course not.' She looked at Grace and frowned. 'I thought you'd realised I will never marry a man. Dora and I are a couple.'

'Oh.' Grace paused, blushing. 'I wasn't sure, I didn't like to assume, or ask what your situation was. I am sorry.'

'Don't be an idiot. Dora and I have been together for a long time now. We love each other like a man and wife, if you get my drift.'

Grace looked away. 'I see.'

'It's perfectly fine. Not everyone agrees with how we are, but that's their business.' She paused, looking across at the steam from the train that was coming into the station, then went on. 'I hope it doesn't worry you.'

'No, not at all. In facet I wonder if I could have a proper talk with you soon. Not today, as you are working, and I'm meeting my sister, but perhaps next week.'

'Next week would suit me. My off duty times change weekly but I am free on Thursday from six in the evening.'

'That would be perfect.' Grace looked across the square and waved. 'And here is my sister.'

Elsie hurried over and hugged Grace. 'I'm not late, am I?'

'Just in time,' Grace said and they climbed onto the tram. 'Let's go upstairs.'

'Wait for me,' Elsie called as she followed Grace to the open air of the upper floor.

'Was that a friend of yours?' Elsie asked. 'You seemed to be deep in conversation together. I didn't know you had a friend who drove a tram.'

'Her name is Georgia and I only met her the other day.'

'You seemed to want to whisk us away rather quickly.'

'Don't be silly, Elsie. I hardly know her at all. I was just flustered as the tram was late in leaving already.'

'Was it? I thought it was early.' Elsie glared at Grace. 'Oh, I can't be bothered with your mysterious stories today. I have news for you. We wanted to tell you together, but I can't keep it from you any longer.'

Grace braced herself for what she knew would be coming all too soon. 'Go on then, don't keep me in suspense any longer.'

'Teddy and I have been getting very close since he came home. I know I should have told you before, but it's been difficult. We are going to be married. As soon as possible.' She looked at her sister's face. 'You are all right, aren't you? I know it seems so quick, especially with the situation between you and Teddy.'

Grace swallowed. 'Of course. I'm delighted for you both.'

'I love you so much Grace. I can't believe you're taking it so well.'

'I made my choice, I suppose, when I took the trainee job.'

'Thank you. And now, as we are going to Handley's we must get the material for my wedding dress. Is that all right?'

'Yes, of course.' Grace squeezed Elsie's hand. 'It will be your day and you deserve to enjoy this.' She changed the subject. 'I love being on the top deck, don't you? We can see all the shops and the people from here.'

'Just like when we were little and Ma would take us shopping.'

'Exactly. Now, do you have a picture with you of your wedding dress? Or are you hoping the store will have ideas for you to copy?'

Elsie took out a sketch from her bag. 'This is my dream dress,' she said. 'Oh, I know it's probably out of my price range, but I'm hoping Ma can modify it to look as near to this as possible.'

'It's beautiful,' said Grace, her heart skipping a little.

'Sorry, Grace. I hope it's not too upsetting for you. After all...'

'Don't say another word about my feelings, Elsie.' Grace looked away.

Handley's department store was somewhere the young ladies rarely visited to actually make any purchases, although they'd often walked through the halls on past occasions doing what Ma called window shopping. Grace's favourite department was haberdashery which was filled with sewing cottons, needles, knitting wool, and materials for curtains and dresses. The hall was filled with colour and even in this time of war, there seemed to be far more than a whole town could use.

Before they reached the haberdashery department, they walked through the perfumery department. This was somewhere Elsie loved. The perfumes were far beyond their budgets but they knew if they walked through the store, they could try out some of those on display. The mixture of all different perfumes as too much for Grace and she was glad to move on through the household department and then to the place where the dress fabrics were on display.

'I've been putting some money aside, Elsie,' Grace said. 'I want to help you have the best wedding dress. I know how expensive things are now.'

'Grace, you can't do that.' Elsie shook her head. 'I won't accept it. I know you were saving for your own wedding.'

'It's not much, and it's no good to me now. I feel bad for not being there for Teddy. Now you're not earning at the moment, things are tough, I know.' She paused. 'Look, I'll be honest with you. It hurts. Of course it does, but you're my sister and always will be important to me. Why should we both be unhappy? So take the gift and stop being stubborn.'

'All right, thank you. And I am starting a new job on Monday.'

'That's good news. I'm glad you're not going back to the munitions factory.'

'I could never do that, could I?'

'So where is it? This new job?'

'Pa has got me a place in the electric shop in the dockyard. I know some of the girls there already too, so I'm hoping it'll be a new start.'

'I'm pleased for you. And the yellow from the cordite will fade in time which can only be a bonus.'

Elsie laughed. 'I never notice it anymore,' she said. 'Now let's have a look at the catalogues of wedding gowns, just to see if there are any ideas I can pinch.' She took out her note-book and pencil as she strode to the counter of catalogues.

Grace followed her, looking around at all the things on display, wondering if she would have been cut out to work in a store like this. She knew the young women lived-in whilst they worked a two-year apprenticeship. The whole place was run on a kind of hierarchy, very similar to working in the asylum, with strict rules for the staff, inspections every day before work, and poor wages but a secure future.

Life for women wasn't so different wherever they chose to work, was it? Men would always be in positions of authority. Mind you, she could aspire to be a ward sister like Biggs, or even a Matron. Even so, they were answerable to the Medical Director, who, of course, was a man. Would things ever change?

Finally, Elsie found what she was looking for and perched on a stool to sketch some idea. 'Ma will be able to do this, won't she?'

'I should imagine she'll have a jolly good try anyway. Are you going to wear white?'

'I thought a pretty cream silk material would be better, to be honest. I know what people will say, but I don't care. Cream is much more fashionable now, and I've seen something perfect on the shelves over there.' She grabbed Grace's arm. 'Come on, let's see how expensive it is.'

The matron-like woman who served them was extremely polite although she appeared to be looking down at them and her smile was not quite natural.

'This one is sixpence per yard, Miss. And how many yards would you require?'

Grace looked at Elsie. 'Well, have you worked out how much you need?'

'I think five yards should be sufficient.' Elsie had put on her posh voice.

'Five yards? Are you sure?' Grace said. 'That seems rather a lot.'

'I have worked it out, and yes, I am sure.'

Grace pulled Elsie away from the counter and lowered her voice. 'How much money do you have?'

'I've got enough. Teddy has given me ten shillings to spend.'

'But that will have to pay for more than the dress, I imagine.'

'Well yes, but it only works out at two and sixpence for five yards.'

'I know.' Grace sighed. 'I will pay for the material. My wedding present to you.'

'Are you sure?'

'I said before, didn't I? Now if you're positive that's what you want, let's have it wrapped and I will pay. And I still have enough left over for a bun in the cafeteria.'

'Thank you, Grace.'

'Then we can plan whatever else you need. I'm sure there will be much more to think about.'

'You are the very best sister, Grace.' Elsie smiled and turned back to the assistant.

34

Rose felt hopeful. Grace had kissed her on the cheek and admitted that she could take it a day at a time, that was surely enough for now? It gave Rose a little more hope to know that Grace had met up with Georgia and Dora, two women she knew were wise and kind and would give good advice if asked. Of course, they would have taken care of Grace.

It made her angry to think about that bully Medford and how he'd thought he could get away with what he tried to do to Grace. If Georgia's dog hadn't found her, she would have been in deep trouble indeed. Of course, no-one would believe a mere woman over his sure denials. Rose hoped that one day soon Grace would see that life with her could be a good thing. Or would it? Rose had doubt about herself. Would anyone ever find her lovable? There had been others in the past, of course, but no-one serious enough to make her feel like this. It was agony.

It was her afternoon off and in order to keep her mind off this turmoil, Rose took herself home to her parents house in Queens Road. The row of dockers cottages looked out across the cobbled street towards the better area of shops. She'd heard all about the Council wanting to clear the area - slums, they called it, where the dregs of society lived. Well, she must be one of the dregs then.

It upset her to think of her parents and how hard they worked to be called that. She worried where they'd go if the clearance happened. So far it had been all talk, with articles in the Evening News. But her Pa worked in the docks - he'd always worked hard at his job and the wages were meagre. As for Ma, she was always on her feet, either washing others' laundry, or ironing, or on her knees scrubbing the flagstone floor in the scullery.

Thoughts of her Ma and all she did to keep the household income topped up, made her even more convinced that Grace wouldn't want to be caught up with the likes of her. Pa's wages often didn't even make it through the door on payday as he went straight to the pub and didn't come in until he'd spent it all. If it weren't for her ma, they'd have starved long ago.

They never entered through the front door. Rose walked down the alley at the back of the row and opened the rickety gate to their yard. She walked through the washing that was always hanging on the line and stepped through the door into the scullery. Steam met her from the boiler which always seemed to be bubbling away and there was Ma, prodding the washing with a pair of wooden tongs. They dripped as Ma put them to one side and crossed the room to hold Rose in a warm embrace.

'My girl,' she said. 'It's good to see you. I'll put the kettle on.'

'I'll do it Ma,' Rose said. 'Come and sit down in the parlour and rest your legs.'

She walked through to the tiny parlour and took the kettle that was always simmering on the range. 'I'll fetch some fresh water, shall I?'

'No need, that's not been on long. You can fill it up before you leave it you like.' Ma sat at the table and smiled at Rose. 'You are a sight for sore eyes, you are. Tell me what it's like, working at the asylum, I mean.'

Rose busied herself with the teapot and two cups and saucers. 'It's different I suppose. Although not that different to being at the Workhouse. I mean, I do a lot more than cleaning and making beds but there is that too. The inmates are interesting to say the least. Some of them are quite a challenge but I can see how we can make a difference and they're not all the lost causes we expected them to be. Well, I did anyway.'

'And the training? Do you have to go into school?'

'Yes, every week day, we're in the classroom for a few hours, and we have to read a lot too. It's hard work, you have to write notes and remember what you've learned. Sometimes I think it goes in one ear and then out the other.' She laughed. 'But the other trainees and the nurses help quite a lot. I think we learn a lot of it on the wards really, doing the job, watching the more experienced attendants and nurses.'

'What are the other nurses like?' Ma asked. 'Have you made any friends yet?'

'They're all pretty nice, those I'm working with anyway.' Rose poured the tea and stirred the cups, handing one to Ma. 'The first day I was there I met two new trainees and we've stuck together more than the others. They're both so different, one is Ethel, she's the brainy one of our group, tall and very posh. She's always well turned out, never a hair out of place. The other one is Grace. We get on really well, spend a lot of time together. She's clever too, but more like me I suppose. Her Pa works in the docks too.'

'Is he like your Pa, then?' Ma sighed and turned her head away.

'Not that I know of. I haven't met him, but Grace talks of him fondly. He works in the Electrical Workshop.' Rose looked at her Ma. 'How has Pa been?'

'Alright, I suppose.' Ma said. 'You know he has his ways. He's not a bad man, you know.'

'So you say, Ma.' Rose sipped her tea. 'I'm just glad I don't have to live with him any more. But if he's treating you badly you will tell me, won't you?'

Ma shook her head. 'He is alright. I don't want you worrying about me. You've got to get on with your own life. Tell me about what it's like in the nurses' home.'

An hour later, Rose filled the kettle again from the water pump in the street and said goodbye to her Ma. Her heart was heavy as she made her way back to the asylum. 'Why should women be treated so badly by men?' She asked herself. 'Surely they weren't all the same, were they?'

35

Once a month on a Friday evening, the asylum held what they almost laughingly called a "Ball". Grace had never been but knew from the other nurses and attendants it was meant to be for the benefit of the patients who were recovering, to help them to re-socialise, particularly with those of the opposite sex. It was true, of course, after being locked away with only women for company, a short time once a month at a dance did help, or at least that's what the nurses were told.

On this particular Friday, Sister Biggs called Grace into her office.

'Now Bennett, This evening and I would like you to escort some of the ladies to the ball. You may take Mrs Smith and Mrs Pullman. They are both settled now, and I think you can manage both of them.'

'Yes, Sister,' Grace said, noticing the neat hair of Sister Biggs and how it was never out of place. She touched her own hair which, as always, was escaping from her cap.

'Bennett, are you paying attention?'

'Yes, Sister.' Grace straightened her back.

'Encourage the ladies to make themselves as presentable as possible and to be ready by six thirty this evening.'

'Yes, of course, Sister. Do you think they'll want to go? Mrs Smith's very shy, particularly around people she's only just met. You know she was mute when she was admitted and although she talks now, she is still very much an introvert.'

'I am quite aware of the behaviour of Mrs Smith when she was admitted, thank you. It will be your task to help her overcome those obstacles. Now, the ladies may have one hour only on this occasion. I think that will be quite enough for the first time, don't you?'

'Of course, Sister.'

'You must stay with them at all times. They may dance but you must keep them in your sight. The male patients who are allowed to the ball are closely monitored too and there will be male attendants with them, but Mrs Pullman and Mrs Smith will be your responsibility once you are off the ward. Do you have any questions?'

'No, Sister, I don't think so.'

'Very well. Now get on with your duties please nurse.'

The two ladies were still in the dining room when Grace went to find them. They both looked up expectantly when Grace spoke to them.

'I have some good news, ladies. Sister has asked me to take you to the monthly ball this evening. It takes place in the ballroom here in the asylum and although it sounds very grand, it really is just a dance for the patients. Staff members go too, and also people of the town who have an interest in supporting the work done here.'

'I really don't think I could.' Mrs Smith was shaking her head, her eyes full of fear. 'I couldn't face it. Do I have to go?'

'I wouldn't like to force you to, but it would be good for you. Sister thinks it would be another step towards you going home.'

'I'm not sure,' Mrs Smith said.

'Oh come on.' Mrs Pullman was keen. 'We both need a bit of a change, don't we? I'm certainly ready to have a little dance.'

'I suppose it might be all right,' agreed Mrs Smith. 'If you don't leave me alone.'

'I won't be leaving your side,' Grace assured her.

'And we can dance together,' Mrs Pullman said. 'I'm used to taking the man's role in dancing.'

'I have nothing nice to wear, though,' Mrs Smith said. 'Have you?'

'Not really,' Mrs Pullman agreed. 'But do we care? We can pretend we have and just have fun, can't we?'

'I have got my blue dress, I suppose.'

'Wonderful, Grace said. 'Now, when you come back from work later, you shall both have a bath, I'll wash your hair and you can put on your nice dresses.'

That evening, once bathed and with their hair styled, each in their only good dress, the two women stood together in the day room.

'You look very fine, ladies,' Grace said as she smiled at them both. 'Now are we quite ready to go to the ball, Cinders?'

'That is not funny, Nurse Bennett,' Mrs Smith retorted.

'I'm sorry. I didn't mean to make light of your situation,' Grace said.

'Well we are like a couple of Cinderellas really.' Mrs Pullman laughed. 'I thought it was funny anyway.'

'Thank you Mrs Pullman,' Grace said. 'Now, let's get to the ballroom and have some fun.'

'Fun? I'm terrified.'

Grace squeezed Mrs Smith's shoulder. 'Please don't be. I'll be there with you both. And you don't have to do anything you don't want to. We can sit and drink lemonade and watch the dancers.'

Grace realised they'd likely never been into the ballroom before. As they made their way to the door, the band had already started playing a waltz. She felt Mrs Smith trembling as they walked, and wondered if this was the right thing for her. Maybe it was too soon? Mrs Pullman seemed to sense it too and linked her arm through Mrs Smith's as they reached the entrance.

Once inside, Grace herself was overwhelmed with the cacophony of noise and the colours of the gowns the ladies wore, the sparkling jewellery at their wrists and draping around their necks. Some even wore fur stoles. The gentlemen were dressed in evening suits, with white shirts and black ties. She had never seen so many wealthy people in one room at the same time before.

Attendants and nurses in uniforms were in groups, some were queuing for drinks, others were with their patients. Some sat at tables on the other side of the dance floor. Female patients were all along one side and the men on the other. The differences between the ladies and gentlemen in their finery and the inmates of the asylum were marked indeed.

Grace wondered to herself whether this kind of event could really be helpful to the patients, or was it all more of a "show" to make the wealthy few feel that they were doing something good.

'Come along, ladies,' she said. 'We'll have some refreshment and sit over there.' She indicated to a table across the room.

The evening was a great success. Mrs Pullman could hardly wait to get out onto the floor and soon swept the more reticent Mrs Smith off her feet and around the room in an elegant waltz. Grace stood at the edge of the dance floor and watched them as they passed by her. She could see Mrs Pullman was smiling, her eyes bright, alive for the first time since Grace had met her some weeks before in the ward.

Mrs Smith at first seemed unsure of herself, although after passing a second time, she looked more relaxed and even broke out into laughter when the two ladies fell out of step with each other.

Grace looked around at the beauty of the room itself. The walls were of pale-coloured brick, decorated with stylish red bricks in symmetrical lines. High up in the walls were stained glass windows which let in the evening sunlight. Grace imagined that when in was completely dark outside the chandeliers which hung from the ceiling would cast brilliant light around the vast hall. The stage, with its proscenium arch, looked perfect and was where the asylum band sat, playing such merry music. You could be anywhere, Grace thought, anywhere but in an asylum.

The hour was soon over and Grace gathered her charges up. They made their way back to M Ward, the two ladies chatting together.

'You enjoyed yourselves, ladies, I think,' Grace said as she opened the door to the ward.

'We certainly did,' Mrs Pullman said. 'Didn't we Gladys?'

'I didn't think I would, Freda,' agreed Mrs Smith. 'But, yes, I did enjoy the dancing. Thank you.'

36

Grace tried to focus on work and study, even though her feelings for Rose were always there in the back of her mind.

The war still waged in Europe and there were rumours now since the American forces had joined the fight, there would be a need for them to use the asylum as a hospital for the injured soldiers who were being brought back almost daily from Belgium. Grace wondered if she'd have to nurse the wounded after all. She recalled her Ma saying that she wasn't cut out for that kind of work and Grace felt inclined to agree. Even though her heart was firmly determined to continue learning about mental illness, insanity and other conditions connected with the mind, she wondered how she'd cope with injured men. She wasn't looking forward to such a change in her life. And where would they put them all?

She found out when the attendants and trainees were all called to Sister Biggs office.

'Ladies. I know you've heard rumours about our friends from America needing to take over the asylum as a hospital for the wounded. This rumour, is, in fact true, and many of our patients will be transferred to other mental asylums in the south of England. We have to prepare them and ourselves for the move. Only the pauper patients will go. The paying patients will be moved to the villas in the grounds here. Some of you will stay in Portsmouth to care for those, but the others of you will go with the pauper patients. Any questions?'

'Which asylums will our ladies be sent to?' Ethel asked. 'The nearest to us is the Hampshire County Asylum near Wickham, isn't it.'

'It is, but it's yet to be decided where our ladies will go. All of the asylums are extremely full so wherever we get sent it will be crowded. This could be a trying time indeed for everyone.'

'What other asylums are there?' Rose asked.

'There is Graylingwell in Chichester, although I am sure they only have room for a few. Some of our ladies may be discharged if they are well enough to be cared for at home. Certainly a few of those private patients who are here will go home. Some will go to the Hampshire County Asylum, but most will go to Brighton.'

'That's a long way,' Grace said. 'But like Portsmouth it's by the sea and more jolly no doubt. I wouldn't mind that.'

'I'm pretty sure that the Brighton asylum is a bit further inland, Bennett,' Sister Biggs said. 'But we shall have to see, won't we.'

For the next week life was to be even more busy preparing the patients for the great move. Grace learned that she was to go to Brighton with the pauper patients, including her assigned lady, Gladys Smith. Gladys had been doing well in the past months, working in the fields with the farm team. Working outside seemed to suit her well and she'd improved quite a lot since the night of the ball. All the same, Gladys, like the other patients, was feeling unsettled at moving so far away along the coast. It was a long train journey and because of the unpredictability of the patients, ambulances were arranged so they were all kept together away from the curious eyes of the public.

All of this organising kept Grace busy but she was still keen to meet up with Georgia again, to talk about her anxieties over her friendship with Rose. She knew Rose wasn't going to be moving to Brighton with the others. She'd volunteered to help with the American nurses.

'Why would you want to do that?' Grace asked when she found out.

'I want to have experience of nursing those with physical diseases and broken limbs.' Rose had said. 'I'm not sure about the men bit, but it'll be an experience, won't it?'

'It'll certainly be that. I'll miss you, Rose.'

'Will you?' Rose looked at her. 'Perhaps it'll be a good thing not to see each other for a while. It'll give you time to decide what you want, too.'

Thursday evening came quickly enough and Grace wandered along Asylum Road again. She reached the houseboat and made to knock on the door which opened before she got the chance. Dora stood there, a huge smile on her face. She wore another loose dress with a voluminous pinafore over the top which was covered in splurges of paint in all colours.

'Sorry, Grace, I was just off to my studio. Excuse the state of my working clothes. You've come to see Georgia, I think?'

'I hope I'm not chasing you out of your own home.'

'Not at all. I was planning to work on my latest masterpiece this evening. Go ahead, Georgia is in.'

'Thank you.'

Georgia looked up from the table where she'd been writing in a notebook. 'Welcome again, Grace.' She stood and pulled out a chair. 'Come and have a seat.'

Grace sat. 'I hope I'm not intruding.'

'Oh, I'm always scribbling away at something. You're not intruding at all. I invited you here didn't I?'

'Yes. Thank you.'

'Would you like a drink? We've got some beers here. Or are you a tea girl?'

'Beer would be perfect.'

Georgia opened two bottles and handed Grace a mug whilst she poured her own. 'Now, what did you want to chat about?'

'I don't know where to start really.' Grace looked at the lacy curtains at the window and wondered which one of the couple was the more feminine one. 'It's hard to know how to talk about this.'

'I suspect it may be about me and Dora? Our... relationship?'

'Well, yes, but no, not really. I know you told me that you were a couple and I can see you have a cosy home here.' Grace hesitated. 'The thing is, it's not you I am wondering about.'

'I see. I think I see anyway. Is there someone you have feelings for? Perhaps another woman? A nurse maybe?'

'There is,' Grace blushed. 'Her name's Rose. We're very close friends and the night you and I met, we got even closer. We kissed. I am ashamed to say I panicked and ran away. That's how I ended up in the mud flats actually. Rose wasn't chasing me.'

'No, it was that brute you told me about.'

'Yes. Anyway,' Grace shuddered. 'Rose wants us to be more than friends. I'm not the first woman she's been close to. She said she knew you and Dora actually. She said you were a nice couple.' Grace took a sip of her beer. 'Look, I'm sorry, I don't even know what I'm asking you. I'm just confused and unsure of how it would work, being with a woman, I mean.'

'My answer to that would be, how does anything work? In a relationship whether it's two women, or a man and a woman, or even two men, it's two people living together, learning how to get on.'

'I've plenty experience of living with other people. I have a sister and two brothers. I know what it's like to grow up in a busy house. But this is different. I'm close to my sister and we've always shared a room. We fight, of course we do, but we love one another and would do anything for each other. But she's my sister. And we don't... you know.'

'I do. And now you live in a nurses' home. Do you have separate rooms in there?'

'We do. We share the living areas, lounge, kitchen and bathrooms but we each have our own private bedroom.' She thought for a moment. 'I get on well with most of the other nurses. We're all in the same boat, working long hours, having to learn so much new stuff. I think there was a spark with Rose from the first day we met. I certainly felt attracted to her. We started on the same day together and it was as though I'd known her for years.' Grace took another drink and sighed. 'Honestly, I have always felt I was different to other women, and have had feelings for women before. But then, I suppose I went along with what was always expected of me, and Teddy was just there. It was the easiest thing to do. With me and Rose, I think I'm afraid of people noticing and making things difficult for us.'

'Look, my advice would be to stop worrying about anything anyone might be thinking about you. Loving a woman is not a crime, even though it's a crime for men to be together, in that way. But I understand how you feel. Not everyone likes the thought of women being independent of men. My own family don't approve of us at all. But there it is. We get along very well without them.'

'I hadn't really thought that far ahead to be honest. I'm still struggling with, well taking the next step.'

'Let's be blunt. Did you enjoy the kiss, or were you disgusted by it?'

Grace squirmed and blushed again. She took another drink from her mug before she answered. 'I'll be honest. I was shocked. I didn't expect it, but I did enjoy it. If I hadn't, I don't think I would have ran away. I was confused.'

'And you still are. You enjoyed something you'd always been taught was wrong, unnatural?'

Grace was on her feet, walking about the room, pacing whilst she thought. When she reached the door to the inner room, she glanced in and saw the double bed, draped with colourful woven cloth. She turned and looked at Georgia.

'You're right of course. Being with a woman goes against all I was made to want as a child. Well, in fact, it was never spoken of. We girls were all expected to grow up ready to be wives and mothers.'

'And you don't need to fit in with any of that,' Georgia said.

Grace sat down again. 'But what about children? I thought I'd be a mother one day.'

'There are some sacrifices indeed.'

'Although if I'm to have a career in nursing I won't be allowed to marry anyway. So I won't be sacrificing anything more than I already am, will I.'

'I would never say never, dear. None of us knows what could be around the corner. Especially in these times.'

'What do you mean? Surely I couldn't have a child if I was with a woman?"

'Maybe not. But there are more and more orphan children since this war began.'

'I don't think I could ever see me taking in an orphan.' Grace shook her head. 'No, I think I'm more clear on my feelings now and maybe how to deal with them. Thank you for being so open about things.'

'Look, I'll tell you one more thing.' She smiled at Grace. 'If you really love a woman and feel attracted to her, I can assure you if the feelings are reciprocated and you let things develop naturally, you will be ecstatically happy together, possibly even more so than you've ever been with a man.'

Grace felt herself becoming red in the face at the thought. 'To be truthful, I haven't had that much experience with a man. I was betrothed to Teddy, but we were going to wait. We kissed of course, but nothing more. Then he came back from the front and told me it was over. He was badly injured, but I would have stood by him, only he changed his mind.'

'I see. Well you have nothing to compare it to then.'

'Not really, and it's even more complicated as my sister and Teddy have now fallen in love and are marrying in a few weeks.'

'No wonder you're in a turmoil. I think the best thing for you would be to take things slowly, but do not be afraid of your feelings or whatever happens. How do you feel about Teddy and your sister?'

'I suppose I made my choice when I told Teddy I wanted to be a nurse first and not to marry before he went away. He did ask me, and I put him off, then I changed my mind. I thought us having a child would make me feel more settled, but by then it was too late. When he came back to Portsmouth he was in the Queen Alexandra Hospital. I went to see him, but he told me not to come again and it was over.'

'I'm sorry.'

'I completely threw myself into my work for a while, and then my sister Elsie got herself into trouble. She was a patient in the asylum for a while. There was nothing wrong with her. She'd been attacked by her boss, Mr Medford.'

'The same brute who attacked you?'

'Yes. Oh, I don't know why I'm telling you all my private things. But you're so easy to talk to. You should be a nurse!'

'Not likely. I'll stick to the tram driving, thank you.'

'Anyway, I'm very happy that Elsie and Teddy are marrying. It means I gain him as a brother and I know they'll both be very happy. It won't be easy. Teddy lost both his legs, but my sister is a determined woman. I've known Teddy since we were children, too, so I'm very glad we will still be close, as brother and sister.'

'Your life has been a bit of a journey so far, hasn't it? How can you bear it?'

'I don't know, really.' They sat in silence for a while. 'Can I ask you one more thing? It's been bothering me all along.' Grace asked.

'Ask away.'

'I'm not sure how to put this, but I have been wondering which one of you is the female and which takes on the masculine role?'

Georgia laughed. 'Good question,' she said. 'Only it doesn't work like that. We are both feminine, through and through. I know you see some women who prefer to dress and act more like a man, but it's not always the case. Oh, I know you're probably wondering who of us is the housewifely type and yes, we do have some things that we prefer to do, like the cooking for example. Dora is a terrible cook, so I take that on, whilst she enjoys the homemaking role. Although we both share the cleaning. We make decisions together, which is how it should be in all relationships I believe.'

'I see. You seem to be very happy together.'

'We are.'

'You've been very helpful. I'd best get going, there's a lot to be done before we leave for Brighton.'

37

There was indeed a lot to do, not only at Portsmouth asylum, but also Brighton needed time to discharge as many of their patients as possible, so there was a delay before the big move. Sister Biggs and the medical officer, Dr Blake, were busy assessing all of the patients on M Ward and within a few weeks there were discharge plans in place for half of them. If the war had not been on, they may have stayed in the asylum for longer, but then, if there hadn't been the war, they might very well have not have needed to be there in the first place. And many of the ladies were improving so much on the moral treatment and in being able to talk about what had instigated their breakdowns, they would have been going home soon enough anyway.

Grace's main charges, Gladys Smith and Freda Pullman, were two who would have been deemed "cured" and both could have been released. In fact Mrs Pullman was to be discharged that morning.

Grace walked to her bed, smiling. 'Are you all packed and ready to go, Mrs Pullman?'

'Well, there certainly wasn't much to pack. Even if I'd wanted to bring more things in, there's hardly room here is there?' She smiled back at Grace. 'I'm sorry, I was only jesting, Nurse.'

'It's good to hear you making light of things.' Grace said. 'I'm sure it hasn't been easy for you over the past couple of months. But I'm glad you're recovered. Soon you'll be back in your own home, with your family.'

'To be honest, I'm not sure I'm ready. My baby won't be so little anymore, and I'll have to learn all over again how to be a mother.'

'You will be absolutely wonderful as a mother. He's been cared for by your nanny, hasn't he?'

'Yes. But he won't know me.'

'It may be a bit tricky for the first few days, but you're well now, and he's your baby so you will love him and he will love you. You'll soon get used to each other again.'

'I'm scared, Nurse Bennett.' Mrs Pullman looked around the dormitory. 'Perhaps I should stay here for a while longer. I haven't seen my babe since I was brought to this place. I've forgotten how to hold him.'

'I know, it must be worrying for you. It's a pity babies aren't allowed to be brought in to visit their mothers, but it's probably a rule for a good reason. Look, I know you're scared now, but as soon as you get home, things will fall into place, you know. Just take it a day at a time.'

'Wise words Nurse,' Mrs Pullman said. 'Anyway, I have to go home so there's no escaping it. Can I thank you for everything you've done for me? It's much appreciated.'

'You don't need to thank me. I only do my job.'

'Not all the nurses and attendants are kind though, are they?' Mrs Pullman looked at Grace.

'Maybe not,' Grace agreed. 'Now, if you're ready, I'll walk with you to the main entrance hall. I believe your husband is waiting there for you.'

Grace's keys jangled as she turned the lock of the ward door. Soon they'd passed down the corridor, the last time for Mrs Pullman. Her pace slowed as they neared the main entrance but as soon as she saw her husband nervously waiting by the front door, she ran the last few steps across the floor to his side. With all nervousness pushed away, she dropped her bag and the two embraced happily.

Grace coughed. 'Well, I will leave you here, Mrs Pullman, Mr Pullman, and wish you both all the best. I trust we won't be seeing you in here again.'

The two turned, smiling. 'Thank you again, Nurse,' Mrs Pullman said. 'For everything.'

Grace's other charge, Gladys Smith, wasn't faring quite as well. She had improved a little after the ball, and perhaps if her circumstances had been better, she would have gone home too. Sadly, with her husband dying and her losing her home in Portsea, things would have to be put in place before she could be released to recover her baby boy from the workhouse. Grace wondered if her fate would eventually be to live in the workhouse herself. There was hope that she might be able to go and live with her sister in Plymouth but because of the war, things seemed to have come to a halt for the time being.

Grace tried to encourage her to stay positive about her future.

'Mrs Pullman leaving must be a blow for you. I know you two ladies were friends and have been a great help to each other. But it will soon be your turn, I'm sure. I hear that Dr Devine has written to your sister in Plymouth so you can be discharged to her home.'

'Yes, I was aware of that, but it's been weeks now,' Mrs Smith replied. 'And yes, I will miss Freda, of course. She has been a good friend.'

'I'm sure that your friendship will endure.'

'Really? I hardly think a lady like Freda Pullman would want to keep a friendship with someone like me. She lives in a grand house in Southsea, whilst my home was nothing much more than a hovel in Portsea.'

'I'm sure that's not important to her.'

'I have heard what people say about the street I lived in, Nurse. And now I'm homeless and have not only been in the asylum, but also the workhouse. How will she introduce me to her friends?'

'Perhaps you're right, but things change with time, and the class system will change too, I'm sure.'

'If you think that, you must be deluded and should be in this dress and not your uniform.' She sniffed and looked Grace in the eye. 'I'm sorry Nurse, you've been very kind to me and to the other ladies in here, but you're hardly a woman of the world, are you? You're still unmarried and have had no life yet.'

Grace laughed. 'I'm sorry, I'm not laughing at you. You're right, of course, I haven't seen much of life yet.' She paused, thinking. 'I have to say, though, when you came in here you had no words at all, and now you talk for England.'

'Charming.'

'No, it's wonderful to hear you talking. I'm only sorry you haven't got somewhere to go yet. Although I'm sure your sister will welcome you to her house soon. And then you can collect your baby and start your life again.'

'We'll see, I suppose, although I don't have much faith in her wanting me there. Her house is smaller than mine was and Plymouth is a long way.'

'Let's be hopeful anyway,' Grace said. 'So, we're going on an adventure to Brighton soon. Who knows what that will bring, eh?'

'I've heard all about Brighton. But we'll be stuck in another place like this so I'm hardly excited.'

'Yes, I know. Hopefully it won't be for long.'

38

It was rare that Grace and Rose were off duty together. Their friendship had remained just that. Good friends at arms-length apart. One afternoon, with only three hours before they were both due back on the ward, they somehow found themselves sitting in the garden together, both trying their best to read their nurse training notes and not to look across at each other.

The July sunshine was hot, only relieved by a gentle gust of wind at intervals. Grace looked up at the white clouds above, shaped like feathers which told her of the high winds which helped to cool the air a little. The gardens were pretty, with a few hollyhocks taking pride of place on the beds. Behind these, of course, were runner beans with the green vines winding their way up the canes, and already a few red flowers were blooming here and there.

Soon we will have fresh beans with our suppers, thought Grace. 'I hope they don't boil all the goodness out of them,' she said out loud.

Rose lifted her head from her reading. 'Did you say something?' she asked.

'Sorry, I was talking about the runner beans.'

'Really?'

'Yes, I was looking at the runners there and thinking about how nice they taste when they're fresh.'

'My dad used to grow them in our garden. Well, it's more of a yard really.'

'It's a pity the cook here boils the veg to death though.'

'That's true but we're lucky to have veg at all really, so don't complain.'

'I know. You're right.' Grace stretched her legs out and wriggled her feet. 'If my feet weren't so sore, I'd suggest we went for a walk.'

'With me?' Rose looked surprised. 'You sure you want to be seen out with me?'

'Don't be like that, Rose.'

'Sorry. I suppose I'm still a bit...'

'I know, and I'm sorry. I didn't want it to be awkward between us. There's a tearoom not far, the one by the farm in Milton. We could walk there and have a cuppa and maybe even a cake.'

'You sure your sore feet can take it?'

'I think I could manage.'

'Don't think there'll be much in the way of cake though.'

'I know - there is a war on!' Grace said. 'Oh how I'm sick of hearing that.'

It was only a twenty-minute walk to the tea room which was quiet at that time of day with only four other tables filled. They sat together in the window, Grace feeling much more relaxed in Rose's company than she'd imagined she'd feel. This was the first time they'd spent time together outside of the asylum.

'They have buns on the menu,' Rose exclaimed. 'We're in luck.'

'That's a relief then,' Grace said with a grin.

Soon they were pouring tea and chatting happily.

'This is a nice place,' Rose said. 'I've never been in here before.'

'Me neither. What a lovely place to sit and watch the world go by.'

The view from the front window faced the barns of Milton Farm. A dairy herd was being walked to the milking sheds. A similar shed was at the rear of the asylum and Grace had noticed how wonderful farm life seemed to be, from the windows of the nursing school, when her attention had wandered from the work in hand.

'Have you ever been on a farm?' Rose asked.

'Only the one at the asylum.'

'Smelly, dirty places,' Rose said, laughing. 'You'd think it was all fresh air, wouldn't you? But it's not. Where there's animals, there's muck. Anyway, I meant a proper one in the country.'

'Have you been to one, then?'

'I did go on a trip once when I was little, with my parents. We rode in a tram all the way to Waterlooville. Do you know where that is?'

Grace nodded. 'I've taken the tram as far as the top of the hill. There's a farm up there. I've seen the sheep, but no cows when I went, although they were probably in another field.'

'We should take a trip ourselves one day,' Rose suggested. 'Might have to wait until the war's over though.'

'That would be nice.'

'Look Grace, I'm sorry you're going to Brighton. And I'm sorry I'm not going with you. I'm going to miss you.'

'I'll miss you too, Rose. And I'm sorry I've been so... uncertain about things.'

'I understand actually, and I am happy to wait until you come back. When the war ends, I mean. I only hope it doesn't go on for much longer.'

Grace reached across the table and took Rose's hand. 'Thank you for being so patient. I've always denied my feelings towards women before, and it's scary,' she said. 'And I'm sure now that the American forces have joined in the fight it'll only be a short time before it's all over. It has to be.'

'Quite,' Rose smiled as she spoke. 'Now, are you going to eat that bun, or shall I? I'm starving.

39

It had been a busy few weeks and there was much excitement around the asylum with the Americans arriving. Such handsome doctors walked the corridors, causing so many hearts fluttering in the trainees and even with some of the seasoned attendants.

Grace had one last afternoon off to spend with her family. Ma had prepared a special meal of pie and mash and they were all squashed around the table: Ma and Pa, Elsie, Teddy and Grace. The brothers were still in Europe and Grace couldn't recall the last time they'd all been together. She'd written to them both with the address of the Brighton asylum and hoped they'd be safe and be able to write to her there.

'I'm proud of you Grace.' Pa took her hand and gave it a squeeze. 'I didn't think you'd really do it, and I admit I didn't want you to, but I'm proud. You take good care, won't you, girl?'

'Of course, Pa, and I'll write as often as I can.'

'You'd better write to your mother. You know I don't know my letters well. You write to her, and she'll read it to me.'

'All right Pa,' Grace said. 'And you take care too. Mind your back in that dockyard.'

'I will.'

'Elsie, shall we go for a short walk? Our last time for a while,' Grace said.

'Yes, and we need to talk about the wedding too. You are coming back for it, aren't you?'

Grace sighed. 'I hope so. It may be a quick visit, but I'll do my best. If not, you know I wish you the very best, don't you? And you too Teddy.' She smiled at them both.

Teddy looked across at her. 'Come and give me a hug, Grace. You are the best sister-in-law to be.'

'Better than I would have been as a wife I think.'

'Don't say that, Grace. I'm sorry it didn't work.'

'You are not sorry,' Grace laughed. 'And neither am I. I'm very happy for you both. It's the right thing for all of us. I will always love you as a brother, and now we'll always be family, won't we.' She looked at Elsie. 'And you got the better sister.'

'Oh get on with your walk, you two.'

'What about a hug for me,' Ma said. 'I'm feeling left out here.'

'I'm coming back, Ma. We're only going for a short stroll.' Grace hugged Ma anyway and left the house with Elsie.

'I am going to miss you, Grace,' Elsie linked arms with her as they walked. 'I don't know how I'm going to get myself ready for the wedding without you.'

'Nonsense! Ma will help and I know you'll be fine at organising your day. I'll be sad if I can't be there but it's a long journey to Brighton and might not be so easy to get the time off now. I'll do what I can, as I've said.'

'How I wish this war was over.'

'Now that the Americans have joined it shouldn't be long, surely.'

'I wish that were the case.' Elsie sighed. 'Such a waste.'

'I can't stop thinking about our boys. I do hope they survive.'

'You hear so many stories about those coming back with mental insanity. What if our brothers get it?'

'They call it "shell-shock". There are a few men in the asylum with it. Most of them are in Netley hospital though,' Grace said. 'It's the effect of the noise and the shock of war. I can't imagine any coming back who aren't affected at all.'

'Such a terrible time,' Elsie said. She suddenly stopped walking. 'Oh Lord. Look who's ahead of us.'

Grace stiffened. 'Mr Medford. And is that his wife with him? They're looking straight at us. Shall we cross the street?'

'Certainly not. We've done nothing wrong. He should be ashamed to walk these streets.'

The couple were almost upon them when Mrs Medford spoke. 'So you are the two hussies who tried to ruin my husband's life, are you? I've been wanting to have a word with you both for a long time now.'

'You want to have a word with us?' Elsie spat. 'Oh, Madam, I have wanted to have a word with you as well.'

'Elizabeth,' Mr Medford said as he gripped his wife's elbow. 'Don't embarrass yourself. They are not worth it.'

'Not worth it?' Grace couldn't help herself. 'Is that what you thought when you followed me to the end of Asylum Road in the middle of the night and left me to die in the mud flats?'

'Shut your filthy mouth. You are a liar as well as a slut.' Mr Medford glared at Grace.

Grace looked at his wife. 'Ask him, then, where he was that night.'

'What night?'

'It was the 25th of March. Ask him where he was that night.'

'This is ridiculous, come along Elizabeth.'

'I don't know how I'm supposed to know where he was that night. It was months ago now and my husband is often out in the evenings, attending his meetings, aren't you dear?'

'I told you not to talk to these two. Now, excuse us, won't you.' He scowled at Grace and Elsie.

'Ask him what he gets up to in the storeroom at the munitions factory, then,' Elsie said. 'And for your information, I am not a hussy. Myself and my sister are respectable ladies. It's your husband you should be looking at more closely.'

'Oh get out of our way,' Mr Medford shoved his way past Elsie. 'Come along Elizabeth,' he said.

Mrs Medford was red-faced. She stood for a moment, glaring at the two young women as she shook her head.

'We are sorry, Mrs Medford, if we've shocked you, but we're telling the truth.' Elsie looked at her husband and continued. 'Your husband preys on young women who are desperate to keep their employment. And you know what happens if he is refused? They are accused of attacking him or worse. You needed to know.'

'She speaks the truth,' Grace added. 'And now, we wish you a good day.' She linked Elsie's arm to hers and they walked together along the street in silence until they reached the corner. Grace took a quick glance back to see Mr Medford and his wife in heated discussion with each other.

'Well done, Elsie,' she said. 'That certainly makes me feel better.'

'Me too, dear sister.' Elsie squeezed Grace's arm and laughed. 'I wonder how their marriage will fare now.'

Almost as soon as the two sisters arrived back home, it was time for Grace to leave. She ran upstairs to the room she'd shared with Elsie throughout their childhoods and looked around, realising the next time she was home, Elsie would be a married woman. Grace felt a shadow of regret that things had turned out the way they had. She ran her hand over the dressing table and said a silent goodbye to her childhood. This time tomorrow she would be living in the asylum at Brighton. Oh, what a new adventure this could turn out to be. Being away from home and more importantly, away from Rose, would give her time to think about what she really wanted out of life and what her true feelings for Rose were.

Downstairs, she said her final goodbyes to the family, hugging them one by one. Ma followed her out into the street and handed her a parcel.

'What's this, Ma?'

'Just something I want you to have, to remind you of us all at home. Don't open it until you get to Brighton. I hope you have somewhere in your room to keep it.' Ma smiled. 'Now get on your way before I cry.'

'Oh, Ma, I will miss you so much.'

'Then write to me every week.'

'I will. I love you Ma.'

Grace kissed her Ma on the cheek and walked briskly down the street to make her way back to the asylum.

Rose was sitting in the lounge back at the nurses home. She stood as Grace came in the main door. Their eyes met and Grace's heart leapt. She wondered why she was holding back and for a moment admitted she longed to kiss those lips again.

'Grace,' Rose began. 'Can we chat?'

'Of course. Are you all right?'

'Not really. I only wanted to say again how sorry I am you're going to Brighton tomorrow. God, I'm going to miss you.'

Grace reached towards Rose and touched her cheek. 'I'll miss you too, but hopefully it won't be for long.' Grace looked around the room. 'I suppose I'll miss this place too. But you the most.'

'I just wish...'

'I know, there are so many things I wish we had time to sort out. But they do say a time apart clears the head. You've said it yourself.'

'And the heart, I hope.' Rose said. 'I know I shouldn't keep on, but I want to say again I do care for you and I believe it could work between us.'

'It's not so easy for me. I have no experience of this. I've been thinking about it and about you all the time. I need a bit more time to get comfortable with it, I suppose.'

'I always believe in following my feelings. Maybe you could do the same. I do think you have the same feelings too. You're just afraid.'

'I agree. I am afraid, but it's not that simple. I have my family to think of. What will they feel about me being - different?'

'We'd manage things somehow. If your family love you, they'll understand won't they?'

'Maybe. I hope so anyway.' Grace took Rose's hand. 'I'll write to you often and think of you all the time.'

'I will too. Let's hope the war is over before long.'

'Yes, indeed.' Grace squeezed Rose's hand, and went to her room to pack her bag, her heart heavy.

40

Rattling around in the front seat of the ambulance, Grace tried to enjoy the view as they travelled. The journey was long, or seemed so, although she was aware of how much further away her dear brothers were, all across the ocean to Europe. How were they faring? They were often in her thoughts of course, but she tried not to dwell on them and usually busied herself to keep her mind occupied. When she remembered how Teddy was when he arrived back home, she hoped and prayed her two brothers would be safe and come back in one piece at least.

The thought of Rose, of course, was in her mind during the journey. To be so far away from each other could only be a good thing, surely? Then her mind grew afraid. What if Rose forgets me, finds someone she likes more than me? How could I have let the chance of being in a loving relationship with her slip away?

Telling herself how ridiculous she was being, she tried to focus on the countryside along the way.

She turned to the ambulance driver, a woman she'd met before when a patient had been delivered from the workhouse to the ward. 'Sorry, I forgot your name. So rude of me,' she said.

'It's Florence, but you can call me Flo. I remember you. You're Nurse Bennett aren't you?'

'Yes, sorry, I haven't been very sociable and please call me Grace. You do a great job. I always wondered if I could drive an ambulance.'

'It's pretty easy. If you can drive a car, you can drive anything.'

'Maybe, but I've never driven a car either. It's not that easy when you come from a family like mine.'

'What do you mean?'

'My Pa works in the dockyard. We don't have much money, just enough to pay the rent and feed us all.'

'Oh, I get what you mean. Yes, I suppose I've been lucky. But still, you're doing a grand job now. Nursing, I mean.'

'I'm only a trainee. And as I work in the asylum, it's not exactly a profession people look up to.'

'People are strange aren't they?'

'Judgemental. Even my own family were against me doing this.'

'Funnily enough, mine were against me doing this too. I was supposed to be looking for a husband, to keep some man's house and breed.'

'Oh dear,' Grace was laughing. 'Isn't that what we're all supposed to want? Us young women, I mean.'

'I thought it was what I wanted,' said Flo.

'This war makes us all think harder about what we want doesn't it?'

'It certainly does.'

Grace looked at Flo and then turned her head to look out of the front window.

'What's up?' Flo asked.

'I was just thinking about all the ladies in the back there. I think half of them wouldn't be in the asylum if this war hadn't lasted so long. And now, to be sent so far away from home. There won't be any chance of many visits for them. Until it's over anyway.'

'Well, your job is to help them get well again, so you'd better work harder than ever to get them discharged.'

'I wish I knew how to, I really do.' Grace sighed.

'You'll find a way,' Flo said. 'And I'm sure you'll find your own way through life, wherever that takes you, as will I.'

'I hope so.'

The two women sank into silence for the remainder of the journey. Grace was settling into a doze when Flo spoke again.

'Here we are, the wonderful Brighton Asylum,' she said.

Grace opened her eyes and looked in amazement at the beauty of the building at the end of the driveway. Instead of the red brick she was used to seeing at the Portsmouth Asylum, this one was of yellow, with red brick banding decorating around the arch-shaped windows. It was a vast building which loomed over them as they pulled up outside the main front door. Although it was named the Brighton Asylum, it was near to Hayward's Heath and overlooked the South Downs miles away from the coast. She was going to miss seeing the sea as well as all her friends and family.

Soon the patients were settled into the ward they'd been allocated to. Extra beds had been slotted into the already crowded dormitories and the nurses were given beds in the nearby nurses' home. Grace was to sleep in a shared room with several others in the converted lounge. She hoped it wouldn't be for long, and she'd get on with the other nurses and attendants she'd be sharing with.

Her nearest neighbour was from Portsmouth too, but someone she'd not worked with before.

'I'm Grace Bennett.' She offered her hand. 'I've seen you at the asylum but don't think we know each other?'

'Nice to meet you. I'm Alice Partridge. I was working on C ward. It's a quiet backwater of a ward and I've been on there for years. What about you?' Her dark brown eyes look straight into Grace's.

'I'm a trainee on M Ward. I haven't been there long, a few months.'

'So, you're one of the new trainee nurses are you? Well good luck with that.'

'Thank you.'

'I've not done any training as such. Just years of hands-on experience.' She shook her head, strands of her sandy coloured hair escaping from her cap. 'There was no training when I started out. And no respect from the public either.'

'I think we are still looked down on,' Grace agreed. 'But time will change that I hope.'

'So, are you learning much?'

'There is a lot to learn. I'm not sure whether I'm keeping it all in though.'

'The best way to learn, in my opinion,' said Alice as she smoothed down her skirt, 'Is on the wards. And coming to this far away asylum will only add to your experience. And mine too,' she added. 'Now, we shall be friends, I hope.'

'I think we shall,' Grace agreed. 'I expect we'll see quite a lot of each other, living in such close quarters.'

'Excellent. And if you want to ask me anything, about looking after lunatics, I mean, then I am here.' She paused. 'And you can ask me anything else you want to know as well. I have been around for a long time.'

Grace smiled as Alice left the room. She looked around. The view from the window beside her bed was of the Downs. It reminded her of times she'd walk up Portsdown Hill, but she knew there'd be no view of Portsmouth on the other side of these hills.

Forcing down her feelings of home-sickness, Grace unpacked her bag into the locker beside her bed. She opened the parcel her Ma had given her and inside was a picture that had been taken at the photographic studio before her brothers had gone away at the start of the war. The family were grouped around her Ma and Pa, each staring into a future they had no idea would be so hard.

'Thank you, Ma,' she whispered to herself before she placed the picture on her bedside locker, wiped away a tear, and made her way back to the ward to find out what her duties were to be.

41

Grace soon settled into her new routine. The days were long and her time off was very short. The Sister on the ward kept reminding the staff that there was a war on. 'As if we don't know that', Grace and the others complained to each other.

A letter came a few days after she arrived, which was a great excitement. It was from Elsie.

Dearest Grace,

I hope you are well, I miss you terribly.

I have some good news for you. I heard today that Mr Medford has been arrested for assaulting one of the young women at the factory. It seems the girls have had enough of him and there were several witnesses. I only wish they had been brave enough to come forward for me. I heard Mrs Medford visited the factory and spoke to some of them and it happened after that. It looks like he will get his just desserts after all.

I am still working on my wedding plans and we are gathering ingredients for a cake. Ma is making a good job of my wedding dress. I wish you were here to see it.

What's it like in Brighton? I've always wanted to go. Perhaps one day, when the war is over we can go there, although by then

I'll be married and maybe have children. Is the beach sandy? Please write soon and let me know how you are getting on.
Your ever loving sister,
Elsie.

Grace read the letter several times. It was so typical of Elsie to jump from one topic to another. She was glad that Mr Medford had been arrested but truly couldn't see he'd get his "just desserts" as Elsie hoped. She knew men like him always got away with things and he was needed to manage the munitions factory so that would be that. However, she was reassured his wife knew what he was like now. At least his life at home might not be as comfortable as it was before.

She was happy to read the wedding plans were going well and of course, she'd write to Elsie to put her straight on where the asylum was. As for Brighton beach, she'd been told it wasn't sandy at all. Grace had always wondered why people set such store on Brighton when the beach there couldn't be any nicer than the one at Southsea, surely?

The following day there was another letter. Grace's heart did a little skip when this one arrived. She recognised the writing she'd seen in Rose's notebook and she slipped it into her apron pocket when it arrived. Today she had time off in the afternoon and would save it for then, when she could be alone.

The sun was shining as she left the ward and stepped through the door into the gardens. Looking around at the shrubs and at the vegetables growing in the beds that were once filled with flowers, Grace smiled to herself. There was a gentle breeze in the air which took the fierce heat out of the sunshine. She walked as she took the letter from her pocket. There was a bench seat underneath the branches of a copper beech tree whose leaves were a deep red. As she made her way to it, looking at the envelope in her hand, Grace suddenly felt a shadow of doubt cross her mind. What if Rose was writing to tell her she no longer wanted to be her friend? Telling herself there was only one way to find out, she reached the bench and sat down, opening the letter before she could talk herself out of it.

Dearest Grace,
I do hope you don't mind me calling you dearest as that is how I think of you. I know I promised not to pester you and I won't. I only wanted to connect with you while you're so far away.

Life here is so different now the Americans are here. The American nurses are fun, although they are strange in the way they speak. Some of the doctors are terrible flirts but of course I am not interested in any of them. It breaks my heart to think of the wounded men when they start arriving. Some of them will be so badly injured but we will do our best to patch them up. I am going to learn so many new skills. I pray I can stand it.

I hope you are settled in at Brighton and it's not too hard. I know the hours will be longer and it may not be as comfortable as being in our nurses' home here but you will make new friends I'm sure. Please write when you can. I do miss you.
Your dear friend,
    Rose

Being called dearest made Grace feel warm inside. Yes, she loved that Rose thought of her like this. Her feelings for Rose were easier to admit whilst they were so far apart. It had only been a few days, not even a week yet, but the distance did help make things more clear. She smiled to think of American doctors flirting with her friend and that the nurses were "fun". She hoped they weren't too much fun and wished she'd stayed behind too. But she knew she'd not be able to cope with nursing injured troops. It would have been too much for her, but Rose would be able to stand it. She was so much stronger than Grace.

Reading the final paragraph again, Grace accepted that Rose would make new friends too and this made her feel uncomfortable. 'Why am I feeling jealous of something that hasn't probably happened yet?' Grace asked herself. 'Rose has just declared she misses me and has called me "Dearest", so why?'

Making her way to the nurses' home, she took out her paper and a pen and wrote immediately to Rose.

My Dear Rose,

I was so pleased to receive your letter today. I have been missing you too, very much. Of course I don't think you are pestering me. We did agree to write often after all.

I am glad you are getting to know new people and the American nurses are nice. I expect you will be speaking with an accent the next time we meet. I can't wait to hear it.

It is busy here and I'm sleeping in a dormitory with several other nurses. I have made friends with Alice Partridge. She's in the bed next to mine and was an attendant on C Ward in

Portsmouth, where all the long-term patients are. Alice never did her training but knows so much about looking after the mentally infirm. The journey here was long and we were driven here by a woman called Florence! How times have changed.

This afternoon is the first time I've been able to go outside for fresh air during the daylight hours. It is a beautiful place, even though it's another asylum. The countryside around us is hilly and no town in sight, nor the coast. I miss that.

I hope we can write often. I do miss you.
Your dear friend,
    Grace.

Then she took another sheet of paper and wrote to Elsie.

My dear sister,

It was so good to hear from you and your news, especially about your wedding plans. I'm glad the dress is going well and you will have a wedding cake.

Thank you for letting me know about Mr Medford and his come-uppence too. I'll bet his wife will make his life a misery from now on and a good job too. I can't imagine he will be penalised though, by the law, I mean. His job is too important with all the men away. Still I am glad that the other women at the factory stood up to him at last.

Please say hello to Ma, Pa and Teddy. I will write to Ma in a couple of days, but give her a kiss from me, won't you? Has Ma heard from our brothers yet? I think about them a lot, don't you?

I laughed when you wrote about Brighton. Only because this asylum is miles away from the town and the coast. I have a lovely view of the hills of the South Downs from my window, but of course there're little time to sit and look at the view. I've only had two hours off duty during daylight since I got here. There is a nice garden just outside the window though and I went for a short walk there this afternoon.

Still, I must get back to my duties now, but will write again. Please keep me informed of everything at home. I miss you all, so much.

Your loving sister

Grace

All too soon she was back on the ward and helping to serve the evening meal, her two letters tucked in her pocket ready to be put into the post-tray in the office. The cost of post would be taken from her wages, and the letters would go first thing in the morning with the general mail.

She spent time that evening sitting with her patient, Gladys Smith, who was finding it difficult to settle. It wasn't easy for any of them, being so far from home, and there had been an incident when another patient had attacked her and now she was sitting apart from the others. She'd been hoping she'd be given work on the farm again, as she had in Portsmouth, but Grace doubted this would be easy to arrange.

'I'm sorry, Gladys,' she said. 'I know you love the outdoors, and of course, you improved so much working on the farm. But it won't be so easy to do the same thing here. I'm afraid you may have to be content with sewing work on the ward for the time being.'

'I knew it wouldn't be easy. I don't mind really, as long as I can go walking in the garden. Would that be possible?'

'I'm sure it will be, and hopefully it won't be for long. You have improved so much.' 'But I have nowhere to go, do I? My sister doesn't want me at hers.'

'I'm sorry to hear that. And your child?'

'Little Jimmy? He's only a baby still. I hate the thought of him still being at the Workhouse but I can't take him can I, until I have a home to take him to?'

'Maybe we can sort something out for you.' Grace glanced out of the window and thought for a moment. 'Let me see. Perhaps I could write to Mrs Simpson, she has helped me before and I know she was planning to visit the patients here as soon as she could.'

'Thank you. But please, I don't want to trouble you.'

'It's no trouble. I'm doing my job, that's all.'

'I think you go beyond your job but I do thank you.'

Later that evening, after her duties were over, Grace sat on her bed and wrote another letter, this time to her old employer, Mrs Simpson. Once written, she sealed the envelope and placed the letter on her locker ready for the morning.

42

Days passed with little change in Grace's routine. The work was hard, there were more times when the patients became irritable and seemed to pick on each other just to ease the boredom. Apart from Gladys, Grace was responsible for several other ladies, some of whom did not necessarily like each other. Gladys was certainly ready for discharge.

This did change after Mrs Simpson came to visit. Grace didn't really expect her to come all this way, but there she was, sitting in the bay window, chatting away with Gladys as though they were old friends.

Mrs. Simpson looked across at Grace and beckoned her over.

'Come and join us, won't you Bennett? We'd like to discuss Mrs Smith's future.'

Grace sat and waited.

'We've solved the problem,' said Mrs Simpson. 'Haven't we, Mrs Smith?'

'Yes, Mrs Simpson said I can have a job and a room as well. And to keep my Jimmy with me, too.'

'It's the obvious answer,' Mrs Simpson said. 'My parlourmaid is going to be leaving us shortly. I'll be sorry to see her go, but I think, Mrs Smith, you will be perfect to take her place. And the house is big enough for a child, I think. It was always our wish to have children in the home. There is what was going to be a nursery and the nanny's room on the second floor. You would be welcome to move in there.'

Gladys had tears in her eyes as she answered. 'It would be an answer, yes. But I'm not sure how I can care for Jimmy and work as a parlour-maid at the same time.'

'We will work something out. While your baby is small, you can manage with some of the duties I'm sure, in between feeding, etcetara, don't you think? And later, we will get some extra help in for you. Don't worry, I am excited for this new chapter in my life, and would be so happy to help you. And my husband and I have discussed your situation and both agree we want to do this.'

'But would I be able to leave here soon?' Gladys looked out of the window. 'It's such a long way from Portsmouth.'

'That will be up to the medical staff here, I suppose.'

'Really? Mrs Simpson you are too kind.'

'Nonsense. My husband is fully behind this as I've said. I can see myself helping young ladies after the war. There is much to be done and I will need as much help as I can get.'

'I hope it can be soon,' Gladys said.

Grace smiled. 'I think that can be arranged. We've been discussing your progress with the Doctor, and he thinks you could have been discharged even before you arrived here. You've managed the disruption of the move very well, and have dealt with the difficulties of living in an asylum better than many would.'

'I can't believe it. I thought I'd never get out of Portsmouth Asylum, and since we've been here, I've felt even worse at times. I miss my Jimmy so much.' She wiped her eyes.

'I knew you'd not be here for much longer.' Grace smiled. 'I'll speak to the Sister and make sure that you can leave as soon as possible. Is that alright with you, Mrs Simpson?'

'It is indeed.'

'But how will I get home?'

'I will organise your rail ticket,' Mrs Simpson said. 'And when you arrive at your new home, I will arrange for us to go to collect the babe.'

Gladys looked at her. 'I can't thank you enough.'

Mrs Simpson looked at the hills outside the window. 'You are most welcome,' she said. 'Now, I will have to get on. There's lots to be done. I will see you soon in Southsea.'

'Thank you. I won't let you down,' Gladys said.

'I know you won't, and I'm happy to help.' She took some coins out of her purse and handed them to Gladys. 'This should help you on your journey to your new home too.'

Grace walked to the ward office with her old employer.

'You're very kind,' she said. 'I'm not sure how Mrs Smith would have fared without your help.'

'Nonsense. I need a new parlour-maid and I'm sure she will fill the role perfectly well.'

'I really didn't expect you to take her in, you know,' Grace said. 'But tell me why Mary James is leaving. I thought she would be a good parlour-maid. Has something happened?'

'Only that she decided she wanted to take a position in Handleys Department Store. I do confess I may have encouraged her. She has been doing some sewing for me and her embroidery is exquisite. I know she will do well working in the haberdashery and needlework department and will learn more about using her skills to produce some beautiful clothing. Now I find myself losing another good member of the household.'

Grace paused at the office door. 'Gladys may have another breakdown in the future, you know that don't you? You're taking a big risk.'

'Breakdowns can happen to any of us at any time. You won't put me off you know. And I intend to be there for her.'

'That is good news, but to take on a child as well.'

'As I said, we have always wanted children in the house, and it never happened for us, sadly. I am quite excited about having a little one running up and down the stairs. And we can afford to help so why not?'

'I don't think many would do what you have.'

'Nonsense!' She smiled. 'How are you getting along now, anyway?'

'The hours are long, and we aren't having any tutorials whilst we're here in Brighton. But I do enjoy the work and find it rewarding, mostly.'

'I think the war will be over before long, then your training can recommence.'

'I hope so. I'm still reading the handbook but I mostly fall asleep before I've read more than a few pages.'

'You must be getting a lot of experience just working on the ward.'

'That's true enough and the gardens here are very pleasant. My favourite time is during the afternoons when I'm off duty and can walk outside. It doesn't happen very often, but there's a lovely copper beech tree I sit under sometimes.'

'Are you happy?'

'I'm happy enough, I've been receiving letters from home which helps, although I still haven't heard from either of my brothers.'

'Is there anyone special in your life?'

'Not really, not since Teddy. He's marrying my sister soon.'

'Oh? Should I say congratulations, or is it something that's painful to you?"

'Not at all, not painful I mean, not anymore. We were sweethearts before he went away, but it didn't work out and I'm glad he's found someone who will care for him properly. I'm committed to nursing now, whatever happens in the future.'

'I do hope you find someone for yourself one day.'

Grace blushed.

'Ah, is there already someone?'

'No. Not really. I have a dear friend back in Portsmouth, a woman friend.'

'Really? I'm glad to hear you have someone you can confide in.'

'I miss her, but we write. She is a trainee nurse at the asylum, too.'

'And she didn't come to Brighton with you?'

'No. She wanted to learn about how to nurse physical wounds and illnesses. She's braver than I could ever be.'

'Well, it's good to have a friend anyway. I expect you'll be working together again after the war is over.'

Grace sighed. 'I hope so.'.

Mrs Simpson looked at her. 'I sense there may be more than friendship between the two of you?'

'Just friends,' Grace said. 'Nothing more.'

'You don't have to hide anything from me, you know. I am a woman of the world.'

'I'm not hiding anything, I just don't know myself to be honest.'

Mrs Simpson took Grace's hand. 'You will find your way, my dear,' she said.

'I hope so,' Grace smiled.

43

It was only a week later when Grace received more letters. The first was from Rose.

Dear Grace,
    Thank you for your letter and letting me know how you are getting on. It sounds like you are already making friends. You will be so glad you didn't stay here in Portsmouth. I don't think I've ever been this tired, and the awful smell of blood and rotten wounds is awful.
    I try not to get emotional about the sights. Everything is red - the blood on the bandages, the blood on the sheets, the blood on my hands and in the bowl of water after washing the poor boys. For they are only boys and remind me of my school pals who went to the front over the past few years. I even see blood on the ceiling of my room in the dark as I lay in my bed.
    Today, I walked to the end of Asylum Road and met up with Dora. She was standing outside her studio and asked me in to see her work. I was impressed. There were piles of paintings lining the floor, leaning against the walls. Two easels had half-finished landscapes of the harbour.

Dora asked about you and sends her regards. She told me you had been chatting to Georgia before you went away.

I think of you often, and miss you very much. Hopefully, it wont be much longer before the world turns back to how it was before and we can get back to our training. I look forward to sharing a cuppa with you again in that lovely tea-room.

I have to get back to the ward now, so will say goodbye for now.

Your dear friend,

Rose

The other was from Elsie and came with a wedding invitation. It was expected, but when Grace opened the envelope and saw the card with the flowers and the careful writing with Elsie and Teddy's names transcribed on the front, she sank down into her chair, her stomach churned with something she wasn't sure she could describe. Wiping away a tear, she put the card aside and read the letter that was with it.

Dearest Grace,

We have been very lucky and have a date for the wedding. It will be next week. We managed to get a special licence so won't have to wait any longer. I am sorry it's so quick but I have to let you know we have found out I am expecting. I know this will be a shock to you and am so sorry. Teddy and I love each other very much so I know you will understand once you've got used to the news. You will be an Auntie, Grace. Please be happy for us.

I would love you to be at the wedding but understand it might not be possible. I'm told the war will be over soon, so we can celebrate properly then.

I love you my dear sister,
Elsie

Why do I feel so shocked at this? Grace wondered. After all, she knew it would happen sooner or later. But it only seemed to be a few months ago that Teddy was her sweetheart and they were planning to marry as soon as the war was over. She kept asking herself what had happened, where had she gone wrong?

Elsie was right, she would have to get over the shock. She was her sister, after all and meant so much to her. She just hadn't expected there to be a child so soon. A child that would have been her own if only she'd not hesitated before. Now she was to be an auntie instead. She asked herself again is this what she wanted?

The door to the nurses' lounge dormitory opened and Alice Partridge came in. 'You all right, Bennett? You look like you've seen a ghost. Not bad news I hope?'

'I'm not sure. Is a wedding invitation bad news?'

Alice sat on her bed. 'Depends whose wedding I suppose. You don't look very happy about it.'

'It's my sister, and I should be delighted, only she's marrying my old fiancé.'

'Oh! Not really good news then?'

'It's a long story. We ended the engagement some months ago, after Teddy came back from the front. He was injured badly and broke off with me then.' Grace shook her head. 'I thought I'd accepted them getting together but now it's here in writing, the wedding's next week, I don't know what I feel anymore.'

'You seem to me to be more of a career woman to be honest. You're determined to be a nurse, aren't you?'

'Yes, you're right. I made my choice and it wasn't to marry, only I thought I would one day. And now my sister is pregnant too.'

'Well! A big shock for you then?'

Grace stood and walked to the end of the room and back. 'Yes, it is, but as Elsie says, I will get over it. She's right.'

'I hope you can. And there may be someone else out there just waiting for you to appear.'

'Maybe.' Grace looked at her hands. 'Or maybe marriage isn't for me.'

'Whatever will be, I suppose. Anyway, we need to get back to the ward, Sister wants to see us in her office.'

'Really? I wonder what's happening now.'

'Maybe it's time to get back to Portsmouth. The war should be over soon.'

'How many times have I heard that in the past four years?' Grace gave out a big sigh. 'Come on then, let's find out what she wants.'

The nurses and attendants were gathered in the small office. Sister spoke quickly.

'It is indeed good news, and what I know we've all waited for. The war is now over and soon we'll be getting things back to normal again.'

A cheer went up in the room.

'Now ladies, please do not be over-excited about this. There is much work to do before the day comes when we can finally get home to see our loved ones, those of you from Portsmouth I mean. We do not want the patients to become agitated. They have suffered enough already. You will all be given your tasks as usual and I will make arrangements as soon as possible for transfers back to the asylum there. Any questions?'

There were lots of questions, but Sister only had the same answer - to keep calm and focused on the work they did from day to day and to gradually prepare the patients for the great move back to Portsmouth.

All of this excitement meant Grace could have no leave to get to Elsie and Teddy's wedding. She was quietly relieved. It would have been too much for her to see them making their vows. It was hard enough to imagine it. She did have time though, to write letters the following evening, after another long shift. The first was to Elsie.

Dearest Elsie,

Thank you for your letter and the invitation to your wedding. I am glad for you and for Teddy too. I wish you all the happiness you both deserve. Congratulations as well on the news of the child. You must be very excited to be a wife and mother. It sounds strange when I write these words as I can only remember you as a wild young woman. I am sure you will be an excellent ma though, and wife, and I am looking forward to being an auntie too.

I am sad that I can't get leave to come to the wedding, but as you say, we can celebrate very soon. I heard today the war is over, as I am sure you already know too. Everything is so busy here but soon I will be home again. I do hope your special day is wonderful and look forward to seeing a photograph of you in your dress when I return. Will it still fit, what with you expecting? I hope so.

Sending all my love to you and to Teddy,
Your sister,
Grace

PS Still no news from Wilfred and Bert I suppose? I wish we had news of our brothers, don't you?

She read the letter to herself over and over, wondering if Elsie would see she'd written it through her tears. Yes, she admitted to herself, she felt as though her heart had broken. It will heal, she told herself. He clearly was not for you.

As she finally put the letter in the envelope and wrote the address on the front, Grace could feel the weight lifting from her. 'It is the right thing,' she said to herself, and as she walked to the post box the following afternoon, she let her thoughts turn once again to her own future as a nurse, and of course, to thoughts of Rose.

44

The next day, Grace took up her pen again.

Dear Rose,

I am so excited that the war is finally over. We are very busy, but really most of my work involves keeping our ladies settled as they are all so keen to be back in Portsmouth nearer to their families, even the ones who will remain in the asylum for a long while yet.

I have a little time to walk in the garden and sometimes even into the village at the end of the long drive to this place. The countryside is quite lovely but I do miss the sea.

I had a letter from my sister Elsie. She is to marry in a few days. I am unable to take time off to go to the wedding and I think it's just as well. My feelings are in such a muddle although a part of me feels good that I am free. Of course I wish them all the best and am to be an auntie soon! I admit this last news made me reel a little.

Being away from you however, has made me realise how much I care for you. There, I have said it and put it in writing. I do care for you very much and think about you all the time. I'm unsure of how to let things develop but I am hoping that if you feel the same way, we can work it out between us when I get back.

I have to finish this now, but hope it won't be too long before I see you in person.

Fondest wishes my dear,
Grace

The very next day brought another letter from Rose, which surely must have crossed in the post.

My Dear Grace,

The Church bells are ringing all over Portsmouth. Such wonderful news - the war is finally over. You must be so excited to be coming home to Portsmouth. Do you know when? We heard today the Americans will be planning to move their wounded out of the asylum as soon as they can organise passage for them to be taken back to the United States. This may take a few weeks though and there are still more injured coming from the continent.

I suppose they'll have to take away all their equipment and make the asylum back as it was before they arrived. I hope it won't take long. I miss you so much and look forward to when we can sit together and share a bottle of beer or two again.

I should have started this letter by asking how you are. Are you delighted the war is over? Have you heard from your brothers yet? Are you managing the work all right? Have you kept up with your studies? I know I haven't. I suppose we will have a lot of catching up to do before we finish our training.

I'd best finish this now as I need to get back to the ward. Please write if you have time.

I hope to see you soon,
Your dear friend Rose

Days passed at Brighton asylum, Grace wondering several times whether she'd revealed too much of her feelings to Rose and when she received Rose's own letter, she'd felt even more troubled. Had Rose cooled off? Perhaps she'd found someone else, not surprising with her working with those glamorous American nurses. Grace had seen photographs of American women and knew they were always portrayed as sophisticated and beautiful. She could easily imagine Rosie falling for one of them. She wanted more than anything to write to her again, but every time she took up her pen to start a letter, something in her heart told her to wait. 'If she really cares about you, she'll write soon enough,' Grace told herself.

When the nurses were told they'd be staying in Brighton for at least another few months, Grace found herself pacing the dormitory and wondering why life could be so cruel. Her escape came soon enough though as a notice went up in the nurses' home for volunteers to go back to Portsmouth to help with re-organising the asylum as the Americans were beginning to clear the wards.

As soon as she got to the ward that morning, Grace knocked on Sister Price's door and entered.

'Well, Bennett, what is it?' Sister Price was quite different from Sister Biggs who had stayed behind in Portsmouth. She was small in stature, but was a force to behold in the ward. What she lost in size, she made up for in her determined and loud voice.

She certainly didn't let anything get past her and made sure everyone knew. 'Come along, out with it!' she said.

'Beg your pardon, Sister, I've seen the notice asking for volunteers to go on ahead of the others back to Portsmouth.'

'Oh, dear, and I suppose you want to volunteer, do you?'

'Yes, please Sister.' Grace stood almost to attention, afraid to move in case she were to annoy.

'Oh, for goodness sake, don't look so scared. I'm not going to bite you!'

'Sorry sister,' Grace said as she fidgeted on her feet.

'Bennett. Do take a seat, you look like you're going to fall over.'

'Yes, Sister.' Grace sank into the chair. 'Thank you.'

'Right, now then, why are you so keen to leave my lovely ward?' Sister looked out into the ward through the small window in the door. 'Are you not happy here?'

'I do love working here, Sister. It's not that. I just want to be back in Portsmouth, where all my family are, and friends too of course.'

'I see. There is probably a young man too, is there not?'

'No young man, no, not now.' Grace frowned to herself. 'I have family though and friends.'

'Ah well, I suppose there will be a lot of young women like you with no young men coming home. I am sorry for your loss.'

Grace swallowed. She wanted to explain what happened to Teddy but hesitated. Finally, she explained, 'My sweetheart did come back, but we called the wedding off. We are still friends though.'

'Well, I won't expect you to explain, and his loss is the nursing profession's gain of course. One day perhaps married women will be allowed to work as nurses, but that I fear will be a long time in coming.'

'Yes, Sister.'

'Very well, I will put your name forward to be transferred back to Portsmouth. I should think it will be finalised in the next week, so you may be home for Christmas.'

'Thank you, Sister. I'm much obliged.'

For the rest of the day Grace kept wondering about her decision. Had she made a mistake in rushing back to Portsmouth? What if Rose had found someone else? How would she ever cope with being back and knowing Rose had moved on?

On the other hand, it would be wonderful to see her parents again. Her thoughts went to her brothers. Surely, they must be on their way home too.

Elsie and Teddy were married now, so that would be another change in life at home. Grace hoped she would be able to keep strong the first time she saw them together, and with a babe on the way, too.

45

The war was over at last and Rose had so much on her mind. Too much thinking made her want to get out of the nurses' home. She had a rare evening off and left the asylum at six o'clock and made her way towards Milton Road. She hadn't given any thought as to where she was heading, just had to walk. The evening was mild despite the time of year. It was already dark but there were people about everywhere. There was definitely a feeling of celebration in the air.

The doors were open to The Milton Arms as she approached and the sounds of happy revellers floated out into the street. Glancing through the window, she wondered if it would be too much for a woman to go through those doors and join in the fun. She could see women inside but there were more men and no women on their own. What a shame she didn't have the courage to go in. A beer would be most welcome at this moment.

Rose turned away from the window, the light, the warmth and the excitement of a world without war, "The Great War" as they were now calling it. She looked out into the relative darkness of the street and began to walk on.

Suddenly a figure lurched from the doorway and stood in front of her, blocking her way. Rose froze for a moment before stepping to one side to walk on, ignoring the man's stare. Before she could move however, he grabbed her by one arm and swung her around.

'I know you!' he said, a glint in his eye. 'I've seen you before. You were with that queer woman at the end of Asylum Road, lives in the boat house. You one of them too, are you?'

'Let me go, you brute,' Rose pulled herself free. She turned on him. 'I have no idea who you are and who I am is no business of yours.'

'Really, pretending you don't know who I am!' He laughed in her face. 'I know your other friend, the one from the asylum. She came to me for a job, silly bitch, and her sister got me in trouble, she did.'

'You! Yes I've heard of you. The low-life you are, Medford. I hope you got everything you deserved. I hate men like you, no better than scum.'

'You'll regret saying that, young lady!' He stressed the word lady whilst curling his lips to a scornful sneer. He looked around the street. 'There's no-one about,' he grabbed her again, forcing one arm up her back. 'Come on then, let's walk.' And he marched her along the path, her arm in such pain whilst they walked. He was strong, too strong to struggle free without risking him breaking her arm. She called out but anyone who was about, ignored her, possibly assuming it was just end-of-the-war high-spirits.

Rosie racked her brains trying to think of how she could get out of this. Suddenly the streets that had been busy, were quiet as he forced her across the nearby fields. Finally they reached a more secluded place where he forced her down to the ground. The grass was still wet from the recent rain, she could feel mud on her face as she lay there face down. She could hear Medford rustling with his clothing. She turned as he exposed himself. Rosie panicked, knowing what must be coming if she didn't fight back. She kicked back at him and sat up.

'You bloody bitch,' he shouted. 'I'll show you what a real man is.'

'You're no real man,' Rosie spat at him. She wriggled away, getting the better of him with his breeches around his knees. But he was too quick in pulling them up again and grabbed her around the waist.

'Now you've made me angry, you silly little girl!' he said. 'Do you think I really want you? How could any man want a woman like you?' He swung his fist back and punched her in the face.

All Rosie felt was a crunch, a sharp pain and then all was black.

46

Grace's release from Brighton came within a few more days. It was a bitter day when she left the Brighton asylum for the last time and the wind cut through her winter coat and sheets of rain like needles attacked her face as she walked down the long drive. It was with relief that she climbed aboard the bus that took her into the town of Haywards Heath. As they drove along the Downs, she looked back at the towering yellow building of the asylum. She felt glad she was finally going home. How she missed Portsmouth, the seaside and even the asylum there.

It was a long journey on the train with plenty to look at as they passed through the countryside. Grace could hardly believe all of this land was so peaceful, and hadn't been touched in all the years of the war. She was so happy it was over at last, but as the train got closer and closer to home, Grace could feel her stomach churning in anticipation. What would have changed at home? Would she be able to bear it?

Not due to report for duty until the following day, Grace made her way from the station to Clive Road. She'd sent a letter to Ma but doubted it would have arrived in time so they would be surprised to see her, and Elsie, now married, was living with Teddy at his Ma's house. She was still afraid of how she'd feel when she went to see them, but at this moment she just wanted to be home.

The look of delight on the face of her mother was all Grace needed.

'Grace! It's so good to see you. A sight for my old sore eyes to be sure. Come in. Pa's here too. We've missed you so much.'

Without wondering why Pa should be home on a Tuesday, Grace dropped her bag in the hall and dashed through to the back parlour. 'Pa! I'm home.' She stopped as she watched him struggle out of his chair. 'What is it? You're not well. Oh, don't get up.'

But he pulled himself onto his feet. 'Grace, dear girl, come here and give your old Pa a hug.'

She could hear the wheeze in his voice as he spoke.

'Oh, Pa,' she said as they embraced. 'I have missed you, and now I'm home, but you're sick? Why aren't you at work?' She stepped back and looked at him. His face seemed older, and there were shadows under his eyes.

'Nothing to worry about. Just a chesty cough. I get them every winter don't I?' As though to prove it, he started coughing, doubling over on each cough.

'Well sit down and rest. And try not to talk. Ma can tell me everything while I put the kettle on. I don't know about you two, but the train journey from Brighton was long and uncomfortable and I'm gasping for a cuppa.'

'I'll do that, Grace,' Ma said as she busied herself. 'The kettle's already boiled. And Pa's not too bad. It's probably all that dust he breathes in at the docks. It don't do him any good does it? And yes, he does get it every winter too. A couple of days rest and he'll be back to work. We can't afford to have him staying off for any longer anyway.'

'I'll take your word for it, Ma.' Grace said. 'I do worry though, there's a flu epidemic isn't there?'

'There's always flu every winter, this won't be any different will it?' She looked at Pa and frowned.

'We can only hope. But please look after yourselves, you two.' Grace took the tea Ma had passed to her. 'What about the boys? Have you heard from Alfred and Bert? I thought they might be coming home soon.'

'They are indeed.' Ma went to the dresser and took a letter off the shelf, tucked behind the clock. 'It's from Bert. You know Alfred never could write very well, and Bert not much better to be honest. It's short and sweet, but I could kill those boys for not writing sooner. I'll bet he was forced to write this one. Even so, I am glad they're both in one piece and coming home.'

Grace took the letter and read:

Dear Ma,

Good news, we are coming home in the next two weeks. Wilfred is with me and we are both all right.

Your son
Bert

Relief swept over Grace and with tears in her eyes she spoke. 'Oh, dear Bert, I thought we'd never see him again, nor Wilfred. I can hardly believe it's all over at last, and they're both in one piece too.'

'Good news indeed,' Pa said before breaking into another burst of coughing.

Grace handed him his tea. 'Here Pa, have a sip of this,' she said. 'You need to get well before the boys come home so we can all have a knees -up.' She looked across at her Ma. 'And the wedding? It went well, no doubt?'

'It was a small occasion, of course, and you were missed. In another time, Elsie would have loved to have you as maid of honour.'

'That might have been too much for me, Ma.' Grace smiled, looking at the window into the yard. 'But I do wish them well, and will go to see them before I leave.'

'You're going back to the asylum, then?' Ma asked. 'I did think maybe...'

'Yes, I am going back. I only have the rest of today off and have to return to the nurses' home in the morning. I'm not sure what will greet me there, whether we'll be helping to clear the wards ready for our patients to come back, or whether they'll expect me to work on some of the wards that are already cleared. I'll find out tomorrow. I will be glad to be back though. I've missed the training sessions and the friends I've made there.'

'So you have made friends then? Well of course you have, why wouldn't you? But are they nice girls?'

'Ma! What a thing to say. I wouldn't be friends with them if they weren't nice would I? Oh I know you're thinking of all the stories about the women who work there being loose. Don't blush, Ma, I know that's what you think. So I'll put your mind at rest, none of my friends are any more "loose" than I am, and I think you know me well enough by now, don't you?'

'I'm sorry, I just worry about you. You've already had disappointments in your life, and I want to know you're happy and safe.'

'I am happy, Ma. And as for being safe, I suppose I'm as safe as any of us can be in this world. Now, I need to take my bag upstairs and then I suppose I should go and wish my sister and brother-in-law all the best in their marriage.'

Elsie greeted her with a warm hug when she opened the door. It felt strange to Grace knowing the last time she'd entered this house, she'd been Teddy's fiancée and now she was his sister-in-law. She confessed to herself she felt nervous but Elsie made her feel welcome and took her through to the parlour.

'Look who's here,' she said as she entered behind Grace. 'Mrs Evans, it's Grace,' she called into the scullery where the older woman was boiling a wash.

Teddy, sat beside the range in the parlour, smiled up at Grace. 'It's good to see you,' he said. 'Come over here for a hug.'

Grace moved towards him and took his hand. She gave him a hug, feeling slightly awkward leaning into him, then she reached across to Elsie and took her hand too. 'I'm sorry I didn't make the wedding, but I want you both to know I wish you so much happiness.' She looked at Teddy. 'I am glad you're my brother now, and you will be good together.'

'You're the best sister I could wish for,' Teddy said.

'And I'm to be the best aunt too, I hope.'

'Oh you will be indeed, Grace,' Elsie said.

'What plans do you have?' I mean will you find a home of your own?'

'We're going to stay here for the time being,' Elsie said. 'Mrs Evans doesn't want to be on her own and it's good to have another pair of hands in the house to help with Teddy. Although,' she paused. 'He hardly needs help with anything now.'

Mrs Evans popped her head around the door. 'It's going to be a busy, noisy household again before long, just how I like it.' She stepped into the room. 'Grace, dear girl, it's so nice to see you again. Are you back in Portsmouth now the war is over?'

'Yes, thank heavens. Oh it was nice enough in the Brighton asylum. It's just another asylum to be honest, like any other, but I missed the sea and my friends and family, of course.'

'Welcome home, then.'

'I'm staying at Ma and Pa's tonight, then back to the asylum tomorrow morning. I'm quite excited about going back actually.'

'You always were strange,' Elsie retorted.

'Thank you very much!'

'Will you stay for cake?' Mrs Evans asked.

'Not for me, thank you. I only popped in to let you know I'm back. I have to get home now. But I'll visit soon.'

After the short walk home, Grace went to her room, once shared with Elsie, and pondered on the changes in her life in the past year. She expected to feel sad, but instead there was a glimmer of hope for a better future.

47

Walking back into the nurses' home the next morning, Grace wasn't sure how pleased Rose would be to see her. Her last letter was more stilted than warm.

Grace's room was waiting for her, recently vacated by an American nurse who'd returned to the United States the week before to nurse her mother. She'd left the room tidy, the bed had clean sheets and the room was dusted.

It was reassuring being back in the familiar environment, but something was definitely missing. After hanging her clothes in the wardrobe and sliding her bag out of the way, Grace changed into her uniform and went out into the lounge, looking around for clues that any of her old colleagues were about. The room was empty as they'd all be on duty already, apart from the night nurses who'd be asleep. She walked along the line of rooms and stopped at Rose's. Listening at the door and hearing nothing, she knocked and entered.

'This is strange,' Grace thought, looking around the room. The bed was neatly made and on it was a bag, she assumed was Rose's. It was full of clothing Grace recognised as her friend's. She looked in the wardrobe and it was empty. 'What on Earth is going on?' she said out loud to herself.

Everything had changed on M Ward since Grace had been away. It was still set up as a recovery ward for post surgery. There were men in the beds which were set along the gallery and in the dining room area. The patient's lounge had been partitioned off into two small areas, one had more beds and the other was a smaller sitting room area for those who were well enough to be up for short periods during the day. American nurses as well as a few of the attendants Grace recognised from before hurried around, fussing with the patients. One or two nodded to Grace and smiled. There was a smell of iodine, disinfectant and festering wounds that made her wonder whether she'd made the right decision to return so soon.

Grace knocked on the door of Sister Biggs' office and waited.

'Enter.' The familiar sound of Sister's voice called her in and she was greeted with a grin. 'Bennett, welcome back. Come in and take a seat.'

Surprised at being greeted so warmly, Grace closed the door behind her and sat in one of the chairs that lined the wall of the office.

Sister sat behind her desk and looked at Grace. 'I am glad to see you. The American nurses are fine enough but I've missed my trainees. I hope you are ready to continue with your career as a nurse here?'

'Yes, Sister, I'm glad to be back, although everything seems to have changed since I've been away.'

'Well, this lot are leaving over the next couple of weeks, and we shall soon be back to normal. We just have to be patient. You know what it must be like with everyone scrambling to sort out the mess the war has left us.'

'I hope it will be soon. I am here to take up my duties, whatever they may be. I know I'll be expected to do work I'm not used to, but I do want to help.'

'I know you'll take in all in your stride. But mostly you will be moving beds and helping to re-admit ladies from the asylums they'll be returning from. As soon as those beds empty in the gallery, and the officers are moved from the side-rooms and on their way home to the United States, we will start to feel happier, I'm sure.'

'Can I ask a question, Sister?'

'Ask away, Bennett.'

'Is Jenkins leaving? We were writing to each other and she didn't say she was planning to leave, but her belongings are packed and it looks like she might be going.' She paused. 'I'm sorry, I know it's none of my business but I'm sure she'd have told me.'

'I am worried about her, to be honest,' Sister said. 'I had believed she would make a good nurse, and she was coping with the change of patients and all the new duties she had to undertake, but it seems she was caught up in the celebrations when the end of the war was announced. She was seen by two of the attendants in the street near the Milton Arms, walking with a man, apparently. She didn't report for duty the next day, I'm afraid.'

'But she wouldn't have done that! Has no-one tried to find out what happened?'

'Her colleagues reported that she regularly went out, and weren't surprised when she was seen. They said she was leaning into him and obviously knew the man. I'm sorry but these things happen all the time to nursing staff. They get caught up in life and just leave.'

'But her things are all in her room. She wouldn't have left them behind. I know she'd have come back for her bag. What if she's been hurt, or in hospital somewhere?'

'Bennett, your imagination is incredible. Besides, we haven't time to chase after every young woman who decides she's not suited to this profession, do we?'

'But you haven't even tried.' Grace was furious.

'We did contact her parents. Perhaps you could call and see them. They may have more news of her. But now, I need you to focus on your duties. Come along, I will show you what is needed on the ward.'

Grace spent the day trying to keep her mind on her work. There was so much that was new and so much needing to be done before the patients returned. She tried to find out from the American nurses on the ward if they knew anything about Rose's disappearance, but no-one could give her a clue. It seemed although Rose was popular enough on the ward, no-one had got really close to her. Whilst Grace was pleased about this on one level, she wished someone, anyone, could tell her what had happened. She wanted more than anything to go on a hunt for her friend but couldn't leave the ward without permission and there'd be no time after her shift either. The next few days were agony for her wondering and hoping Rose was alright.

48

Darkness flowed in colours of grey and black through Rose's head. All was swirls of clouds and brief thoughts, memories of something terrible. Sometimes a shaft of light would enter her eyelids but she always pushed it away, it hurt so much. There was no symmetry to anything in her life any more. There was pain and then no pain, flashes of something she couldn't grasp hold of and a deep fear rolling over and over every moment of the day and night. But there was no day, only night now. She was held down, couldn't move, then she was pushed and pulled about. She may have vomited - there was a smell of vomit, or was it?

Someone was washing her face, terrifying her, soothing her, gently wiping her lips with a sponge. But she couldn't open her eyes to see who it was. She couldn't hear anything and then she heard so much loud noise, and talking and laughing. They were laughing at her, stabbing her with pins, asking her to sit up, to lie down, rolling her over to wash her and change the damp sheets she lay upon. In the middle of the darkness she heard footsteps coming closer but then they carried on walking past her, voices getting angry in the distance.

Once she did wake up, at least she thought she had. A nurse spooned something into her mouth but it was too hot and burnt her tongue. She spat it out and fell back down onto the pillows. Then it was darkness once more. When she woke again, there was no-one there. She was all alone in a long empty room with a window at the far end. The urge to escape was so strong, to get to the window and call for help. She was being kept here without any way to get out. But she couldn't make her legs move and slipped back into the darkness and shadows in her mind again.

She must be getting better. After another long time she woke with the nurse offering her soup again. 'Too hot,' She mumbled.
'It's not too hot, I tested it,' the nurse assured her. 'Please try a little, it will make you strong again. You need to eat.'
'Where am I?'
'You're in hospital - The Royal. You had a nasty knock on the head and have been asleep for a long time,' the nurse said. 'Now, come along and try a little of this.'
She managed to drink four spoonfuls of soup before the feeling of extreme exhaustion came over her. 'Tired,' she said.
The nurse stood and offered her no more. 'That's a good start,' she said. 'Now go back to sleep and I'll bring you something more to eat later.'
Expecting the room to be empty, she looked around, but who was she? Her name seemed to slip away. And why had she thought she was all alone in here? There were rows of beds - a long ward, and all the beds were filled. There was coughing and wheezing from the bed nearest to hers, and crying from across the way. And there were windows, lots of windows all along the

wall above the beds. Nurses hurried about, some carrying bedpans, the metal shone in the sunlight that was forcing its way through the window opposite.

Shaking her head was painful, moving any part of her body was painful. Her chest was sore, as though she'd inhaled a bonfire. There was only one thing to do. She sank slowly onto the pillows and closed her eyes. She felt the churning inside as the soup lined her resisting stomach.

In her dreams she was running across a field in the middle of the night. An owl hooted an alarm call and then she was falling into a bottomless pit of black.

It was the touch of a gentle hand that brought her into the world again. She opened her eyes and looked up at the nurse. 'Where am I?' she asked.

'You're in the Royal Hospital,' the nurse said, smiling at her.

'I remember, you said before. Why am I here?'

'You've been very ill my dear, but I think you'll be on the mend now. I'm going to bring you something to eat and a drink. You're very weak.'

'I don't feel hungry.'

'You won't. Your stomach isn't used to food, but if you take small amounts, we'll soon build you up again.'

'What happened to me?'

'You were brought here by a young couple who found you unconscious in a field. You were lucky they found you.' The nurse smiled again. 'We know nothing about you, not even your name. We've been calling you Grace. You mumbled the name several times in your sleep.'

'I'm not Grace, no. She's my friend.'

'Really, well, we must change our notes then. What is your name?'

'I, I really can't remember.'

'Alright. Do you remember anything else about your friend Grace? If we can find her we can find who you are, can't we?'

'How long have I been here?'

'Three weeks now. You had the influenza on top of the injury from the fall. It looked as though you'd been attacked. Can you remember anything about that?'

'I think I was running away from someone. Yes, he was wrestling with me. That's all I remember. I don't want to remember.'

'What about your friend, Grace? May we contact her? It would help.'

'Yes, of course.' She thought for a long moment. 'I don't know. Yes - Bennett, her name is Bennett. We work at the asylum, only she doesn't any more. I remember now. She went to work in Brighton whilst the war is on.'

'But the war is over now,' the nurse said.

'Is it? I didn't know. Look, I'm sorry. I can't think straight, I'm so tired. Please let me rest.'

'You are right, you must rest. I'll just bring you a drink and later you can try some food.'

49

It was nearly a week before Grace could go in search of Rose. The most obvious place to start would be at her parents' house, just off Queens Street. It was a tram ride away on the other side of the island but Grace had all day. She forced herself to believe she'd find Rose and felt her spirits lifting as she alighted the tram and walked back along the wide road, now busy with shoppers.

The narrow side street was more of an alleyway, dark and quite dingy in contrast to the main thoroughfare. She remembered Rose had said her home was the third one of a row. She'd described it as a hovel and said she'd be ashamed to take Grace there. It was certainly smaller and more dishevelled than Grace's home in Clive Road. She knocked on the door and waited.

It seemed like an age before the door was opened. There stood an older version of Rose. She had a lined face, her hair was untidy, a mixture of dark brown with grey streaks, but her apron was clean and the smile she gave Grace was pleasant enough.

'Mrs. Jenkins? I'm a friend of Rose's. Is she in please?'

'No, dear, she's working at the asylum. We haven't seen her here for some weeks now. You should try the asylum.'

'Sorry, I should have explained. I work with Rose at the asylum. At least I did until some months ago when I was transferred to Brighton. I'm back at Portsmouth now and Rose seems to have disappeared. I'm worried about her to be honest.'

'You'd better come in then.' Mrs Jenkins led the way into the tiny house. 'I don't know, that girl gets up to things I know nothing about. I dread to tell her Pa.'

'I'm sure she didn't disappear because she wanted to. We've been writing to each other and I know she was reliable as a nurse and wouldn't have left without permission or at least without telling people.'

Mrs Jenkins looked at her suspiciously. 'Have you known her for long then, Miss...?'

'It's Grace, and we met when we started the training at the beginning of the year.' Grace looked around the room. 'But we're good friends, as I said, and I know Rose was doing well in her work so I can't imagine why she would leave without saying anything.'

'I'm afraid you don't know her as well as you thought, then. I'm sorry to say, that one is a flighty one.'

'But she would have taken her things with her, wouldn't she? I've checked in her room and her bag is still there, with all her belongings in it.'

Mrs Jenkins frowned briefly and shook her head. 'Well, I don't know, I really don't. Look Miss, Grace, I can't help you. I wish I could but...' She looked to the back door as it opened, a look of fear flickered across her eyes as a man entered the room.

'What's this?' He was short and chunkily built, his clothes filthy, an unshaven shadow on his face. 'Visitors?'

'This is a friend of Rose's. Grace works at the asylum too.'

'How d'you do? Mr Jenkins, I'm pleased to meet you,' Grace began.

'Never mind all that 'ow d'you doin's. You one of them women? You're not welcome 'ere.' He glared at Grace and turned his back on her. 'Where's me dinner Missus?'

'I just wanted to ask if you've seen Rose,' Grace said. 'She's missing.'

'Is she still 'ere?' He spoke to his wife, sat down at the table and pulled a tobacco pouch from his waistcoat pocket.

'I'm sorry.' Mrs Jenkins took Grace by the elbow and steered her to the door. 'You'd best go now. Mr Jenkins ain't the best of hosts.'

'I can see that, and I'm sorry to intrude but surely you must be concerned about Rose. She's your daughter.'

'I can't, not anymore. She's a grown woman now and has chosen her own way, so I have to let 'er be.' She opened the front door and they stepped outside. 'Look, of course I care about her and wish I could do more. But I have to keep him 'appy don't I? A woman on her own in this world can't survive, and anyway I love him, but he'd not be 'appy if he thought I was helping Rose in any way.'

'But that's wrong, isn't it?'

'Maybe it is, maybe it ain't, but it's the way of things around 'ere.' Mrs Jenkins smiled ruefully. 'But if you do find her, tell 'er I love 'er, won't you?'

Grace walked along Queens Street to The Hard and sat looking across the ferry to Gosport. She remembered when she'd been across to the munitions factory and thought about what had happened that day and since then. It did occur to her everything had started to go wrong the day Mr Medford assaulted Elsie. Or was it earlier, at the beginning of the war? She reasoned life could always throw things at you and some of those things were hard to overcome. Sometimes you just had to come to terms with the bad things and to get on with it.

Perhaps Rose had decided nursing wasn't for her, and she hadn't meant the things she'd said to Grace about her feelings. Rose knew a lot of other women - perhaps she'd fallen in love with one of them and had thrown in her lot, doing a midnight flit from the asylum. But why would she leave her belongings behind? Why would you do that? Then she answered herself - because she has found herself a wealthy woman who's promised to buy her new clothes, and a beautiful home to live in. Grace had heard the lesbian fraternity in London was thriving now since so many of the men had disappeared and women were looking for love. The excitement of the night life there may have been enough to tempt Rose away.

It was cold and a wind whipped across the water, making Grace feel chilled to the bone. High above, gulls were screeching at her. She hoped life in Portsmouth would start to go back to how it was before the war. One day, before long, she hoped families would stroll along the seafront again, without having to wonder if their loved ones were safe, or that there would be a future for their children without war.

She stood and walked across to the tram stop. There was Georgia, standing on the front platform. 'As I live and breathe, it's you!' She greeted Grace with a grin. 'You're back in town, then?'

'Georgia, it's certainly good to see you.' Grace climbed aboard the tram. 'I've been back a week now but been working and this is my first day off. How are you?'

'So far so good, but I've been told not to expect to keep my job now the war's over.'

'That's a shame. What will you do?'

'I don't know, and that's the truth. I thought I'd just wait and see what turns up.'

'I'm a bit worried actually,' Grace changed the subject. 'You know I told you about my friend, Rose? We were starting to work things out before I went away. Then we were writing to each other. She never gave me any clue she was going to leave the asylum but when I got back I found she'd gone, left all her things behind and just disappeared. No-one at the asylum knows anything about her wanting to leave. I've been to her parents' and they've not heard from her. I don't know what could have happened.' She paused and sighed. 'I don't suppose you've heard anything?'

'No, sorry.'

'I don't know why I thought you would. It's just me, I wish I knew where I could look.'

'Do you know anything more about when she left?' Georgia asked.

'She was last seen going out on the day they declared the end of the war. Some of the nurses think she went out to celebrate and found herself a man to go off with.'

'Not very likely?'

'No. But I did wonder...?'

'Look, I hardly think that would happen, she's a good woman. Dora and I, we met her at a party a couple of years ago. And even more recently, about a month ago, she came along to Dora's studio and they had a good old chat apparently. Maybe about you?'

'Oh? She talked about me?'

'Only anything good, I'm sure. Look, we have to get this tram moving now, or I'll get the sack sooner than I'm ready, but have you checked the hospitals?'

'No! Do you think something's happened to her then? That's the last thing I thought.'

'It's possible and if you've tried her home and her things are all still in her room at the asylum, I would say that's the best place to look.' She took the controls of the tram and started it up. 'I agree with you, I wouldn't have thought she'd have gone anywhere without letting someone know. But try not to worry.'

50

As she walked along Fratton Road she noticed the shop windows were decorated with flags and some already had Christmas paper chains hanging inside. Grace wondered if they were having early Christmas this year, or was it more to do with the end of the war fever. Everywhere she looked there were people milling about, looking in the shops, but their faces were lined. So many loved ones were missing, so many others were home, or on their way home, but would never be the same again.

The papers were making a big thing out of celebrating The Great War and the "War to end all Wars". She shuddered to herself wondering if this would be true.

About to turn off into Clive Road, she almost collided with a figure who'd been on her mind that morning: Medford. An electric chill of fear flashed through her for a second, then she saw he was with his wife. She stood behind him looking into the window of a fabric store and hadn't seen Grace. Turning to her husband, Mrs Medford began to speak.

'Ernest, dear,' she began, then stopped, seeing Grace standing before them. 'Oh? We do not want any more trouble, young lady, Now if you would move out of our way, we will leave you alone.'

Grace stared. 'Trouble? I am minding my own business, walking home. I want nothing to do with either of you,' she said and then raised her voice. 'I am surprised you are not still locked up, though, Mr Medford, after your assault on my sister.' She turned to his wife. 'And you, Mrs Medford, you need to be careful. This man is dangerous.'

Mr Medford, now red in the face, somehow found his voice. 'How dare you attack us in the street.' He glared at her. 'Such common behaviour, to be expected of someone like you, one of those women, aren't you?'

'You are disgusting and cruel, one of those men,' she paused, 'who only cares about themselves.' She looked at his wife. 'Are you sure you know what he's like, and what he was doing on the 11th November?'

Mr Medford coughed. 'What on earth is she on about now?' He laughed in her face.

'The night my friend disappeared. I wouldn't be at all surprised if you didn't know exactly what I'm on about.'

'Really, young lady, you are taking this too far.' Mrs Medford took her husband's arm. 'Come along dear, we need to leave, now.' And she marched him away.

Grace stood watching them, the feeling he was something to do with Rose's disappearance growing more and more. But was she just imagining it?

She talked to Ma about her meeting with the Medfords as soon as she got home.

'I'm only stopping for a quick cuppa, Ma,' she said. 'I want to get along to the Royal Hospital to check something before I'm due back at the asylum this evening.'

'Why you going there?' Ma asked. 'Isn't one hospital enough for you?

'I'm a bit worried Ma, about my friend, Rose. We were writing to each other while I was away but she's now disappeared. Left all her things behind and gone. I don't know but I've got this horrible feeling it's something to do with that man, Mr Medford. I've been to Rose's parents' and she's not been there. And then when I bumped into the man and his wife just now, I had a thought he might know more about Rosie going missing than he would admit.'

'You didn't have a go at him in the street, did you?' Ma looked horrified. 'Not in front of his wife, too?'

'I did, Ma, and he deserved it. And as for her, she should be careful around him. He's a dangerous man.'

'Why do you say that?'

'For goodness sake, Ma. He assaulted Elsie and then got her certified. And if that wasn't enough, he then attacked me and left me stuck in the mud flats.'

Ma looked shocked. 'I knew about Elsie, but you never told me he attacked you too!'

'Sorry Ma, I didn't want to tell you. I was lucky someone came along and I got out. Anyway that's all in the past now. I'm just worried about Rose. No-one knows where she is so I thought I'd check with the hospitals.'

A loud bang on the front door brought Grace to her feet. Her Ma was already at the door before she could give any thought as to who it could be. None of their friends would ever knock like the world was at an end.

It was her father, brought home from the docks by a work pal of his. Pa was wheezing and could hardly walk. His face was the grey of the sky and his lips blue. Between them, Ma and Grace managed to help him into the parlour.

'I gotta go back to work, sorry mate,' his friend said. 'Hope you get well,' and he was gone, terrified no doubt, of catching whatever it was Pa had, who couldn't speak to say thank you.

He fell back into his chair beside the range, the only sound coming from him was the wheezing of his chest as he tried to breathe.

'We need to get him upstairs to bed,' Ma said. 'I knew he should have stayed there this morning. It's that flu, it's going round the town faster than the plague.'

'Oh, Ma, don't say that. I know the flu is about and it's bad, but Pa's strong, aren't you? A few days in bed and you'll be right as rain. Can you get up?'

They helped him to bed, struggling up the narrow stairs together. 'Now try and sleep,' Ma said. 'I'll bring you some broth later. Do you need a glass of water or anything? There's tea.'

He shook his head and laid back on the pillows to rest.

'Ma, why didn't you tell me Pa was so ill. You let me prattle on about my worries and said nothing. If he hadn't been brought home while I was here, I'd still not know.'

'I didn't want to add to your troubles, and I really hoped it wasn't as bad as it turned out to be.' She took out the big pot and went into the scullery to fill it with water. 'He'll feel better after a rest and some of my broth.'

'Is there no medicine he can take?' Grace asked. 'Or at least honey and lemons?'

'And where do you think we'll be getting lemons, or honey at this time, eh?' Ma laughed. 'No, we've got a bottle of that onion cough medicine, and he's been having that, but he's just going to have to ride through this. He's strong, he'll be back to work before your next day off.' She took out an onion and some carrots from a basket.

'Is there anything I can do to help? He'll be losing pay won't he? I've got a bit saved up if you need anything.'

'We'll be alright. Now, stop worrying about us. You have enough to worry about as it is. Are you going to check the hospitals, like you said?'

'I can't just go off and leave you with Pa like this, I have to go back to the nurses' home this evening but I can stay and help you, or just keep you company for a few more hours.'

'That would be nice, but I'm sure we'll be fine.'

'Let me chop something, at least.'

'If you really want to you can peel and chop the onion. That's a job I hate doing, I can't stand the tears.'

'Give it here then, Ma,' Grace laughed. 'Who likes tears?' she said, rolling up her sleeves and taking a sharp knife from the drawer in the dresser.

Grace worried about her Pa, but her thoughts were also on Rose, wondering where she might be, thinking about her feelings for her friend, could they have a future together

She wondered how it would work, would they ever be able to be together like Georgia and Dora were. What would her Ma and Pa think? But you are taking your thoughts too far into a future that may never happen, she told herself. You don't even know where Rose is; it's possible she has just decided to run away and start a new life somewhere. But Grace knew in her heart that couldn't be true. Rose must be somewhere near, and she could be in trouble.

51

'Wake up dear, it's time for some more broth.' The nurse was standing beside Rose's bed with another bowl of something. This was the routine, sleep, eat, sleep and more sleep.

Rose struggled to sit up and looked around at the ward. 'How long have I been here?' She asked.

'Several weeks now. You've improved a lot but you've been very ill.'

'I can't remember anything much. The days and nights just flow into one another.'

'You will get stronger, the flu took it out of you, I'm afraid, and of course the injuries of when you were attacked.'

Rose shivered. 'I remember parts of that. It was at night, I think. I was walking, people were celebrating. The end of the war, wasn't it?'

'Yes. Can you remember anything else?'

'It was dark, but the lights in the pub were bright, I was followed.' Rose looked at the nurse. 'I don't know, but I think I was being followed by someone I knew.'

'It seems whoever followed you ended up attacking you. You were found in a field away from the road. Had you been running away from someone?'

The feeling of fear she'd held at arm's length for so long, started to rise as Rose remembered the face of that man, the grab of his hands on her. She remembered kicking at him as he had her on the ground, her trying to scrabble away, but then nothing more.

'Are you alright, my dear?' The nurse took her hand. 'You're shaking. What have you remembered?'

'I don't know,' Rose whispered. 'I think, yes, I was attacked. I remember fighting him off but then everything went black. I'm not sure, but I think he was trying to rape me.'

'I suspected as much. You had bruising, you know, on your legs and, places.'

Rose felt the tears forcing from her eyes. 'I didn't know! Why didn't I know?'

'I'm so sorry. I think you may have blocked it out. Sometimes we do when things are too terrible to face. It's nature's way of allowing us to heal. Now you are stronger, your mind will start to remember in it's own time.'

'Yes, you're right, of course,' Rose agreed. 'I did learn that at training school.'

'But you still can't remember your name?'

'No. Oh, I hate this. Why can't I remember a simple thing like that?'

'I don't know enough about how the mind works, I'm afraid. I'm just a nurse, used to caring for the body, not the mind. Now, eat some of this before it's completely cold.' She offered the bowl to Rose who took it gratefully.

Left alone once she'd finished her meal, Rose thought about the memories coming back to her. She did remember a man confronting her outside the pub and marching her into the field. She knew she'd tried to fight him off but there was no memory of her being raped so why did she think he had? Maybe she was wrong. But then the nurse had said she'd seen bruising. There was no bruising now but it had happened weeks ago and would have healed after all this time anyway.

What if she was pregnant? She'd have to leave her training behind, give up nursing altogether. How could she work and look after a child? And it would be his child, the child of a rapist! She tried to work out when she'd had her last monthly, it was at least a week or maybe two before the war had ended and she knew that was the night she'd been attacked. She must be overdue by now. But, she told herself she'd been ill and that could effect things couldn't it? Only time would tell, when she got back to normal. But what if she was pregnant? How would she cope?

Stop thinking ahead! It's not happened and won't be happening, she told herself. There was no way she could have a child at all. She wasn't the kind of woman to have babies, was she? She'd decided long ago, even before she was an adult. The very thought was unbearable. She blocked it out of her mind, as she'd blocked out her very name.

Of course, she could easily recall her name if she wanted to, she remembered Grace didn't she? And she knew she was training to be a nurse for the insane, it was only the denial of what had happened that was stopping her mind from letting her know who she really was. It was easier to block it out, as she could block out her future and not have to face what was likely to happen to her next. If Grace didn't want her, she couldn't face anything else, especially not a child.

She was pregnant. Her breasts were sore and she felt sick all the time. They'd wanted to discharge her, needed the bed for other patients but where could she go? She now gave up all hope of a life as a nurse, and although the thought of that man's child growing inside her made her feel even more sick, she knew she couldn't lose this baby.

52

'Sister wants to see you, Bennett,' Ethel Lang called to Grace as she came out of the dining room the next morning.

'On my way. I wonder what I've done wrong this time.'

'No idea, but you'd better get in there, she's in a right old flap.'

Grace had stayed with Ma for the rest of the day before. Pa didn't seem to improve as the day wore on. She'd sat with him for a while beside his bed whilst Ma went out for more groceries and then it was too late to get to the Royal so she'd made her way back to the nurses' home where she'd tried to get some sleep with still no idea if Rosie was in hospital or had disappeared somewhere.

She knocked on Sister's door.

'Come in, Bennett.'

'You wanted to see me, Sister?'

'It's a bit of a puzzle, you may be able to help. I have had a message from the Sister on G ward at the Royal Hospital. They have a patient in the ward who they think has your name. At least they don't know her name, as she can't remember it herself, but she said your name when she was first admitted and so they thought that's what she was called. Only now, she's told them Grace is not her, but her friend. It doesn't take an idiot to work out this mystery patient could be Jenkins, although why she can't remember her own name, but can remember yours, is difficult to understand. What do you think?'

Grace could hardly keep up with the convoluted explanation, but her heart did leap with hope when she realised Sister Biggs must be right.

'It must be her,' Grace said. 'I'd planned to go to the Royal yesterday to see if she was there, but my Pa was brought home ill and I stayed to help Ma so never got to go.'

'But why your name?' Sister looked askance at her.

'Perhaps because we spend a lot of time together, helping each other with our studies, or at least we did before I went to Brighton. And we had been writing to each other whilst I was away.'

'Good friends then?' Sister asked.

'Yes, Sister.'

'I suppose you will want to go and find out if it is her, then.' She looked at Grace. 'Well you must go and visit her after dinner then. You may have time off to go.'

'Thank you, Sister.'

'You'd better get your jobs done before you go and no hanging about when you get there. If it is Jenkins, you'd best put her in the picture as to who she is straight away. And tell her she's needed back here as soon as she can get herself out of bed. We can't have her missing any more of her training, can we?'

'Yes, Sister, I will.' Grace was smiling when she left the office, and she kept finding herself grinning at nothing in particular the rest of the morning.

As soon as the lunchtime medication was administered, and all the dining room cleared, the ladies of the ward were taken back to their places of work. The ones who stayed on the ward were setting about their afternoon tasks, some with sewing, others were allowed to read or draw and Grace was able to go on her mission to find Rose.

Quickly donning her overcoat, she left the front of the building and briskly walked to the tram stop which would take her to the Royal Hospital in Commercial Road. Grace could hardly believe she would be seeing her friend at last. She had to keep reminding herself it wasn't completely certain it would be Rose. But it just had to be her, she thought as she looked out of the tram windows into the streets where shoppers were out and about. With Christmas just a week away now, everyone was trying to make up for the terrible years of the war.

The journey seemed to take an age, but eventually it was her stop. The red brick buildings of the Royal Hospital were in front of her as she walked through the main gate. Her heart couldn't stop itself from fluttering in an unsettling way as she looked at the signs for G ward. She hoped they'd let her in at such a time. There was only visiting on a Sunday but she was there as a nurse, she told herself.

Sister was waiting for her. 'You must be Bennett. Come into my office.'

Grace sat in the chair offered.

'Now, I expect you are keen to see your friend, if it is indeed her. It seems strange to me she could remember your name but not her own. I wonder why and think perhaps there is something stopping her to admit her own name. She seems to remember much else of her life and what happened to bring her in here.'

'If it is her, then her name is Rose Jenkins. I can't imagine why she used my name though, nor why she cannot remember her own.'

'Well, to be truthful, we assumed her name was Grace, as it was the name she kept calling out. She was unconscious for a long time before we could have a proper conversation and so called her Grace for want of any other name. She does have family in Portsmouth, does she?'

'She does, and I have visited them thinking she may have been there. She went missing from the nurses' home on the evening the war ended and some people are saying she just went out and was too busy having a good time to come back. I didn't believe that. She was seen with a man, which isn't like her.' She paused. 'Her parents didn't seem to be very concerned about her, but I am.'

'I wanted to warn you before you see her, she's had a very traumatic time. I expect she'll tell you all about it if she wants to, but be warned, she is still unwell, although getting stronger every day.'

'What was it, concussion?' Grace asked.

'She arrived here with concussion and then contracted influenza shortly afterwards which set her back, and she has been very unwell. We thought we might lose her for a while. Luckily, she is recovering, as I have said, and I believe she'll be well enough to leave here fairly soon.'

'Thank you Sister. May I see her now?'

Rose's bed was halfway down the long ward. Grace was dismayed to see how frail she looked. Instead of the jolly, rounded figure of her friend, there lay a shadow of the woman. Of course she would have lost weight, Grace thought, and would soon be back to her old self, but at the moment it was shocking to see her looking like this.

Rose opened her eyes as Grace drew near. At first there was a puzzled look on her face which soon broke into a whisper of the grin that Grace knew so well.

'Is that really you, Grace?' Or am I seeing things again?'

'Oh, Rose! Thank goodness I've found you. I thought...'

'Thought I was dead and gone?' Rose shifted herself up on the pillows. 'Not yet, anyway.'

'No, I didn't mean that. But no-one knew where you'd gone and I had no way of knowing what was going on in your head. I wondered if you'd just decided to move on and had upped and left.'

'As if I would go without telling you. Honestly you are an idiot. Anyway, you're supposed to be in Brighton. I didn't think you were coming back, at least not until the spring.'

'I'm sorry, I didn't have time to write and let you know. They wanted us back as soon as possible, to get on with the training programme. Apparently they need us!'

'It's good to see you.'

'You too. But what's all this about you forgetting your name?'

'I did. At least I suppose I was just blocking it out, but when you spoke to me I realised who you were and then when you called me by my name, I knew it was right. Yes, I am Rose Jenkins, of course I am.'

'Sister says you should be well enough to leave here soon. It will be so good to be working together again.'

Rose looked past Grace at the beds all along the other side of the ward. 'I don't know, though,' she said. 'I'm not sure if I'll come back.'

'Why ever not? You must come back.'

'I don't know if I want to.' She looked up at the ceiling and back at Grace. 'Look Grace, it is good to know you're back in Portsmouth and still see me as a friend, but I've been thinking a lot about us whilst I've been stuck in this bed, and I honestly think it'd be best if we stopped it going any further. I can't be your lover,' she whispered.

'I don't understand. I really care about you. I wrote to you before, didn't you read my letter?'

'I did, and it was nice to hear, but it can't go any further. I'm sorry.' She turned her head away. 'I'm tired now, please go.'

Grace frowned, hardly believing what she was hearing. This was like history repeating itself. First Teddy, then Rose, all from a hospital bed. What was it about her?

'I can't believe you, Rose,' she said.

'You must. Just go. Please.'

The journey back to the asylum was filled with pain.

53

It was a long day on the ward for Grace and her colleagues. There had been a lot of sickness amongst the staff on other wards as well as their own and everyone was expected to work harder and to move on to other wards when they were needed. Grace hated the thought of having to work somewhere else. She had so much on her mind. It was bad enough working where she knew where everything was, and the patients' ways. Luckily, she had been left on M Ward so far, but it still meant you were responsible for more patients and more of the daily tasks. She longed for the Americans to be gone and for life to go back to some kind of normal. But nothing would be the same again, now that Rose was gone. Nothing would go on as normal because there was no normal anymore. So many lost in the war and now, so many more dying of the flu epidemic. She could hardly bear it.

It had been two weeks since she saw her Pa and so far, there had been no news from home, so Grace assumed he'd recovered well enough to go back to work. It was a shock when she was called by the Sister to go to the front entrance to meet her Ma. The last time this had happened was when Elsie had been in trouble, all that time ago. Looking back, Grace realised it was only just over a year ago. So much had been happening in her life since then, it seemed like several years.

Ma's face was grey when she greeted Grace. 'Pa's gone,' she said, as she fell into Grace's arms. 'He passed away last night. I wanted to be the one to tell you. I'm so sorry Grace.'

Grace held her Ma and gently helped her into one of the chairs along the wall. 'Oh, Ma,' she said. 'Poor Pa, I thought he would get better, I really did.'

'He was tough, I know. But that flu was stronger. I wish I'd gone with him.'

'Don't say such things, Ma, I know you must feel that now, but I need you. We all do. Me and Elsie and the boys.'

'Elsie's settled now she's wed, and Wilfred and Bert, they'll be all right too. You know they're coming home in two days' time. I don't know how I'll tell them.'

'Ma, they're grown men now, used to people dying no doubt. They'll look after you, won't they, when they get back.'

'I suppose, but I've seen some of those boys who've come back already and few of them are all right. They might be strong and healthy in their bodies, but war does terrible things to a man.'

'But they get over it in time, don't they?'

'I do hope ours do.'

'What about the funeral for Pa? And will you get a widow's pension?'

'His funeral's covered by the insurance. He paid a few bob a week, and there will be a small pension from the docks. It'll be tight but I'll manage. It's not me I'm worried about, as I can always get work. Oh, Grace, I feel so sad and miss him already and he's not even left the house yet. Me and Mrs Jennings next door laid him out this morning and Teddy and Elsie are sitting with him till I get back.'

'Ma, you are such a strong woman, always practical and getting on with things. But please take care of yourself, and let yourself have time to grieve over Pa. I know how close you two were and what a good pa he was.'

'Now don't you start me off in here, young lady.' Ma wiped her eyes with her handkerchief and put it back in her bag. 'I'll have plenty of time to grieve once we've sorted out his funeral properly. I'll be on my way now as there's lots to be done. I'll let you know when the funeral is. You will be able to take time off, won't you?'

'I don't know but I will do my best to be there. We've lost a lot of nurses to the flu here and several patients too. But I will do my best, I promise.'

'I'll write then,' Ma said and they hugged goodbye.

Back on the ward, Grace's head was reeling. One thing after another, the world was such a cruel place sometimes. She would miss her Pa so much, even though she only saw him occasionally these days. To know he'd not ever be there again when she called back home was hard to think about. Her Ma would be lost without him. Grace hoped she'd be all right and her brothers would take care of her. She wondered if it was a selfish thought as she hoped Ma would be fine without her having to leave her work in the asylum.

Sister Biggs called her in for a chat, asking her about the funeral.

'You must let me know when it is, Bennett,' she said. 'I will make sure you have time off to go, even if it's only for the service. Do you know what the plan is yet?'

'No Sister, and my two brothers are coming home from Belgium the day after tomorrow. They'll help Ma organise it, I expect. But I was hoping I may have a few hours off to be at home when they arrive. Would that be possible?'

'I can't promise anything, but we shall have to see on the day.' Sister looked at her watch. 'Now you'd better get on with your work. I know you have much to do, don't you?'

Grace went through the motions of working over the next two days. Every time she thought of Pa, she felt pain in every part of her body. When she wasn't thinking about him, Rose was on her mind. How could it have come to this? In the end, she allowed a numbness to sink into her as she pushed away any thoughts of what might or might not be and focused on her work. It was easy enough as she knew the routine inside out now and working was the only thing that kept her going.

Soon enough, it was the day her brothers were due to be home and Sister, as promised, had given her the afternoon off to meet with them.

'Don't expect this kind of treatment every day, Bennett,' she said. 'I'm only giving you this time to welcome home your war hero brothers.'

'Thank you, Sister.' Grace dashed out of the ward, keen not to waste a minute more before she saw them.

Flags were out in the street when she arrived, and despite the cold weather, people were milling about, hugging each other and laughing. Her brothers weren't the only boys home today and there, in the middle of the crowd, they were, waving at her and grinning. She broke into a run and flew into the open arms of Wilfred, then felt Bert's arms around her too.

She couldn't speak as the tears were streaming from her eyes. It was a wonderful feeling having them home at last. Then relief turned to anger.

'Why didn't you write? I longed for letters from you two. Surely you could have at least answered mine.' Then she hugged them each again. 'Oh, it is so good to see you both.'

'Oh, Sis, don't make such a fuss,' Wilfred said. He was the eldest and taller of the two, even though they were both grown men now. 'We were a little bit busy, fighting a war, you know.'

'I'm sorry I didn't write Grace,' Bert said. 'You know I struggle with my writing.'

'Serves you right for joining up before you finished school then, you idiot!' Grace looked at him and laughed. 'I can't believe you both got home. Oh, it's so good that you're here at last.'

Wilfred looked at them both and frowned. 'It's a good job too, now Pa's gone,' he said. 'Ma told us as soon as we got here this morning. It hasn't really sunk in yet, to be honest. After all the terrible things that have happened, I at least expected it to be the same once we got home. Losing Pa was the last thing I expected. How has Ma been?'

'I'm not sure, to be honest. She came to tell me when Pa passed away and said she'd manage all right. I've been on duty since then and couldn't get away until today. I've only got a couple of hours off now and have to be back by five o'clock.'

'You're still working in the madhouse, then?' asked Wilfred.

'Don't call it that,' Grace said. 'And yes, I am doing my training.' She looked around. 'Anyway, where is Ma?'

'She's in the house baking for Pa's funeral tomorrow and no doubt making our dinner at the same time.'

'Shall we go in then?' Grace made her way to the door.

'Just going to say hello to some old friends,' Bert said as he wandered across the street.

Grace shook her head, smiling. 'I know where he's going. Remember how he used to moon after Aggie Jones?'

Wilfred laughed. 'He's grown up now, hasn't he? Bet he's been dreaming about her while we've been away.'

'Good for him, I say,' Grace said as she went into the house.

Ma was there, in the back parlour, baking a seed cake for the funeral tea.

'Grace, dear girl, you got away then?' Her eyes were red but she smiled at her daughter.

'I've only got a couple of hours, just to see the boys and check you are coping.'

'Oh, you know me. I cope with whatever the dear God above throws at me. And now the boys are home, we will be just fine, won't we Wilfred?' She looked over at him as he entered the room.

'We will, Ma,' he agreed.

The afternoon was all too soon over and Grace was back on the ward for the evening meal. Sister welcomed her back and said she could have the morning off for Pa's funeral as long as the breakfast was all cleared up and the morning tasks completed.

'It will be a sad day for you, I know, Bennett, but I can't spare you for the whole day. Make sure you are back by twelve.'

54

The first stop for Rose after leaving The Royal had to be the asylum. She needed to collect her belongings and speak to the Matron about her situation. Her stomach was doing flips all the way as she walked along Asylum Road at the thought of seeing Grace again and knowing this was definitely the end for herself as a nurse. Both thoughts were making her so sad but she knew she'd have to bear it and get on with things the best way she could. Her first stop was Matron's office.

As she entered the revolving doors at the front of the asylum, Rose looked up at the windows of the place she'd thought would be her home and work place for most of her life. But it wasn't to be after all. There was no way a woman with a child could work here. Apart from it being against the rules - nursing was only for single women - it would be too hard to do both.

'Well, nurse Jenkins,' Matron looked her up and down. 'I'm so glad you've decided to join us again. I understand you have been a patient in the Royal Hospital? You are fully recovered I take it?'

'Yes Matron, I am. But I won't be able to continue my training now. I have decided that nursing isn't for me after all.'

'Oh, you have, have you?' Matron sniffed and then went on. 'I must say, I am surprised. The reports I've had about your work have been very good. You fit in well here, and managed the transition with the American nurses and medical men very well.'

'I am sorry to leave Matron.'

'Then why on earth are you doing so?' Matron looked at her sternly. 'Everyone has doubts from time to time, but you will get over it.'

'Sorry Matron, but this isn't like that. I am certain I can't be a nurse after all.'

'Well! You certainly seem sure of what you want, although I can't imagine why.' She stopped and looked Rose up and down. 'Unless, something has happened since you've been away. Let me look at you, stand up girl.'

Rose stood.

'Hmm, I thought so. You foolish girl, you are with child. I won't ask how that happened. I'm not a complete fool, but it seems you are. So, are you to be wed?'

'Sorry Matron. Yes, I am pregnant but I don't want people to know, and no there is no man to wed.'

'A night of passion, then? These things happen, especially at times of celebration.'

Rose blushed. 'There was no passion Matron. Sorry Matron.'

'Well, you are unfortunate, but what will you do?'

'I don't know exactly. I know I can't keep nursing with a child, but hope I can find some work and a place for us to live. I have some friends I can ask.'

'Your parents won't take you in then?'

'No. Their house is tiny and there wouldn't be room.'

Matron gave her another look, this time with raised eyebrows. 'I see. That's the way of the world of course. Well, I am sorry to see you leave, Jenkins. But you are right, you can't be a nurse and a mother at the same time. I only wish you all the best and hope you find somewhere safe to stay and a way to make a living.'

'Thank you Matron. And I am sorry.' Rose moved to the door before turning. 'Please Matron, I wouldn't want any of the other nurses to know about the baby.'

'Your secret won't come from me, Jenkins, but remember, you may need your friends once the baby is born.'

Crossing the yard to the nurses' home, Rose hoped she wouldn't bump into any of her friends. They should either all be on the ward, or visiting their families if they had a day off. She just wanted to be able to drop-in quickly and collect her things.

Opening the door as quietly as she could, she stepped inside. The gallery was empty and no-one seemed to be about so she stepped along past the dining area and the lounge to her room. She passed Grace's room and stood by the door for a moment, wondering if she was inside, but could hear nothing, so walked on to her old room. She already was thinking it as her old room, but it was with regret as she opened the door and went in.

Her bed was neatly made, as she'd left it, her bag sitting on top of it. Someone must have packed her things into the bag. She wondered if it had been Grace as she looked in the bag and saw her uniform dress on the top, tidily folded. I won't be needing that any more, she thought, sadly.

The wardrobe was empty and the desk had been cleared. She looked in the bag again, and there underneath her uniform was her notebook and the dreaded Handbook for the Attendants of the Insane. Her eyes were damp now, as she held back her emotions. 'I won't be seen crying here,' she told herself sternly.

Taking the bag up and with a long last look out of the window into the orchard beyond, she sighed. The trees were bare and there wouldn't be any sign of spring buds for a few months yet. As she looked she saw the first flutters of snow falling. Usually a romantic sight, she felt it was echoing the coldness in her life now. She'd lost everything - her career as a nurse, her Ma and Pa, and her new love, Grace. But there was new life inside her and Spring would come around soon enough.

Ethel Lang was the last person Rose had ever thought would be her saviour. It had been by pure chance she'd seen her in Charlotte Street the afternoon she'd left the asylum with her belongings. Ethel's face had lit up when they'd met and although Rose had tried to duck into an alleyway, Ethel strode up to her and gave her the kind of hug Rose had never expected the woman to be able to give.

'Jenkins!' Ethel shouted, all traces of her elegance disappearing. 'Where have you been?'

'I've not been well,' Rose admitted. 'I was in the Royal for a while, I'm better now though.'

'So are you coming back to work, then?' Ethel asked, looking at the bag Rose was carrying.

'No, I'm not coming back. I've resigned.'

'Whatever for? You're the best nurse I ever knew.' She turned to speak to another woman who was with her. 'Winnie, this is my friend from the asylum, Rose Jenkins. I told you about her.'

'Pleased to meet you, Rose,' Winnie held out her hand.

'But why are you leaving?' Ethel asked again. 'What is it? You're not...?' She looked Rose up and down, her eyebrows shooting up as she realised she was right. 'You are! Oh my dear, that's why you're leaving.'

Rose could feel her face getting redder and tried to keep herself from crying.

'How will you manage?' Ethel asked. 'Will you get married?'

'Yes, of course. I mean, no. I mean, I don't know,' Rose was stumped for what to say. She'd hoped she'd get away, disappear somewhere that no-one knew her. She hadn't thought about what she could say to anyone who'd be curious about her.

'There is no man, is there?' Winnie asked quietly. 'Or at least, not any more. Did he die at the front?'

'No!' Rose snapped. 'Look, I'm sorry but I can't explain. I don't know what to do, to be truthful.'

'What about your parents? Are they standing by you?' Ethel asked.

'No. But don't worry about me, I will be perfectly all right.'

'You are not all right, dear,' Winnie said. 'Now listen to me. My husband isn't coming back home and there's only me and two little'ns in the house. We've got room for you and your baby when it comes, if you like.'

'But you don't even know me. Why would you do that?'

'Your a friend of Ethel's and that's enough for me. I was wondering how I'd manage anyway and if you move in, you can help with the rent and then when your baby is born, we can both look after the kiddies. I expect you can turn your hand to something to earn money, can't you?'

'I can sew and clean, so yes.' Rose said. 'And there's work going, I know, at the corset factory. I'll try there.' She smiled. 'You are so kind though. I would have managed somehow. I was going to get lodgings and see how I went from there.'

'Well, you won't have to now, will you? My Winnie and you'll get on like a house on fire. And her two are a bit of a handful so you'll be kept busy enough.'

'Thank you both.' Rose said, then turned to Ethel. 'Can I ask you to keep quiet about seeing me. I don't want people at the asylum to know that I'm, you know, like this.'

'Don't worry, no one will hear anything from me, if that's what you want,' Ethel agreed. 'But I'm sure your friends would be there for you.'

'Please. Promise me you won't tell anyone.'

'Fair enough, if you're sure, I promise.'

Winnie's house was in Arundel Street, a terraced two up two down, much more roomy than Rose's old home off Queens Street. Winnie welcomed Rose in and showed her around.

'The grand tour,' she announced. 'Won't take long though. You can have the front parlour. We never did use it for much even when my Charlie was home before the war started. It seems such a waste to me, having a room that's not used. You'll be alright on the sofa for a while, won't you? Then when you're settled we'll get you a bed, get rid of that sofa, and you can make it your own. There's room for a crib as well.' She opened the door wide and stepped inside. 'Just about room, anyway. What do you think?'

'It's perfect. More than I could wish for, thank you so much.'

'Right, that's sorted then. Now, the rest of the house.'

Rose was shown the back parlour where they'd all live together, sharing meals, the cooking, the scullery with the boiler and running cold water. They went upstairs to look at the two bedrooms. Winnie's sons were at school and their bedroom, although tiny, was cosy with one double bed against the wall.

'They're only little yet and sleeping together keeps them warm at night. I know it looks tidy in here, but that's only because I worked hard this morning in clearing up their mess. You wait until you meet them later.' She laughed. 'Still love 'em though, don't I?'

Winnie's own room had a sadness in the air. Rose imagined Winnie and her sweetheart in that bed, happy and contented before the war took him.

Downstairs again, she was shown the back yard with the outhouse and the coal shed and the gate leading to the path along the back of the houses. 'We are lucky here, we've got a proper flushing lav',' Winnie was proud to say. 'Now that's the grand tour done. You must make yourself properly at home and I know we will be great friends.'

'I am so grateful, you don't know.' Rose felt the tears brimming again.

'No need for that, girl. We women must look after each other in these times, don't you think?'

55

Christmas came and went. This time it was another different Christmas for Grace. Her brothers both home but a big gap without Pa. She thought back to the day of his funeral, only a week ago. How could she ever enjoy Christmas again without her Pa? All she could think about was the day they put him in the ground. It was good to have her two brothers home, of course, and everyone put on a cheerful face. On Christmas morning, Grace walked with Elsie, Teddy, Ma and the boys to St Mary's Church and they all stood around the still newly laid grave of Pa, before going inside for the service. It seemed wrong somehow, being there with such mixed emotions in her heart.

Back home for Christmas dinner, Grace tried to be happy. And she supposed she was content with life, rather than happy. But there was, underneath it all, sadness, the loss of not having Rose in her life anymore. Sometimes she couldn't discern between the grief she felt for her father and the pain she carried in missing Rose. Watching Teddy and Elsie together was bittersweet too. Grace knew they were happy and married life wasn't for her, but would she ever recover from the love she'd lost? So many losses in such a short time.

Bert drank too much beer and Wilfred had to get him up the stairs to his bed at three o'clock. Later Bert was cross and blamed Wilfred for making him miss a visit from Aggie Jones.

'You should mind your drink, then brother.' Wilfred just laughed at him.

Ma worked hard, keeping herself busy, to keep her mind off Pa, Grace thought. She helped her Ma with the dinner and the washing up and all too soon it was time for her to get back to the nurses' home. Christmas was over.

And so the New Year came around and the long month of January was plodded through with Grace back into her training. As time passed the thoughts of Rose were still there, although she was learning to get on with life without her being around. She became closer to Ethel who had started the training again with her. They helped each other in swotting before the tests that kept coming along, revising methods of laying trolleys for wound cleaning, enemas and mundane things such as ear-syringing.

At the end of April all the Americans had left and the post-war euphoria had settled down in the town. The influenza epidemic seemed to be abating and life went on. Grace visited her family once a fortnight, and she sometimes popped in to see her old friends in Craneswater Road.

She was becoming used to the idea of being a spinster aunt. Elsie was due in a few weeks and everyone was excited for her. Grace had been knitting baby clothes on her short hours off after duties. She knitted in pink but Elsie laughed at her and said, 'What if I have a boy?' Then Grace went out and bought some blue wool and knitted more of the same, just in case.

Ma did what she'd always done, and got on with things. Alfred was happy enough to go back to the dockyard and work at his old job welding metalwork, and Bert was busy courting his young sweetheart, Aggie, and was working at the Post Office.

Now and again, Grace wandered along Asylum Road to the old lock gates and called in on her friends there. Dora sometimes was in her studio whilst Georgia was out at work. They'd enjoy a good old chat together, drinking tea made from water boiled on the little paraffin stove.

It was a warm spring afternoon on this particular day and they sat outside the studio in the sunshine.

'We never hear anything about Rose anymore. Do you?' Dora asked.

'I don't. I haven't seen or heard from her since I got back from Brighton and that was months ago now. Life has moved on I'm sorry to say.'

'It's strange. I can't imagine where she went. None of our old pals have seen or heard from her either.'

Grace felt the sadness descend. 'I still miss her, and wish I knew what had happened. I thought we had some kind of a future together, but obviously I was just fooling myself.'

'I don't know. I thought she had feelings for you,' Dora said. 'Oh God, I'm sorry, I didn't mean to upset you. Something must have happened to make her push you away. Perhaps she'll turn up again one day.'

'I doubt it, and anyway, she made it quite clear she didn't want me in her life. I've come to accept that now.'

'Do you think you'll ever find someone else? Another woman, or perhaps a man?'

'No. I'm a committed spinster aunt now, and a nurse. No more relationships for me.'

Elsie and Teddy's child was born in early June and Elsie was delighted to inform Grace she'd given birth to a boy. 'Good job I made you knit those blue romper suits, eh Sis?' she said.

'Well, now you'll have to get on, and have a girl won't you?' Grace retorted.

'Not yet thank you very much. Now say hello to your nephew, Auntie Grace. We're calling him Archie.'

'That's perfect. Hello, little Archie,' Grace smiled as she kissed his tiny hand.

56

Rose was sick to death of carrying around all that weight in her belly. How much longer would this last? Each day she climbed out of bed dreading the long hours ahead. The baby wasn't due for another three weeks and the weather was getting hotter and hotter. So when the pains came early, although she was fearful, there was a part of her relieved it would be over before long.

Winnie called the midwife and the two women bustled about between the scullery and the front parlour, now Rose's bedroom, getting things together - hot water, towels and a soft blanket she'd crocheted over the darker days of winter and early spring.

Rose knew labour could be difficult. She'd seen enough of it in her childhood in Portsea. She'd heard the women screaming too, through the open windows of the cottages near her home. But experiencing it herself was something else. Waves of pain, unimaginable pain, washed over her until she thought she could bear no more, then times of relief when it seemed it was all over, only to allow the pain, like fire, to rush over her again and again. The midwife left at some point, to visit another birth along the street. She'd be back later, she'd said.

Time passed. It must have done, she realised, although there was no sense of time for her, only the darkening of the sky outside the window to blackness and then again to the early sunrise, casting red shadows on the wall behind her.

'You should eat something,' Winnie told her. 'The midwife will be coming in soon to check how you're doing. Look I've made porridge.'

'I can't eat,' Rose said. 'Feel sick.'

'You can't be sick. Hold onto it and eat some of this. You feel sick because your body needs food. You can't keep going without getting your strength up.' She handed the bowl to Rosie and stood over her until she'd taken a few spoonfuls of porridge.

'It's good,' Rose acknowledged. 'Thank you.'

There was a bang as the front door opened and closed. 'That'll be Ethel,' Winnie said. 'We're in here Ethel,' she called. 'I've asked her to take the kiddies today, to give us some room.'

Ethel stood at the door and looked at Rose. 'How are you doing, then?' she asked.

'I've been better,' Rose said as another pain began to squeeze her in that vice as her body prepared itself for the birth. She screwed her face up and tried not to make a noise.

'Take deep breaths when the pain starts,' Winnie told her. 'I find it helps a bit.'

Rose tried but it was too much and she let out a low, long groan.

'Is there anyone I can fetch?' Ethel asked.

'The midwife is due round in a while,' Winnie replied.

'What about your Ma, Rose?'

'No Ethel. I don't want her here. She won't come anyway, so leave it.'

Ethel thought for a moment. 'Before you go mad, I haven't told her, but I know Grace is still missing you. She talks about you all the time, drives me mad actually, but don't you think she'd love to see you? Once the baby is born I mean.'

Another long scream stopped Rose from answering and before she could recover, the midwife had let herself in. 'What is going on here?' she asked. 'Now ladies, off you go, and give me some room. Put the kettle on Winnie, and make me a cup of your best tea.'

The day wore on with no sign of a baby. Rose was completely exhausted, thinking it would never happen. Ethel had gone back to the nurses home and the children were in the parlour with Winnie, eating their supper.

Winnie knew how long labour could take so she thought nothing much of it, and spent time watching the children playing, reading them stories to keep their minds from the sounds coming from Rose's room.

It was late in the evening when she finally heard the sound of a baby's cry. She made a sigh of relief and knocked on the door before entering. 'Is everything well?' She asked.

'Come in and have a look at this bonny girl,' the midwife said with a smile. 'Mother needs her rest now, but I have to finish off first.'

The baby was a red-faced shrivelled pea, too small really, in Winnie's mind. Rose lay back on the pillows, her face red too, and covered in sweat, her straw-like hair, damp and plastered to her forehead.

'Well done, Rose,' Winnie said. 'You must be so tired now. But you have a beautiful baby girl.'

Rose could hardly speak. She smiled weakly at Winnie. 'Thank you, for everything,' she whispered and fainted into a deep sleep.

57

Ethel was the last person Grace expected to have news of Rose. She'd been carrying the secret all those months and now was the time she'd need to break it.

'I need to talk to you, privately,' she said, as they sat in the dining room eating breakfast. It was Grace's day off but she was always up early whether on duty or not.

'Really?' Grace looked surprised. 'Here, or in the garden?'

'The garden, I think,' Ethel stood and made for the door.

'Right.' Grace followed her.

They sat together on the bench outside in the early morning sunshine.

'It's about Rose,' Ethel began. 'I am so sorry, but I've known where she is all the time and although she made me promise not to tell anyone, I know she'd want to see you now.'

'What?' Grace felt a stab of pain in her chest.

'Please don't be angry with me, nor with her. I can understand why she didn't want anyone to know, and I only found out because I bumped into her one day. She's been staying with Winnie, my sister, and her kids. I wouldn't have told you now, either, but Rose is with child and she's about to give birth and…'

'Stop! With child? How could she be?' Grace looked at the roses, now fading in the garden.

'Well, I suppose the way it usually happens.'

'But she doesn't like men. It doesn't make sense.'

'I don't know, but I thought you should know. She's on her own now, that's all I know about it.'

'Do you think I could visit her? Where does your sister live?'

'Well I would,' Ethel said. 'But that is just me. You must do what you think is best.'

By the time Grace had reached the address in Arundel Street, and knocked on the door, she was frantic, wondering what she could say when she was face to face with her dear friend. Her thoughts were rushing. How would Rose would react to seeing her? Would she be angry, or delighted? Would she just look at Grace and tell her to leave? What about the father?

The door was opened by a tall woman who had the look of Ethel. 'You must be Winnie, Ethel's sister,' she said.

'And you must be Grace,' said Winnie. 'Come in please.'

'How did you know me?' Grace asked, puzzled.

'It was obvious. I knew Ethel would tell you about Rose and the babe. I was expecting you.'

All Grace heard was "Rose and the babe". 'Is she, has she...?'

'Yes, the baby was born this morning early. It was a long labour and poor Rose is exhausted. She's sleeping now.'

'And the baby?' Grace asked.

'A little girl, came too early but healthy and strong enough.'

'Do you think Rose will want to see me?' Now she was here, in the house, she wasn't so sure it was a good idea. 'Should I go?'

'Don't you want to see her, then?' Winnie asked. 'I had the impression you two were close, if you get what I mean.'

'We were, at least I thought so, but Rose told me she didn't want to see me anymore.'

'Look, between you and me, I think something bad happened to Rose the night she ended up in The Royal. It was after that she found out she was pregnant. I think she was afraid you'd judge her, or not want her, the state she was in. We've got fairly close over the past months, and she never said, but I wouldn't be surprised.'

'Oh, my poor Rose.'

'So, yes, you should go in and sit with her. She's asleep anyway and the baby's asleep too. I imagine they're both worn out from the birth.' She paused. 'Well, are you going in or not?'

Grace nodded and opened the door.

Rose looked so beautiful, lying there, her straw-like hair all over the pillow, her eyes closed peacefully, the few lines that appeared on her face in the past year, making her look even more like the strong woman she was.

Grace gazed at her, the feeling of love growing as she acknowledge it to herself. How could I live without this person in my life?

A whimper came from the nearby crib. She stepped closer and looked down at the child. 'Hello little girl,' she whispered. 'Aren't you beautiful too, just like your mother.'

'Grace, is that you?' Rose's voice was low.

Grace took Rose's hand. 'It is me. I'm here, and before you say anything, I'm not going to go anywhere.'

'I'm sorry.' Rose had tears in her eyes. 'I was so ashamed.'

'Ashamed? You are a brave, wonderful woman, and you have a beautiful daughter now too.'

'I'm calling her Peggy. A pretty name for a pretty girl.'

'That's lovely, Rose. She is perfect.'

'But, aren't you angry with me?'

'Only for not telling me sooner. Can I ask you a question? Do you want me in your life or not? Or is there a man?'

'No man, and I do want you in my life, but now I have a child? You can't want me now, can you?'

'Why wouldn't I? I've always hoped to have a little girl one day.' Grace thought for a moment, looking at the crib. 'Look, I know I'm new to all this and I'm not saying it won't be hard sometimes but I want to be more than friends with you and now I think we can be a family, can't we?'

'I love you Grace.'

'And I love you too.'

Over the next few weeks, Grace and Rose spent every spare moment together. So much time had been wasted. There were moments in the past months that Rose just wanted to forget, but gradually, most of what had happened to her came to the fore, and she was able to talk about some of the dark times.

Grace didn't want to keep asking questions, so she allowed Rose to talk whenever she needed to. No doubt it would be painful, although she realised how healing talking about things could be.

One evening, Rose began to talk about the day the war ended. She told Grace all she could remember of that night.

'You were very ill,' Grace said. 'It must have been awful.'

'I wasn't the best patient, I'm afraid.'

'I wish I'd known. I would have been here for you, if I had.'

'I was in and out of consciousness for a long time, and couldn't remember who the hell I was. By the time I'd started to recover, I was ashamed to realise that I'd been raped and was pregnant. I couldn't let you know.'

'I wish you had told me when I came to see you in hospital.' Grace said.

Rose smiled. 'That would have been too easy, wouldn't it?'

'Well, at least we're talking now,' Grace agreed.

'Whatever happens, I'm sure we can work it out. So much is changing in the world, isn't it? One thing I'm sad about is my mother. She came to see me once. I was so pleased to see her but she made it clear she didn't approve of my being pregnant. She said she couldn't turn her back on me, and then she did just that. She told me I couldn't ever come home again. As if I'd want to.'

'Your father wasn't exactly nice to me when I went searching for you.'

'You went to my old home?'

'I was worried about you.'

'I'm sorry. I can't blame Ma for being like she is,' Rose said. 'You must think my parents are awful.'

'Not really. I felt sad for your ma, though.'

'She's burnt her bridges with me, that's for sure.'

'Give her time, Rose,' Grace said. 'I can't imagine she'd stay away from you and lovely Peggy.'

58

Grace was grateful for the broad brimmed hat she wore. The sun beat down and glistened on the water out in Langstone Harbour. The picnic rug on the grass was littered with crumbs of pastry left from their lunch. Peggy and Archie had abandoned their toys - a doll with a dirty face and a teddy bear with a ragged ear, both much loved, but with the beach so close there was far too much to see and do that was more exciting.

Such a lot had happened since the end of the war. Both Wilfred and Bert had married and moved out into their own homes with their new brides. Ma, no longer wanting to live alone had taken in Rose with her baby Peggy, and Grace was able to stay whenever she was off duty. Ma had welcomed their loving relationship with the understanding that times would never be the same again.

Grace closed her eyes and allowed herself to enjoy the peace for a moment. Rose and Elsie were beach-combing with the little ones, dropping all kinds of interesting things into the buckets they carried. Grace knew they would be decorating the windowsills in their bedrooms once they were taken home.

A warm feeling of contentment drifted over her. Now she'd completed her training and was on the register as a fully qualified mental nurse, Grace was happy she'd achieved all she'd hoped for. Now it was Rose's turn to finish her training and Grace would stay at home to look after their little daughter, Peggy. They hoped they'd both be able to work as nurses soon enough. After all, they weren't married women, were they? Ma had offered to look after little Peggy, but Ma wasn't so young now and it wouldn't be fair to expect her to do it all by herself.

Elsie and Teddy were settled, still living with Teddy's ma, and very happy with their little boy, Archie, who was a bundle of energy and kept them both busy. Elsie was the perfect mother and Grace had never seen her so content. Even Teddy had gone from strength to strength as a husband and father, and his work in the dockyard office kept him busy, working in the accounts department. Grace laughed to herself to think Teddy would have ever been working with figures when he'd been so bad at sums in school.

You never knew what life would bring you, she thought as she drifted into a dreamy sleep.

'Wake up lazy bones.' Elsie was standing over Grace, casting some welcome shade from the sun as Rose plumped herself down on the rug beside her, laughing.

'It's time to get the little ones home, Grace,' said Rose. 'There's so much to do before I move into the nurses' home. I don't want to be late tomorrow.'

'Back to school for you, eh?' Grace replied. 'I know you're excited.'

'I have to admit, I'm nervous, going back to the beginning again, with new trainees. It's not going to be easy for me.'

'You'll be fine, you know that. You're already a good nurse, with lots of experience and you'll soon get used to the wards, the hours and the people again,' Grace said. 'It'll be like going home for you.'

'I will miss being at home with Peggy.'

'You'll see her whenever you're off. It won't be so bad.'

'I couldn't do it without you, Grace.'

'We are a proper family, aren't we?'

'We are. And Peggy is lucky to have two mummies.'

'Come on, then. Let's go,' Elsie said as she began to pick up the toys and the debris from the picnic.

'All right. I'm coming.' Grace stood, and pulled Rose to her feet before they gathered up the children and made their way home.